AFTER ALIENATION

AFTER ALIENATION

American Novels in Mid-Century

BY MARCUS KLEIN

Essay Index Reprint Series

 BOOKS FOR LIBRARIES PRESS
FREEPORT, NEW YORK

For my mother and father

&

for my ladies

INTERNATIONAL STANDARD BOOK NUMBER:

0-8369-1969-6

LIBRARY OF CONGRESS CATALOG CARD NUMBER:

70-128267

PRINTED IN THE UNITED STATES OF AMERICA

CONTENTS

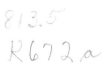

Our joy will be in love and restoration, in the sensing of
humanity as the concrete thing, the datum of our cultural
existence. It will lie in the creation of a new capacity,
proof against terror, to experience our natural life to the
full. What has once been transcended cannot be repeated;
already we live without morality, though hypocrites study
the old deceits. Men will go on to seek the good life in
the direction of what is joyous; they know what is terrible.
May the knowledge of joy come to them, and the knowledge of
terror never leave!

So who is alienated?

ISAAC ROSENFELD, "The Meaning of Terror"

ACKNOWLEDGMENTS

I am indebted to the many friends and colleagues who have given me counsel. To two friends, Herbert Gold and the late Richard Chase, I owe extraordinary gratitude.

It was in conversation one summer afternoon with Herbert Gold that I began to order my ideas for this study. I thank him for initial encouragement, for the refreshment of good argument, for many reassurances, and for no small number of what accuracies of insight may have survived into the finished book.

Were the finished book worthy of his example, I should like to say that it was Richard Chase who taught me both intellectual adventure and critical responsibility. As the book is, I may express only, and too late, my gratitude for the time and care he gave to portions of my manuscript.

I am greatly indebted also, for their free gifts to my thinking generally and for their attention specifically to this work, to Aaron Asher, Robert Brustein, Robert Gorham Davis, Albert Hofstadter, Lewis Leary, Robert G. Olson, and to Robert Pack. I have been provided with particularly useful suggestions for the improvement of my manuscript by Leon S. Roudiez and Barry Ulanov. My former student Miss Mary Solimena gave me help with some translations.

I wish to thank Barnard College for its award to me of a Faculty Research Grant for the purpose of pursuing this study, and Columbia University for its award to me of a University Fellowship.

A portion of this book has appeared in the pages of *The Kenyon Review*. I am grateful to its editors for permission to reprint. I take this advantage finally to thank Marian for patience far beyond the stipulation of her contract.

MARCUS KLEIN

February, 1964

INTRODUCTION

Current history is inevitably blurred by the rush of events, and one has scarcely room or time to see it. For that reason, among others, I have not intended this book about a current literary history to be anything more definite or complete than an introduction to a study.

The time I refer to has not yet come to order, and for that matter it has not come to an end. I discuss a period beginning about 1950 and extending to just this moment, and I regard it as a period because one must set end stops somewhere and because I do not want to be forced in some even more mechanical way at every moment to act the spokesman for a generation, at every other moment to predict and proclaim the future. But of course it is merely a convenience to assume that these few years do or will in themselves constitute an epoch in our literary process. Perhaps because the 1920s and the 1930s were marked off by a series of terminal events which did make a great difference to our literature— the end of a war, the Depression, the beginning of a greater war—for this reason we have got used to having our modern literature in tidy historical packages, and incidentally we have got used to a rule of decimals. Obviously such custom misleads. And indeed it is perfectly clear, because the future is quick and one can see something of it, that this time in our literature, since mid-century, is not epochal nor discrete nor self-enclosed. A kind of literary journalism always listens for the first murmurs of significant revolutions and there are always literary revolutionaries to proclaim new partisanships, but truly there is nothing this year to indicate an imminent *terminus ad quem* or *terminus a quo* to anything. Art, says Joyce Cary's Gulley Jimson, keeps on keeping on. What has been going on recently, anyway, is still going on and defining itself.

Our best and our most serious novelists have in the years since mid-century, I believe, been engaged by an agony different from that which our best and our most serious novelists just before them typically knew, and that is the reason for this book, but our novelists' response is not yet shaped, and the agony itself is still fresh and challenging for everyone. Furthermore, the few novelists whom I study here are each still in mid-career, and summary statements about them will be not only tactless, one hopes for some time to come, but clearly impossible. Except that it can be said that when their response is fully shaped, their careers will be over.

But there is something *new* in the work of these writers, something that seems to have got started just a little more than a decade ago. It is something that everyone seems to have felt—it has been called variously, and in various voices, the new nihilism, poetic naturalism, radical innocence, a new concern for final matters, the rule of personality, the disappearance of manners, the death of dissidence, the end of social engagement, the age of accommodation. The epithets are informative especially, perhaps, as they dramatize an antagonism between the programmatic expectations of critics and the probationary, current discoveries of novelists, but they also signify that novelists in the last few years have been working within a sentiment that is generally felt to be different. It is only a sentiment or an attitude or a motive, with some consequences in technique. It is something that is not yet a message or a program or even a deliberate theme—and therefore the novel in these years has seemed to disappoint those who prefer clear sermons only tricked out with exempla. It is something that can be felt but that by its nature will not be available to precise definition until it has defined itself, until what is sentiment or mood has become an idea.

An attempt at definition seems to me nevertheless worth some effort. The recognition of the seriousness of serious contemporary fiction is itself always important. What is more important, this contemporary fiction appears to be not only new and therefore subject to clarification, but in as many instances as one could hope it seems to be large, exciting, and peculiarly serious.

To describe the mood in which it has been written, I have in the following pages most often used the word "accommodation," and to describe the historical mood which it replaces I have used the word "alienation." The words themselves want a word of explanation. They are cant terms of contemporary criticism which have become standards in a battle, and therefore there is a certain risk of bombast in them. I have used them because they are available, because better than other terms they do describe what I think is to be seen, and I have used them precisely because they contain a usage and a tradition. They describe now not only historical circumstances, but parties and powers. On the other hand, as is the case with political yelps, they have come to comprehend a vagueness of partisan reference in which all issues may be lost.

As I find an excitement in a literature that I have called

accommodationist, I should not want to be thought to be defending *Marjorie Morningstar* against *Moby Dick*. If the distinction between these novels were one between "accommodation" and "alienation," then the terms would mean on the one hand everything that is slack and factitious and supine and cowardly and merely imitative of seriousness, and on the other everything of extensive awareness and intelligence, everything great and true and courageous. Marjorie in her novel accepted Mamaroneck, as she was doomed to do, in the same way that Sloan Wilson in our years accepted his tailor, and what took place in both instances was an adjustment to social realities which, to be sure, might be called accommodation, but which was really a constriction of awareness amounting to retreat. Melville, on the other hand, was in his time alienated, certainly, but "alienation" wasn't his accomplishment. The word "alienation" means, or should mean, something less than *Moby Dick*. Nor does it refer to that dissident outsideness which is simply the constant and the most conspicuous tradition in American literature.

I use the word alienation as in fact it is used by the critical laity—deriving on the one hand from a usage by Hegel and Marx, on the other from nineteenth-century theology, but come to refer really to a particular time in our history.* I

* Professor Sidney Hook points out that the word alienation actually has little appropriateness as applied to writers. "Hegel understood by self-alienation the process of dialectical development by which the individual consciousness progresses from innocence to maturity. . . . Marx's notion of self-alienation is historically circumscribed and . . . applies primarily to the worker who is compelled to labor at something which neither expresses nor sustains his own needs and interests as a person." See Sidney Hook, in "Our Country and Our Culture: A Symposium," *Partisan Review,* XIX (September-October 1952), 570–71, and "Marx and Alienation," *The New Leader,* XLIV (December 11, 1961), 16–18.

The word has become larger and less exact. Professor Joseph Brennan has recorded a discussion by a lady vice-president of the

mean by the word to speak of a certain attitude having to
do with the social position and function of the novelist, an
attitude that succeeded another at the beginning of this century, toward the man of letters as Brahmin or at least as
genteel, benevolent, wise, composed, and if separate from
his society, then separate by reason of being above the battle.
In the first years of this century and for almost half a century
the novelist worked typically, it may be said, within a mood
—though not necessarily a conviction—of usefulness, and his
usefulness was precisely that he was outside this Philistine,
this commercial, this restrictive American society, and therefore in a position to be its critic and a rebel. "Alienation" I
take to begin in that deliberate strategy of discontent, almost
a program, which was enunciated just before World War I
by Van Wyck Brooks and Randolph Bourne, which informed
if it did not entirely account for famous episodes in our
modern literature like the *Risorgimento,* and the Lost Generation, the Younger Generation, and Disillusion, which then
was inherited and put to the uses of revolution by the proletarian 1930s, which finally was the dominant mode of our
literature until just yesterday, some time after World War II.
It is the theory, not necessarily enunciated, of something more
than a generation of our *avant-gardes.*

"Poets and novelists and critics are the pathfinders of society," said Brooks in 1918, some time after he had recovered
from the romantic insouciance of his own earliest critical
work,[1] and it is Brooks's vast importance in the literary history of this century that before and more than anyone else

Institute for Motivational Research on the psychology of litterbugging.
The cause of litterbugging lies in a sense of anonymity and estrange-
ment found in litterbugs. "This sense of alienation," said the lady,
"loosens the individual's sense of social responsibility. . . ." See Joseph
Brennan, "Alienation of the Modern Artist: A Problem of Social
Context," *The Paumanok Review* (Spring 1962).

in this century he created a sense that the American writer
as a writer had a social engagement. The writer's business was
"the vision without which the people perish." The American
writer, according to Brooks, was to "precipitate" the American character, or he was by the inspiration of his personality
to pull this country together into an organic unity, to unite
the sense of personality with a sense of the social ideal.[2] In
fact just *what* the American writer was to do was, like the
socialism to which Brooks also lent his own personality, left
vague, but what is important is that the writer was to consider that his special, peripheral place in this society gave
him a business in this society. "In the best of circumstances,
and considering all the devils that beset the creative spirit,
a strong impulse is scarcely enough to carry the writer
through: he must feel not only that he is doing what he
wishes to do, but that what he is doing *matters.*"[3]

Writers in this country fall by the way for lack of respect
and self-respect, and for lack of what Brooks called, quite
in a medieval sense, a literary guild. Brooks discovered that
this was the time to make one. And if the positive goal of
this literary guild was vague, its feel, its composition, its idea
of literature, its antagonisms—all these things were not.
Writers were to be organized and activist. The literary guild's
recruiting was addressed specifically to the "younger generation." Literature was to be a current and a constant force.
And literature was to be organized against that acquisitive-
ness, that prudery, that complacency, that bloodless high-
browism—all the appearances of the enemy that Brooks named
Puritanism.

Brooks was the theoretician of an *avant-garde.* Its agent
may be said to have been Randolph Bourne, that young man
who took it upon himself in the years just before the first
war to *be* "the younger generation" and who in the same

moment called himself a "literary radical." The literary radical
was the young man who had been educated in all the cautious
orthodoxies and who made it his business now to explode
them. Bourne in his short life undertook radical causes—
socialism, John Dewey's theories of education, and then, with
the coming of the war, pacifism. But it was radicalism itself
that he stood for, radicalism pure, the duty for intellectuals
of alienated dissent. The reigning intellectuals had failed,
Bourne said, "as value-creators, even as value-emphasizers." [4]
The allure of fresh ideas could not come from them. And
what Bourne wanted was a zest, a flair, and a quality of life
that could not possibly be discovered in assent. "Whence can
come this allure?" he asked.

> Only from those who are thorough malcontents. Irrita-
> tion at things as they are, disgust at the continual frustra-
> tions and aridities of American life, deep dissatisfaction
> with self and with groups that give themselves forth as
> hopeful,—out of such moods there might well be hammered
> new values. The malcontents . . . will be harsh and often
> bad-tempered, and they will feel that the break-up of things
> is no time for mellowness. They will have a taste for spir-
> itual adventure, and for sinister imaginative excursions. It
> will not be Puritanism so much as complacency that they
> will fight. A tang, a bitterness, an intellectual fiber, a verve,
> they will look for in literature. . . . Something more mock-
> ing, more irreverent, they will constantly want.

That programmatic malcontentedness, irritability, danger-
ousness, that "deep dissatisfaction with self and with the
groups that give themselves forth as hopeful," together with
the adventure in it—may be taken for the definition of what
a later socially oriented criticism called alienation. And our
literature passed, quite simply, into the hands of a younger

generation composed—Randolph Bourne was a true messenger—of malcontents. The breakup of things, of things that obviously needed breaking up, was, in one area of endeavor, the energy of Menckenism, and in another it was the whole spirit of Ezra Pound's *Risorgimento*. It was the motive for a generation of little magazines. It was the fervor in something more than a generation of literary factions. "A more skeptical, malicious, desperate, ironical mood," Bourne called it, and the epithets apply to everything in our literature of this century that is distinctly modern.

Iconoclasm is the note of the years just before and after the First World War. There was to be an assault on a rhetoric that had become soft and merely literary, and at the same time on a society living within anachronistic pieties, and there were to be assaults on prudes and boobs and Babbitts and on the village virus, on Attorney General Palmer and Prohibition, on evangelical Christianity and Calvin Coolidge and Dayton, Tennessee, and Anthony Comstock, on the words "sacred," "glorious," and the expression "in vain"— the icons of both great and small substance were all to be tumbled down. And then, after a decade and a half of iconoclasm, there was, in the 1930s, an opportunity for writers to participate in a revolution that obviously mattered, a revolution the process of which was thoroughly defined, a revolution which allowed writers at the same moment to be alienated from, and integrated into, the society outside.

The novelists of the largest achievement of these years— Hemingway, Fitzgerald, Faulkner—were not simply iconoclastic, of course, nor rebellious nor alienated. But the literary direction of these years was toward what may be seen as an organized isolation, one that would be related to this society and useful, its function being rebellion. That is the defining attitude of our "modern" literature, and it is an attitude that had its obvious uses. For so many years there was apparent need for just the sort of social demolition that literature might initiate. Brooks and Bourne, Mencken and Sinclair Lewis and Sherwood Anderson and E. E. Cummings and John Dos Passos, then, and James T. Farrell, and Steinbeck, and the many others didn't, after all, invent the enemy, and they could do something about him. At the very least they could, as Randolph Bourne suggested, oppose to complacency their malcontentedness.

And that is to say that the land was rich in irritants, rich in enemies who could be irritated, and the writer could, in some fairly obvious way, be dangerous. There was war and laughter enough to go around. The time was when a writer really could secure a promise of major achievement by exposing the drinking and kissing going on at Princeton. There was shock in it, and value in the exposé. And when Hemingway announced a deliberate retreat from Caporetto, that was really an act of sabotage, immediately and profoundly meaningful because, even in 1929, war was for many Americans still Lord Tennyson rushing the guns at Balaklava. And then there was the time when writers didn't necessarily have to write novels and stories and poems in order to participate in the thing that literature was doing—it was possible to believe that to be sophisticated in a revolutionary partisanship was to be a writer. Our modern literature is a history not only of a rebellion at hand for the writer, but of a choice among rebellions.

But then came the Second World War and it left us, obviously, with a social situation different from that of the 1920s and 1930s, different in small and in great matters. On the one hand, the boobs were not now so dumb. The likely truth about the village was that it was an industrial suburb. The prudes had yielded their virtue, and what went on at Princeton was returning veterans. The lost generation had quite evaporated into its own success. That insular inertness against which all the *avant-gardes* of the 1920s had had the opportunity to rage was simply no longer the significant social fact. And on the other hand, the urgency of the Marxist revolution had all but disappeared with the political misfortunes in the United States of the Communist Party, and Marxists who survived the war foundered in a general prosperity, in a nation which was becoming more and more a welfare state, and then they foundered in the superior urgencies of the Cold War. Then came the overwhelming time, which is with us, of the prospect of absolute catastrophe. Given that common prospect, the posture of malcontentedness was not relevant. Not only that; in these years it has been the nature of this political matter that alone matters supremely that it leaves little room for individual choice. One might have been partisan against the Bomb, but so was everyone against the Bomb, and that affected matters not at all. What cold frustration there was in this overwhelming politics is measured, indeed, by the fact that no novelist of significant talent has written about it.

New terrors have perforce settled some old issues, and incidentally deprived the writer who would be a malcontent of that negative usefulness which should be his justification. Revolutions perpetuate themselves, however. What happened to our modern literature just after the Second World War the critic John Aldridge clearly enough indicated in 1951, by calling his book about it *After the Lost Generation*. "For some reason," he said, "those of us who began to take a serious interest in literature in the first years of the second war felt an immediate kinship with the Lost Generation." And he went on, in that book, to measure some strictly contemporary writers according to their ability to get lost again, and found them all wanting. "Negation and loss" were, he said, no longer means of communicating social value.* And Aldridge was quite right, in all of his instances, to use Hemingway and Fitzgerald and Dos Passos as the measure for his selection of what he called "small, confused, and mis-guided talents." The whole point of the Lost Generation had been that everybody had known exactly where it was. That is the apparent "reason" for Aldridge's sense of, or long-ing for, kinship. The locale of his contemporary novelists' striving was not so easy to determine. And the general pros-pect of our literature just after the war is of a number of young-to-middle-aged novelists—just those whom Aldridge named: Norman Mailer, Vance Bourjaily, Paul Bowles, Gore Vidal, Irwin Shaw, Truman Capote, and some others—try-ing to find themselves anew in a situation where they would be conspicuously lost. They were moved, all of them, in one way or another, by the impulse to dissidence, through a formula of negation and loss to shock a public, to set things astir.

John Aldridge himself was forced eventually by the logic of his criticism to declare that outside New England and the Deep South there was in America no possibility for the novel. But from the perspective of a subsequent decade one may say that the novel of critical revolt, in the years just after the war, and in the years since, was entirely possible, and that

* In the Preface to his second book, *In Search of Heresy,* Aldridge, still the spokesman, with a greater poignance located the greater problem. His dissident point of view toward what he thought a new intellectual conformism was, he said, "now anachronistic, unwork-able, and quite without adherents, except for a few mavericks like myself who have not yet learned to reconcile the contrary teachings of their heads and hearts. I mean the ideal of creative independence and free critical dissent which has come down to us in the central tradition of American thought. . . ." (New York: McGraw-Hill Book Co., Inc., 1956), pp. 7–8.

was one of its troubles. The corollary of its lack of immedi-
acy, its lack of distinct relevance, was its acceptance by the
public. A modern history of critical alienation comes almost
to an end with Paul Bowles and Truman Capote. Bowles in
The Sheltering Sky, Truman Capote in *Other Voices, Other
Rooms,* the one in that amoral Algeria which had already
been discovered by Gide and Camus, the other in what
seemed the interior of the womb, dramatized an extremity
of alienation—and what happened was that their talent was
approved. Their daring was neither shocking nor dangerous
to anybody. It had merely the look of danger. What happened, one may guess, is that a literary, an intellectual revolution that was to encourage sinister imaginative adventurings
had outlived its context and had retired into a solemn literary
tradition, concurred in by both writers and readers. The
Americans after the Great War were not suddenly ancient
and European and decadent and cynical. Such a development
might have made a palpable issue. But after a generation of
propaganda almost everybody knew that the posture of rebellion was in literature and in intellectual matters generally
a healthy, cheerful thing. It was taught in Midwestern col-
leges. And so the more wicked were Paul Bowles and Truman
Capote, the more bracing and generally delightful they were.

At this perspective they seem to betoken the mere inertia
of a revolution. There is more vivid proof, in a symposium
sponsored in 1952 by the *Partisan Review,* that by the turn
of the half-century "alienation" was no longer an obviously
relevant intellectual position. The symposium, called "Our
Country and Our Culture," addressed to its participants a
number of questions derived from an observation taken as
fact, that "For better or worse, most writers no longer accept
alienation as the artist's fate in America." Not all of the
participants, it turned out, did accept that historical judg-

ment as a fact, and not all of them seem to have known what the editors of *Partisan Review* had in mind, but the editors themselves knew and thought it necessary to have such a symposium, and that is the event's significance. They first of all, of course, addressed themselves, on the reasonable assumption that they thereby spoke to the intellectuals. But the intellectuals to whom they spoke in the first place shared, after all, not only some common assumptions about the function of the intellectual, but some common history. They were the veterans of the wars of rebellion. In a later elaboration of his own response to the symposium, Lionel Trilling observed, simply by way of an introduction, "The editors of *Partisan Review* have long been thought to give a rather special credence and sympathy to the idea of 'alienation,' particularly to the alienation of the modern artist, most of all to the alienation of the American artist." And Lionel Trilling, himself an advisory editor of *Partisan Review,* in that introductory statement tells the whole story of the rebellion and of its embarrassment in current circumstances. That "rather special credence and sympathy" to the idea of alienation, already so much less than a conviction, has the odor of nostalgia; it is the intimate memory of the terms of modern literature come to the point where honesty requires a sad reappraisal. To say that the editors of *Partisan Review* "have long been thought" anything was to say that the generals were at least at that critical point where they might become elders and statesmen. Times, politics, our country, and our culture had changed. The symposium, perhaps it is not too much to say, was a kind of vocational retraining for warriors, to forestall premature retirement.

This happened: the revolution in behalf of an alienated engagement found itself ancient, respectable, and irrelevant to the social reality. The critical warfare of our subsequent

years has been largely in a battle between critics who remember the revolution and are true to it, and writers whose
field for exploitation must always be contemporary circumstances. The critical battle has been between the forces of
alienation and the forces—although they are hardly organized
into forces—of what a current critical vocabulary often names
"accommodation."

For the critics the process of the battle has meant a certain
removal from contemporary books, and at worst such a
hardening of the arteries, such dogma, that criticism is not
and refuses to be informed by literature. Something of that
order has happened when so good a critic as Alfred Kazin
complains of the lack in our novelists of a "social intelligence"
and discovers in their works only repeated assaults on his
compassion. Something of that order has happened when
Philip Roth, a writer of so nice a talent, turns critic and tolls
the bells for the writer in America: "The news I wish to
bear is . . . a loss of subject; or if not a loss . . . then let me
say a voluntary withdrawal of interest by the writer of
fiction from some of the grander social and political phenomena of our times." The observation to be made about this
news is that social engagement, the situation and the function
of the individual with regard to "the grander social and
political phenomena" of our times and every time, is the
interest precisely and the dilemma at the center of our most
serious contemporary fiction. Social engagement, whether
one is for or against "accommodation," is the meaning of
"accommodation." But this social engagement is not a simple
matter—not so simple a matter, for instance, as whether the
novelist is for or against TV antennae on the roof, sit-in
demonstrations, guided missiles.

It is perfectly true that something has been lost, an opportunity for direct social, not to say political, antagonisms, for

deliberate mutinies, for rousings of the multitude. The spectacular proof of it is in those novelists who have at all costs in these years preserved the spirit of the rebellion, those novelists precisely in whom a dogmatic criticism of alienation should find its realization. The most deliberate and the most intelligent of them is Norman Mailer, who once, in *The Naked and the Dead,* owned a personal war that was also the public's, a war that had—to his good fortune—been left over from the 1930s, that was about native fascism and about the failure of democracy of which the World War was a convenient, catastrophic, and an ironic expression. It was—Mailer has said so himself—an easy book to write. It was easy in part, certainly, because it took place within a public battle, because there was available to it a revolution of obvious significance. And it was, there can be no doubt of it, a major novel within a contemporary tradition.

But, there can be no doubt of it, the tradition ran out on Mailer. He couldn't—he has said so himself—make a career of the materials of *The Naked and the Dead.* There came *Barbary Shore,* a political and a dissident and a most engaged novel, but a peculiarly parochial one. Then came *The Deer Park,* inventing a pornography of politics. Then, most revealingly, *Advertisements for Myself,* a sad book. None of them easy and none of them major. And each of them, successively, more obstreperous, more intentionally rebellious, more nakedly a groping for an alienation that, like that of *The Naked and the Dead,* would mean something. Nothing is more revealing of the futility and the anachronism of a dogma of alienation, and nothing is more pathetic, than the record of ten or twelve years of fever that Mailer compiled in his *Advertisements.* There Mailer is, with all his seriousness, with all his insight, with all his discipline and his subtle talent, for years running off in every direction after any glowworm that has the glow of villainy. There he is, glowing himself in his villainy, exhorting the Mongols, urging war now on American journalism, again on David Riesman, then on the movies, then against the Un-American Activities Committee, then against television, flexing his muscles, urging war on behalf of murder, suicide, and such sexual freedom as is beyond not only conventional standards but ordinary human ability, the captain of troops as the first philosopher of Hip, against so much, so frequently, so extremely and so uselessly, that finally his one worthy and responsive enemy becomes himself. And so the *Advertisements,* a record of Mailer's radical public gestures, becomes finally cranky, subject to tics, an exquisite's record of failures and disintegrations. And the book that was to be a universal protest is about, finally, Mailer's fatigues, breakdowns, self-analyses, bouts with narcotics, the effort to break the cigarette habit—a private affair after all.

"In a time of peace," said Nietzsche, "the warlike man attacks himself." This is not a time of peace, but it is a time apparently confusing to old soldiers. They attack themselves. Mailer is not alone. There are novelists like William Burroughs and Alexander Trocchi, Jack Kerouac and John Clellon Holmes, whose public rebellions turn out also to be private affairs. But Mailer is much better and he is exemplary. That thrashing about, his always bloodier excesses, his romantic and showy self-torture, exemplify as well as anything can the end of a theory of dangerous malcontentedness. One sees Mailer, and with him the consecutive editors of every consecutive little poetry magazine dedicated to spontaneity, the crusaders against the academy, the poets of obscenity, the strip-tease homosexuals, the young critics who are self-declared orphans of the Lost Generation, the young critics who have educated themselves into a nostalgia for the 1930s—

one sees them frustrated in an act of piety, among the idols
that are already fallen, searching through the potsherds for
something still substantial enough to smash yet once again.
One sees them pounding finally at their own toes. Or one
sees them, at worst, and like Mailer, captivating an audience
which they had meant to threaten. The end of "alienation"
would seem to be merely paranoia or mere entertainment.

The years since mid-century outmoded a literary attitude
which had become a tradition. The time demanded something
else, and what it has got from those most serious of our
novelists who have made their major reputations in these
years is that response which may indeed be described, just
as alienated critics would have it, as "accommodation." The
act of accommodation, of adjustment to the social fact, has
been sometimes, just like instances of alienation, a recoil of
timidity and a refusal of intelligence. But the act of adjustment to the social fact as it has been recorded in the novel
in these years has included more, and much more strenuous,
possibilities. By "accommodation" I mean to refer to a mood
in the best of our contemporary literature, the mood that
occurred when rebellion had exhausted itself, when suddenly
the manner in which the individual—the intellectual, the
writer, any man—might meet society was no longer so certain, when there was no politics to speak of and when there
were no orthodoxies to speak of to restrict one's freedom,
and when all theories of society had been shattered.

The novelist has in these years been free, in what Jean-
Paul Sartre has taught everybody is a "dreadful freedom."
He has not therefore, like Sartre, pursued a duty of engagement. Simply, he has tried to meet the small, bitter necessities
of engagement. The novelist has this advantage over the
philosopher, that he knows that the confrontation of self and
society begins at home, and he knows that one loves or doesn't

love one's mother, wife, friend—to speak of "engagement" in its initial instances—not according to any philosophy. But it is just in that tricky distance between the sense of one's self in one's freedom and the sense of society out there that this novelist seems to have found himself.

The novel has been accused in these years of exploiting personality and it has been accused of quick surrender to the community. Contradictory accusations, and the truth would seem to be that our best novelists have discovered their work within the contradiction. "Accommodation," that is to say, is an enterprise of acrobatics, an achievement that lasts something less than a moment and requires then a new balancing. By "accommodation" I mean to suggest that simultaneous engagement and disengagement which is the characteristic movement of the novel in these past years. The hero begins in freedom of the self and discovers that he is isolated. The hero chooses community—he assumes racial obligations, or he declares himself a patriot, or he makes love—and he discovers that he has sacrificed his identity, and his adventures begin all over again.

The goal is the elimination of the distance between self and society, the perfect union of self and society, but the issue of this novel is at best a lesson in the perpetual necessity of killing adjustments. What is at best to be achieved in this necessary marriage is a cautionary, tentative *accommodation,* and that is the method, in this world, of social engagement. The technical term for this mood is comedy. The hero exercises his wits and thereby lives within his dilemma, and managing to live within it he proposes the possibility of living.

The mood of this novel is comic, and its strategy is accommodation. In the chapters following I have intended to elucidate the matter, and that intention has required some extended examination of the work of a few novelists. It is a

matter of mood that is my concern, not of expressed motive
or goal or ambition. And it is something that runs through
these novelists' works, not quite a theme, but a principle in
their development as writers, and so I have found it impossible simply to point to a collection of novels and to consider
the point thereby proved. A survey wouldn't answer my
purposes. The evidence is as often as not outside the novels.
The novels themselves don't yield up their evidence at the
first knock. And because this is the case, I have dealt with
fewer novelists than otherwise I might have. Moreover, there
are very few serious novelists among those who achieved
their major reputations within the last decade or so who have
yet produced quite enough substantial work to yield in any
systematic way to the kind of analysis that I have wanted to
do.

For this further reason, I have not intended that this book
be anything more than an introduction to a study.

My selection of these particular novelists—Saul Bellow,
Ralph Ellison, James Baldwin, Wright Morris, and Bernard
Malamud—has been not quite arbitrary. They are, first of
all, important, and there is a general critical assent to their
importance. They are good craftsmen, and they therefore
disoblige me from commenting on what Alfred Kazin once
called the "question of frigid correctness." More important,
they represent a breadth of technique and subject. I have
thought that I could get a more extensive proof from their
work than I might find in that of another selection of novelists, and at the same time I have thought that I might avoid
repeating cases.

There are other novelists nevertheless whom I might have
considered, who have accumulated a substantial work, whom
a general opinion holds at least as important as those novelists
I have chosen. There is Norman Mailer. I have not concerned

myself with his work at any greater length than I have done in these pages above because it seems to me the informative end of something rather than an example of the mood peculiar to the past several years. There is J. D. Salinger, who everybody for a while thought was everyone's favorite. Despite the great complications of his later fiction, Salinger has remarkably little to say, it seems to me, and I have not wanted in this book to examine his or anybody's reputation. Salinger's later mysticism, as in the stories "Zooey" and "Seymour," is one with his stance earlier as a connoisseur of the "phony." In both instances what he dislikes is the moral complications of real, living experience, and there is an end to the matter.

There are other novelists—William Styron, Vance Bourjaily, Harvey Swados, R. V. Cassill, George P. Elliott, Flannery O'Connor, John Cheever, John Updike, Herbert Gold—whose work one might at least estimate. If I haven't discussed their work it is, once again, for no better reason than that I have not here concerned myself with making a critical sampler or a survey. It is not my purpose to discover contemporary fiction; I am concerned with its history.

I have concerned myself, and at some length, with two writers who are Negroes, Ralph Ellison and James Baldwin. Their work too, I hope to have demonstrated, indicates an impulse toward accommodation succeeding a history of alienation. But the meaning of "accommodation" in their work has a special complication, and the history behind the work, both literary and social, has a special intricacy. Therefore I have added to my text one more word of introduction. It will be found in the first pages of my chapter on Ralph Ellison.

～II～

SAUL BELLOW

A Discipline of Nobility

The social progress of the sensible hero of our time has been from a position of alienation toward accommodation. Accommodation has meant in all cases an impossible reconciliation, a learning to live with, and at the same time a learning to deny, what has been plainly there: the happy middling community of these years, the suffocating suburbs, the new wealth, the fat gods, the supermarket, the corporate conscience, and also one's own conscience. That was after all the effort of Sloan Wilson's man in his gray flannel suit, of Marjorie Morningstar, and of David Riesman's "autonomous man" and deliberate patron of the supermarket. Riesman's social prescription became part of the language, and there is evidence in that fact that Riesman accomplished what the many sensible heroes have wanted to accomplish. He discovered in "autonomy" the technique of a togetherness that was perfect and yet, for the spirit's ease, salvaged a tic of nonconformity. But when for novelists, after the effort, the retrieved awareness was small, less than one had when one began, and whenever the progress toward accommodation was most successful, then accommodation has looked like retreat.

Saul Bellow's novels, altogether the most exciting fiction in these years, have worked, too, within the motion from alienation to accommodation. They were shaped of course by the forces all lined up and waiting for all novelists and for everyone in these years, by the same conflicts existing within the same terms, and Bellow's novels find their definition indeed as a systematic exploration of the concerns of all the Wilsons and all the Wouks, except that—of course it makes all the difference—they are more aware, more imaginative, and more severe.* Bellow's characters, for all the variousness of mood and style of the novels, remain much the same: a youth and a fat man, with a quirky philosopher loitering near-by. And they face problems which are reducible to a single problem: to meet with a strong sense of self the sacrifice of self demanded by social circumstance. Alienation, the sense of separate and unconciliating identity, must travel to accommodation. Bellow's inspiration is perhaps finally in other, deeper sources, but as the novels have worked themselves out, they have dealt in the terms presented by the history in which they have found themselves, and they have traced a clear progress within those terms. The dialogue between alienation and accommodation is what the novels first of all are about.

The sensitive youth of Bellow's first novel, Joseph in *Dangling Man* (1944), awaiting induction into the army,

* Everyone has tried to put Bellow back together again. I find myself in substantial agreement with Mark Schorer, who, in his review of *The Adventures of Augie March*, said: *"Alienation, relation, assimilation:* the thematic progression is something like that. And *regressive, intensive, expansive* are words that will define the psychological no less than the stylistic and structural correlatives." Moreover, Schorer is exactly right in anticipating at this time that the next work will be toward "integration." "A Book of Yes and No," *The Hudson Review,* VII (Spring 1954), 136, 139.

suspended in a strange moment of complete freedom, watches his freedom become isolation. He is alienated. He believes that accommodation to ordinary social reality has terrible consequences. He is part of the historical moment when rational political enterprise has erupted into chaos—Joseph is, as is to be expected, an ex-member of the Communist Party— and he has, significantly, abandoned an essay on the philosophers of the Enlightenment. But he knows as well that alienation, secession from current society, is both psychologically and logically impossible:

"What if you declare you are alienated, you *say* you reject the Hollywood dream, the soap opera, the cheap thriller? The very denial implicates you."

He entertains in the beginning a desperate belief in the possibility of a "colony of the spirit," of "a group whose covenants forbade spite, bloodiness, and cruelty." But Joseph discovers in a series of test encounters during his seven wintry months of dangling that the colony of the spirit is not possible either. His associations in formal categories of love, with his wife, with his mistress, with his family, with friends and with neighbors, those whom he might make colonists of the spirit, are steeped in real spite, spite in which Joseph shares, and so he is shunted back again and again into the imprisoning self. Nor, as a last shift, is it possible either, he discovers, to live in an "ideal construction," in a principle of action which has been invented despite chaos and by which chaos is to be met. There is inevitably a gap between ideal constructions and the real world, and principles which have become obsessions are exhausting. Alienation and accommodation, both impossible, are, it turns out, the spirit's only choices. Joseph must give himself to idiopathic freedom, and that way is madness, or submit to the community's ordinary,

violent reality. He hurries his draft call. He surrenders. And
he says to his journal:

> I am in other hands, relieved of self-determination, free-
> dom canceled.
> > Hurray for regular hours!
> > And for the supervision of the spirit!
> > Long live regimentation!

Joseph's capitulation, though made in great awareness, is
the consequence merely, finally, of his fatigue, and it is total.
In *The Victim* (1947) the matter is pursued another way,
not yet to resolution, but to a provisional balance in a problem of responsibility. Asa Leventhal is called upon to make a
nice adjustment in his guilt, to pit what he owes to another
against what he owes to himself. Asa, the Jew in what is at
its first level a novel about anti-Semitism, is confronted suddenly by an anti-Semite who accuses him of malice and an
obscure crime which he may or may not have committed.
Having every reason to deny his culpability—not only is the
crime ambiguous, but his putative victim is himself a vic-
timizer and he is as well his own betrayer—Asa is gradually
displaced from his isolated rectitude. Kirby Allbee penetrates
his solitude, his apartment, the domestic secrets of his marriage, invades his bed, the intimate habits of his cleanliness,
finally the last stronghold of his being, to the point where
Asa must admit his implication in the fate of Allbee, of all
men, all-being, no alibis permitted. To do less is to deny
compassion and it is to be less than human. But on the other
hand, compassion brought to a certain extreme is more than
human. Pitched to a certain extreme, compassion is death.
When Allbee, turning on the gas in Asa's apartment, would
have Asa share his grief to the point of sharing his suicide,
he compromises the moral injunction for which he stands.

The components of the problem are the same, still the individual and the community, and there is still the basic conflict between the self that demands preservation and the society that demands self-sacrifice. The terms are, however, deeper than alienation and accommodation, and they are less abstract. In each succeeding novel these public terms have become more personal. Asa Leventhal, a middle-aged fat man and not an intellectual, is involved in a situation the intensity of which commands his complete participation and constant practical decision. That makes the difference in *The Victim* of validating the conflict, and it as well eliminates the possibility of the romantically ironic gesture of surrender. The plot of *Dangling Man* provided a pretext for intellectual play, but it was not sufficient to test the play in action. Asa's situation (which is, it happens, precisely that of Velchaninov in Dostoevski's *The Eternal Husband* *) forces him to moral realizations which mean life and death. And the very weight of domestic detail in the novel, its very ordinariness—Asa's going to and coming from work, his eating, his sleeping, his washing and dressing, his subway riding, his complete occupancy of his days and nights—reinforce the importance of his realizations.

The Adventures of Augie March (1953) reaches much the same provisional equilibrium, but reaches it the other way

---

* Velchaninov becomes the victim of a man whom many years ago he had wronged. The parallels between *The Victim* and *The Eternal Husband* are in fact numerous and detailed, and there can be no doubt that Bellow had this Dostoevski novella in mind. Velchaninov finds himself one sultry summer alone in St. Petersburg. He becomes aware suddenly that he is being haunted by a man he faintly recognizes. Pavel Pavlovich, whom he had once victimized, gradually intrudes himself into Velchaninov's intimacy and at last moves into his apartment with him. It is when Pavel tries to murder him that Velchaninov can begin to unravel the complications of guilt and expiation that bind him to Pavel, and thereby free himself.

around and in a mood of ebullient hopefulness. Augie is, or was in the time that he is engaged in remembering, an inverted Joseph, a constantly accommodating youth, plastic and submitting, a ready participant in other people's projects. Augie is "susceptible to love." People are adoptive toward him, and there is, as he says, something adoptional about him. He is an adoptee. He is his society's most willing recruit. But at the same time Augie has "opposition" in him and, fallen again and again midst theorizers and absolutists and universalists, enticed by glitter and wealth and glamour, engaged by social causes and by lovers, he remains loyal to his sense of his own distinctness and to his clouded prevision of what he calls a good enough fate. Augie's dozens of high adventures are, all of them, engagements in a battle which forces him always back to himself, which imply to him the virtue of disengagement. Like Joseph, Augie is caught, but now at the level of impulse, between community and individuality. "Kindly explain!" Augie says. "An independent fate, and love too—what confusion!" Like Joseph, Augie rejects the last shift of ideal constructions. Humanity is made up of millions of artists and inventors all inventing versions of the real. "But the invented things never became real for me," Augie says, "no matter how I urged myself to think they were." And like Joseph, who had wrestled with the question of "a separate destiny" and found it insoluble, Augie is unable to find a principle of reconciliation between himself and others.

But unlike Joseph, Augie is provided with quick emotional responsiveness, with equipment for experiencing the universe and others, and that once again makes the difference of precluding either romantic isolation or romantic surrender. Augie is feelingly alive, and, like Asa Leventhal, he is ineluctably a part of an ordinary, felt social reality. Because he is alive, he must live and live with his confusion. If the principle of reconciliation is not at hand, still the act of living demands that its possibility be always considered. The hope for reconciliation, finally, is the principle of Augie's livingness, and it is his fate. After many adventures in hard usage by the world and then within a marriage that is an incomplete compact, that hope is his last word:

> Look at me, going everywhere! Why, I am a sort of Columbus of those near-at-hand and believe you can come to them in this immediate *terra incognita* that spreads out in every gaze. I may well be a flop at this line of endeavor. Columbus too thought he was a flop, probably, when they sent him back in chains. Which didn't prove there was no America.

The reconciliation is effected, but in quite another mood, in *Seize the Day* (1956). Tommy Wilhelm is, like Asa Leventhal, a suffering fat man, but he is a man this time at an extremity of isolation—a perfect slob, unkempt, unsanitary, a hippopotamus, and emotionally a slob too, full of whining, demanding pity and the world's love, nursing his hurts. He is so repulsive to the world that not to find a means of involvement in it will at the next turn mean death. All the obvious means—living in the world's assigned role, with marriage, family, money—have already failed him. He has in the past been an actor, provided, as his agent had advised him, with an opportunity to be the world's lover—cast by his agent as the type that loses the girl—but such extravagant saintliness, such loving so removed from his privacy, and such a denial of his inescapable self, were beyond his capability. He did not become a Hollywood star. His marriage has ended in separation. His father dislikes him.

Moreover, he has lost his job, and on this day of days in

which the novel finds him, he will lose the last of his money
and his place therefore in the world's business. A stranger
even to his hotel clerk, cast as a swine before Mr. Perls, beyond rapport with Mr. Rappaport, a stranger to everyone he
meets, displaced, baffled, rejected, and shamed, no more now
than a soup of flesh and whisky—he speculates at the Com-
modities Market in the futures of lard and rye, which is to
say in his own future—he encounters this day all the broken
ends of his attempted engagements with the world. He has
precisely Augie's confusion, but he has tested its terms more
desperately and he is face to face now with loss of the whole
world and of his own soul, too. His salvation is Dr. Tamkin.
Tamkin, another theorizer, overbears Tommy anew, with
metaphysical rant in amalgamated English. He is an oddball
and a crackpot, a jerk, an operator, and a swindler, but he
knows well what gives, and the truth is in him.

That truth is threefold. It begins in the realization that
every man has to love something or somebody. "He feels,"
says Tamkin, "that he must go outward. 'If thou canst not
love, what art thou?' Are you with me?" Tommy is with him
and he learns secondly that a kind of love, the most usual
and the kind in which Tommy has dealt, is inverted vanity
and death to the true soul. That is the love, says Tamkin,
that is "the same as the interest of the social life, the society
mechanism." It panders to the love of the dying, and:

> The love of the dying amounts to one thing; they want
> you to die with them. It's because they love you. Make no
> mistake.

The third and final stage of the truth is the possibility of
loving, and living too. It is a matter of necessary belief in
the beneficence of life, if not in that of the universe. Augie
before this had discovered in himself a feeling about "the

axial lines of life, with respect to which you must be straight," and Tamkin pronounces:

Creative is nature. Rapid. Lavish. Inspirational. It shapes leaves. It rolls the waters on the earth. Man is the chief of this. All creations are his just inheritance. You don't know what you've got within you.

The final truth is in the simple giving way to one's humanness, accepting the doom of one's burdens but seizing the indisputable lavish life within one here and now. That giving way allows life in a dying humanity, and the seizing of existence confers value upon life.

Seizing the day is, moreover, as Tommy learns in the last resonating adventure of his day, the principle of reconciliation, an act of love itself. Finding himself shuffled into someone else's funeral, and now after intimations of death all day long face to face with the thing itself, he weeps at the bier of a stranger. Heavy sea-like music pours into him, he sinks deeper than sorrow, and through torn sobs he moves "toward the consummation of his heart's ultimate need." That need, the whole of the novel comes to reveal, is the need not to die. The corpse is the tutelary Tamkin's last appearance or it is his successor, and it forces Tommy to a moment of *Angst:* at the point of death, he realizes existence, the "true self," the vitality which all men share, and which defines men. Tommy's weeping is an acceptance of life and therefore an act of love toward life within an acceptance of death. And the acceptance presents Tommy with a place in the world.

The progress of Bellow's sensible hero from alienation to accommodation has become in *Seize the Day* a progress of the soul through its freedom, from isolation to affirmation of ordinary life in the world. Joseph too had struggled within his "freedom" and had, tentatively, found a ground of community in what he assumed to be a universal quest for pure freedom, but it is not until Tommy weeps for his corpse that the strong sense of existence chosen becomes the condition for life itself.

The soul's progress toward life is recapitulated in the first movement of *Henderson the Rain King* (1959), once again in terms of a suffering fat man who comes upon a quirky philosopher. But the fat man is now lifted to gigantism (collar size twenty-two) and provided even in his suffering with burlesque and also with Augie's sprawling exuberance. "I am to suffering what Gary is to smoke," Henderson says, "one of the world's biggest operations." Full of suffering, full of violence and death, and surrounded by annunciations of death, Henderson goes off to a fantastic Africa to find a cure for the spiritual disease that has made him a pig among men and, in the words of the chorus always at his lips, despised and rejected, a man of sorrows and acquainted with grief. The disease is death itself, and it has many symptoms. "Oh, it's miserable to be human," Henderson wails. "You get such queer diseases."

> Just because you're human and for no other reason. Before you know it, as the years go by, you're just like other people you have seen, with all those peculiar human ailments. Just another vehicle for temper and vanity and rashness and all the rest. Who wants it? Who needs it? These things occupy the place where a man's soul should be. . . . Lust, rage, and all the rest of it. A regular bargain basement of deformities. . . .

A voice in the basement, Henderson's soul, meanwhile cries out, "I want," and it is the first part of Henderson's cure to be told by an ancient African queen, *"Grun-tu-molani,"* man wants to live. When he hears that message, Henderson's heart fills with joy.

It is the monition, now explicit, that moved Tommy Wilhelm to his heart's ultimate need. But Henderson is a hero. He is huge, ridden by high energies and lofty ambitions, and equipped therefore for the discovery that the principle of reconciliation is not enough. He needs further adventures, as the principle needs extension. Man wants to live, but in what shape and form? The communal principle fails Henderson as soon as he learns it, when, in an impetuous gesture of good will, attempting to rid a cistern of frogs, he blows up his host's water supply. The idea of community imposes the idea of service and Henderson possesses that idea fiercely. He would make men better, and free them from the law of decay. His passion for service must, however, be chastened and trained, and his further adventures under the tutelage of an African king, who is part Wilhelm Reich, part Zarathustra, and part King David, provide him with just that spiritual exercise. He is put by King Dahfu of the Wariri to lessons in self-transcendence. He must learn to contain humiliations. He must overcome fear, and finally, in a dungeon, set on all fours by King Dahfu and made to roar like a lion, he must give issue to the soul's bellow thus to rid himself of the demanding self. Like Zarathustra descending from the mountain, he must empty himself in order to become a man again. Having done it, Henderson can return to Connecticut, to his wife, and he can make plans to enter medical school.

It is to some Nietzschean terms precisely that the dialogue of *Dangling Man,* between alienation and accommodation, will come. The terms now, fifteen years after *Dangling Man,* are not strictly the same terms, but they are clearly consonant with their originals. They refer to the same problem, and the five novels show a remarkably strict struggle with it. An insoluble problem in alienation and accommodation yields in *The Victim* to a more tangible problem in responsibility. Its provisional resolution lies in acceptance of experience and it finds its comic expression in *Augie March*. *Seize the Day* locates and solves the problem in an existential conception—*Angst*—and *Henderson* brings the isolated hero into functional activity in the community. The problem since the beginning has been in the distance between the individual and others. It is a problem, that is to say, when given wide social significances, in the bases of social conduct. When given immediate significances, it is a problem in love.

To say so much is to define Bellow's achievement thus far as a coherent progress in a strenuous formal speculation. The problem, in these years when "conformity" has become a malediction even in popular literature of self-help, and "alienation" has become a critical directive, has been conspicuously available and Bellow has made hard fiction out of it.

But the novels are not logical constructs, nor are they "philosophical" novels in the way that *The Magic Mountain* and *La Nausee* * are philosophical novels. The fiction is not made for the sake of the argument. With the exception of

* I am in agreement with an Italian critic, Piero Sanavio, who in the course of a general article on Bellow makes a detailed comparison between *Dangling Man* and *La Nausee,* and then finds it necessary to emphasize that for Bellow the novel comes before the philosophy. "The relevant thing, however, is that while Sartre's character moves first of all among 'metaphysical' situations, where for example the 'sordid' is not part of the 'human element,' but a projection of a philosophical dimension (that is, a symbolic translation of it), in Bellow's book . . . it is the same philosophical dimension that becomes a human fact: indeed, the 'suspense' of the protagonist is first of all physical, a real and temporary fact, his isolation is provoked from the outside, not obtained by his own choice. . . ." "Il Romanzo di Saul Bellow," *Studi Americani,* No. 2, pp. 263–64.

The Victim, the novels are not even well-made. They spill over on themselves, they work themselves out according to the demands of character, and if they deal finally, with great subtlety, in a conspicuous issue, it is not because Bellow has studied the issue as such. The novels have their novelistic failures—*Dangling Man* is enclosed and short of action, Augie's exuberance runs down in the middle and becomes repetitive, Henderson suffers turgidity among his other sufferings—but they are never either journalistic or pedagogic. They work themselves *out* toward thematic statement. Indeed, Bellow's work has been exciting precisely because at every turn it has been shaped by a pressure of personal commitment, by an imagination confronting human needs which spill all over themselves and which yield to clarity only after heavy labor. Before the work has been about the alienated individual struggling toward accommodation, it has been about the individual personality filled with its own chaos and set down in the chaotic circumstances and the obscure obligations of the ordinary world. It is his large awareness of the chaos and his powerful intimate response to it that has first of all given Bellow's work its life and its importance.

The alienated hero before he is alienated is a terribly oppressed individual, and it is with the feeling of his oppression that Bellow's fiction begins. Human beings crowd upon Bellow's hero and attempt to subjugate him. Human beings threaten his freedom, his self, and become burdensome to him. And, indeed, it is not only those others who directly assault him who threaten his freedom. He begins in a condition of individuality imperiled and his career is a series of adventures through a metropolis of perils. Bellow's hero lives among clutter, boredom, distraction, things—as well as among the constant solicitors and recruiters. "Things done by man overshadow us," says Augie. "And this is true also of meat on the table, heat in the pipes, print on the paper, sounds in the air, so that all matters are alike, of the same weight, of the same rank, the caldron of God's wrath on page one and Wieboldt's sale on page two." Augie's complaint is diagnosed as *moha,* opposition of the finite, a curious complaint which is the beginning of Augie and of all the other Bellovian protagonists.

It is the sheer weight of chaotic existence that first of all defines Bellow's hero. "The novelist is distracted," Bellow says in an essay called "Distractions of a Fiction Writer." [1] "There are more things that solicit the attention of the mind than there ever were before." The novelist is menaced with "death by distraction," and not only the novelist, but everyone on every level is exposed to the danger.

It is out of that sensibility that the hero is born.

We are menaced by the sheer distraction of sheer wealth. "The world is too much with us, and there has never been so much world," Bellow has said elsewhere. We have so much money now and we are offered so very many possessions. "Love, duty, principle, thought, significance, everything is being sucked into a fatty and nerveless state of well-being." [2] The fat gods of the new materialism are all about us demanding our energies, and the truth about the reign of the fat gods, Bellow has said in still another instance, is that "it destroys and consumes everything, it covers the human image with deadly films, it undermines all quality with its secret rage, it subverts everything good and exalts lies, and on its rotten head it wears a crown of normalcy." [3] When that false-seeming has overborne all that one would want to call reality, the refuge of reality is in poverty. Indeed, scarcity is "the foundation of a system of reality which the rich share with the poor. . . . The lives of the poor move us, awaken compassion, but improvement of their lot merely by

the increase of goods and comforts deprives them of the sense
of reality. . . ." [4] In a more hopeful mood, Bellow has said that
we are only "temporarily miracle-sodden and feeling faint," [5]
but the lesson under the hopefulness is the same. We are
menaced by the clutter of things, and of humanity, too.

It is to the point that Bellow, unlike the past masters
Hemingway and Faulkner, is entirely a city writer. (*Henderson* takes place mostly in Africa, to be sure, but not in the
green hills of Africa. It is an Africa teeming with people and
political intrigue and with furniture, an Africa urbanized.)
In the city there is much more to contend with. Things and
others both are close and thick in Bellow's novels and, though
Bellow is not without affection for nature, there is no escape
into rural simplicities. In urban circumstances the rites of
love are enormously difficult. Bellow's cities—Chicago and
New York—are dense with neighbors and noise, with street-
cars, subways, families, friends, soot, and filth. Joseph, living
in a six-sided box within a Chicago rooming house, is victimized by the old man next door who coughs all night, leaves
the door to the toilet open, steals socks, and throws empty
whisky bottles into the alley. *The Victim* begins: "On some
nights New York is as hot as Bangkok," and then all the
gagging heaviness of a New York summer, the light of the
sun like "the yellow revealed in the slit of the eye of a wild
animal," the subways, the sweat, the listless crowds in the
parks, the invincible dirt, the struggle for air, bears down
upon Asa Leventhal's burden of guilt.

Augie's Chicago, while it spawns heroic vitalists, is what
he calls it in his first sentence, a "somber city." Those vitalists are all Machiavellians,* omnipresent, dangerous, reaching

---

* A fragment of *Augie March* which appeared in *Partisan Review* in
1949 is identified as "the first chapter of a novel entitled 'Life Among
the Machiavellians.' "

out with too many clever hands. The somber city provides neither a recollection of Edenic childhood nor expectation of heaven. Augie is set down into "deep city vexation" and "forced early into deep city aims," and "what," he wants to know, "can that lead to of the highest?" His initiation into love is of the kind the city affords, love paid for and second-hand. "That's what city life is. And so it *didn't* have the luster it should have had, and there *wasn't* any epithalamium of gentle lovers. . . ." The character and the fate which are Augie's study are located first in his response to the enormity and complexity of Chicago. "Crusoe," he says, "alone with nature, under heaven, had a busy, complicated time of it with the unhuman itself, and I am in a crowd that yields results with much more difficulty and reluctance and am part of it myself."

The clutter of the city weighs upon and shapes Tommy Wilhelm and Eugene Henderson too. His existence lies upon Tommy Wilhelm like a hump, and he is "assigned to be the carrier of a load which was his own self," but it makes a difference that he must carry it along upper Broadway on a summer's day. On a day after sleepless, noisy New York nights, through the dust of the street and the fumes of buses, through "pushcarts, accordion and fiddle, shoeshine, begging, the dust going round like a woman on stilts," and talking to himself because there is no one else to talk to among the millions of a city like New York. "The traffic seemed to come down Broadway out of the sky, where the hot spokes of the sun rolled from the south. Hot, stony odors rose from the subway grating in the street." And when Tamkin, the confidence man, a deity of this inferno, tells Tommy that the world is full of murderers, Tommy answers helplessly that "there are also kind, ordinary, helpful people. They're—out in the country."

Henderson does go out into the country, first as gentleman
pig farmer, then as an African explorer, but the spirit, the
heat, the humanity, and the junk of the city are always
at his back. His farm becomes a pig kingdom swarming with
grunting animals. The city's steaming pavement becomes the
strange, obscurely threatening "calcareous" rocks of King
Dahfu's country. The heat of the city becomes the boiling
African sun, felt as the jungle fever which oppresses Henderson throughout his spiritual adventuring. Tamkin is re-
created in Dahfu, king of the warlike Wariri, another prince
of darkness. The clotted Broadway crowd becomes the
frenzied savages who batter Henderson to his knees in the
ceremony in which he becomes the Rain King. Henderson abandons things and people to make the trip into
Africa.

It is the idea of junk, indeed, that is the immediate motive
of his going. Climbing through the rooms of an old lady
just dead, he is overwhelmed by her collected rubbish:
"Bottles, lamps, old butter dishes, and chandeliers were on
the floor, shopping bags filled with string and rags, and
pronged openers that the dairies used to give away to lift the
paper tops from milk bottles; and bushel baskets full of but-
tons and china door knobs." And he thinks, "Henderson,
put forth effort. You, too, will die of this pestilence. Death
will annihilate you and nothing will remain, and there will
be nothing left but junk."

He puts forth effort to escape, but the city stays with him
none the less. In Africa he talks city talk: "Now listen, Your
Highness, don't sell me down the river. You know what I
mean? I thought you liked me." He thinks, in Africa, in
city metaphors and of city events. The city maintains its
pressure, and alive within his other speculations is the city
idea of other people, nameless, faceless, billions of other

people with whom no communication is possible. Tommy Wilhelm was condemned to talk to himself in a city where every other man spoke a language entirely his own, and Henderson is brought to the vision of Babel raised to include the universe: "This planet has billions of passengers on it, and those were preceded by infinite billions and there are vaster billions to come, and none of those, no, not one, can I hope ever to understand. Never!" He goes on to reflect that this matter of quantity, come upon in another view, need not bury you alive, that it is marvelous and not depressing, but that reflection comes of his struggle and not of his primary condition.

Under the mass of such quantity and confronted by such chaos in the external world, Bellow's hero in his first motion moves toward unburdening and sloughing off. Civil society is too much, and indeed, in extreme moments, even the cultural accumulations, the very history and wisdom of civilization, are too much and are rejected. Most emphatically by the aging wise man, another Zarathustrian prophet, of Bellow's monologue called "Address by Gooley MacDowell to the Hasbeens Club of Chicago":

Around our heads we have a dome of thought as thick as atmosphere to breathe. And what's about? One thought leads to another as breath leads to breath. By pulling [it] into universal consciousness, can [we] explain everything from Democritus to Bikini? But a person can no longer keep up, and plenty are dying of good ideas. We have them in the millions, in compilations, from the *Zend Avesta* to now, all on file with the best advice for [one] and all human occasions. . . . Look at us, deafened, hampered, obstructed, impeded, impaired and bowel-glutted with wise counsel and good precept, and the more plentiful our ideas the worse our headaches. So we ask, will some good creature pull out the plug and ease our disgusted hearts a little? [6]

It is a prayer Augie, too, records: "Anyway, there's too much of everything of this kind, *that's* come home to me, too much history and culture to keep track of, too many details, too much news, too much example, too much influence, too many guys who tell you to be as they are, and all this hugeness, abundance, turbulence, Niagara Falls torrent. Which who is supposed to interpret? Me?" Then Tommy Wilhelm is overcome by the sheer quantity of information in Tamkin's discourses, and Henderson, a millionaire, fills beautiful pieces of architecture with pigs and then, seeking Eden, makes a safari to the pre-civilized past, "the real past," he says, "no history or junk like that." And if all history and culture are rejected in a style that borrows widely from the world's accumulation of literature, that fact is more than an irony. Bellow's style, which beginning with *Augie March* has become a racy vehicle bearing great freights of knowledge, is a thing that simultaneously admits and dismisses clutter. All its process of literary echoing goes to lend the rejection authority.

Since the beginning all Bellow's heroes have started in a gesture of escape from burdens, an extreme romantic gesture. It is a gesture which, it happens, in its extremity brings Bellow into touch with one of the defining impulses of American character, into touch with at least all the classic Redskins of American letters, from Leatherstocking to Whitman to Mark Twain to Hemingway, all those who light out for the woods, the open road, the Territory. (And perhaps he is in touch with the Palefaces, too. The extreme need to escape burdens, to be free of all the clutter, it may be argued, is as well a distinction of Hawthorne and Henry James.) Bellow's hero is tempted frequently to epiphanies of love for mankind in general, though never for things, and his motion is brought to various thematic significances, but he is in the first instance activated by the need to rid himself of the weight of the chaos and clutter outside.

He might escape into harmony with natural laws vaguely realized as beneficent, or he might escape into himself, locate all value and reality in his person, or he might in various ways attempt to reconcile himself with external existence in all its chaos. And it is from these three possibilities, the first two stretching toward the last, that all the action of Bellow's novels has come.

Nature is not ever, either as a metaphysical conception or in the allure of its phenomena, dominant as a motif in the fiction, although it has become more emphatic as the novels have succeeded each other. Bellow's city imagination is not comfortable with the natural laws. He has little nature to bring to them. But his hero entertains a yearning for them and a provisional trust that they are good, because the circumscription of the possibility of escape demands it. Joseph dismisses "nature" when it is presented to him by a friend who complains of the treelessness and the too-human deadness of New York—dismisses it as nostalgic sentimentality. Nevertheless his whole struggle toward what he calls the "facts of simple existence" is involved in a turn of the seasons toward fruitful harmony. The death and disorder of winter submit to spring. Joseph begins his journal in the dark Chicago December and surrenders himself, relieves himself of his freedom, in April. Bellow accents the matter by having Joseph look forward throughout his winter to walking in the park in his spring coat on the twenty-first of March, and he shifts the mood of the novel toward resolution with the coming of spring.

Asa Leventhal, next, locked in New York's inhuman heat,
has moments of freshness and deep breathing at sea on the
Staten Island Ferry, and the plot of the novel moves him
toward the relief that will come with Labor Day. Allbee's
attempted suicide on the eve of that day makes possible
Leventhal's birth into a possible world and the day itself
brings cooling breezes. Nature as transcendent reality brushes
Leventhal lightly once—for a brief moment of half-sleep he
feels the whole world present to him and about to offer him a
mysterious, it would seem redeeming, discovery. But the discovery blows by him and at the end of his action, having
abandoned ultimate questioning and now re-entering a dark-
ened theater with his wife, he is no closer to a notion of
reality.

But Augie comes, if not conclusively, at least wholeheartedly
to the natural laws, his "axial lines" called "Truth, love, peace,
bounty, usefulness, harmony!" which, he says, quiver right
through him when striving stops. They excite him in the next
moment after his perception of them to pastoral ambitions.
He wants to own and settle on a Midwestern farm, to marry,
and to teach orphans. His adventures carry him, however,
into complexities which won't permit cessation of striving.
The axial lines, he says, are "not imaginary stuff . . . because
I bring my entire life to the test." There is no doubting his
sincerity, but this is one of the moments when Augie's hopefulness becomes shrill. His whole life does not validate the
perception. The novel does not earn that leap into faith. In
fact the novel is honest beyond Augie's knowing and it does
not permit him so easy an escape. Nor is it an escape that
Tommy Wilhelm, so strictly confined by authentic troubles,
can practically afford to take. He cannot, anyway, take it
in its romantic simplicity. Tamkin's offer of eternally creative
nature, rapid, lavish, and inspirational, is of itself no solace

to a middle-aged slob rapidly and lavishly dying in the middle of New York City. Tommy is simply confused by the offer.

It is Henderson who most clearly moves toward harmony with the natural laws. He goes among noble savages and to live with the beasts in the field, and if his Africa has the feel of Chicago and the smell of New York, that is apparently despite Bellow's first intention. On the other hand it is Henderson who most clearly demonstrates the naïveté of the escape into nature. That is by no means the total meaning of his safari, but he does make a journey into the heart of darkness to discover the horror of it. He goes to Africa to discover Reality, Reality as an Idea. That is what the voice within him that says "I want" ultimately wants. "Truth" and "Reality" are ambitions always at his lips. His soul's progress is marked by a succession of emblematic beasts.* At first a porcine pig farmer in a sty of piggish phenomena, he comes in the first stage of his journey upon a motley tribe of pious

---

* Fables perhaps can't be novels. *Henderson* sacrifices some density of dramatic texture to its emblematic play with beasts, as it sacrifices some sound and smell to an elaboration, throughout, of symbolic constructs. It was perhaps Bellow's own apprehension of this certain thinness for the sake of symbols that led him to publish, in the week of *Henderson's* appearance, an assault on symbolic reading and readers. "Perhaps," he said, "the deepest readers are those who are least sure of themselves. An even more disturbing suspicion is that they prefer meaning to feeling. . . . Novels are being published today which consist entirely of abstractions, meanings, and while our need for meanings is certainly great our need for concreteness, for particulars, is even greater." "Deep Readers of the World, Beware!" *New York Times Book Review*, Feb. 15, 1959, pp. 1, 34. Nevertheless, *Henderson* remains a book made of symbols, shot through with meanings and abstractions, and having some consequent lack of concreteness. Indeed, the book cannot be understood, as some of its reviewers pointed out, except symbolically. See Elizabeth Hardwick, "A Fantastic Voyage," *Partisan Review*, XXVI (Spring 1959), 302; Keith Waterhouse, "Literary Lions," *New Statesman*, LVII (June 6, 1959), 806.

cow-worshipers, and then he tries to do what none of them
will do, to deal at first hand with a plague of frogs. He
fails, but in failing he has pursued nature to a certain depth.
His next, and most important, stop, with a tribe of lion-
worshipers, brings him face to face with the thing itself. Under
the tutelage of Dahfu—himself a refugee from civilization
come home to meet Reality—Henderson is put to the task
(following disciplines derived from the somatic psychology
of Wilhelm Reich)[7] of assuming and absorbing Dahfu's pet
lioness. She is all lion, Dahfu observes. "Does not take issue
with the inherent. Is one hundred per cent within the given."
She is the way to Being, the end of Becoming, the unchanging
truth prior to the cycle of desire and fear. She will force
Henderson to the present moment. "She will make consciousness to shine. She will burnish you."

She *is* Being—or, as it turns out, penultimate Being—
itself. And Henderson has some small success in overcoming
his fear of the lioness and then in absorbing lion-ness. He
meets the inhuman thing, in the same way, it happens, and
within the same image as previous Bellow heroes had met it
—Asa had seen the yellow of the sun like that in the slit of
the eye of a wild animal, "say a lion, something inhuman
that didn't care about anything human and yet was implanted
in every human being, too," and Augie had had adventures
with the lion's American equivalent, his eagle with "the
pressed-down head, the killing eye, the deep life of its feathers.
Oy!" But Henderson goes further. The lion is pure fire, he
says, which forces him to close his eyes. So are the stars pure
fire, he realizes, and not small gold objects. He develops his
consciousness of the matter beyond ways that are permitted
Asa and Augie. He discovers that the inhuman fire is at the
center of his humanity too.

With that discovery he should achieve harmony. Here is the

very principle of Augie's axial lines. But Henderson is hurried to a further pitch of Reality. Dahfu's lion is a pet lioness after all. Henderson is now made to confront the authentic lion, male and wild:

> Then, at the very door of consciousness, there was a snarl and I looked down from this straw perch . . . into the big, angry, hair-framed face of the lion. It was all wrinkled, contracted; within those wrinkles was the darkness of murder. The lips were drawn away from the gums, and the breath of the animal came over me, hot as oblivion, raw as blood. I started to speak aloud. I said, "Oh, my God, whatever You think of me, let me not fall under this butcher shop. . . ." And to this, as a rider, the thought added itself that this was all mankind needed, to be conditioned into the image of a ferocious animal like the one below.

That lion castrates and kills King Dahfu. The voice of the lion is the voice of death itself. And this Real, far from being an escape from chaos, is chaos and old night itself. To submit to the harmony it offers, on the principle that the lion outside is inside too, would be to accept the inhumanity of the inhuman Real. Henderson had in one of his discourses with Dahfu parried Eliot by saying that humankind could not stand too much *un*reality, but Eliot wins the point. Henderson now reflects on the great inescapable rhythms of life, Augie's axial lines once again, but he reflects that he can't afford to worry about them. The old queen's advice, "*Gruntu-molani*," man wants to live, comes to mean going about the business of living despite the death-dealing, chaotic Real.

That is very much, if not explicitly, the ground upon which Augie had finally mounted his optimism. If Augie is only incidentally concerned with the nature of the real Real, he is completely engaged with the natural laws as they impinge

on his larky and boisterous freedom, and the *animal ridens*
rises in him despite their influences. His adventures are
escapes from all determinisms, human and superhuman. And
that is the ground upon which Tommy Wilhelm, also made
to confront ultimate reality as death, had been able to choose
to live. The escape from under the weight of external chaos
into the natural laws does not work. It is no escape at all.
At the center of the universe are violence and death, and
the vague yearning for the natural laws lucent in the earlier
novels is quite extinguished when the fiction works it out to
the test.

There is an alternative dodge for Bellow's oppressed hero in
the assertion of his own character as the locus of reality and
value. In the face of cluttering chaos and with a swagger, he
can assert personality broadly. "A man's character is his fate,
says Heraclitus," says Augie with relishing approval, and if
at the end he learns that a man's fate is his character, why,
that is a fate good enough for him. Tamkin, besides being
something of almost everything else that it is possible for a
man to be, is a most minor poet, and he advises Tommy:

> Seek ye then that which art not there
> In thine own glory let thyself rest.
> Witness. Thy power is not bare.
> Thou art King. Thou art at thy best.

It is advice under which Tommy staggers. The hero of one
of Bellow's short stories, "The Trip to Galena," [8] a young man
engaged in a war against the overburdening boredom of
things and people, proposes that "a man is bound to do everything in his lifetime." He will conduct war by the simple
exertion of personality. And Henderson, whose person is explicitly reflected in his body, is great and joyous in his body.
His very suffering delights him because it is an exercise of

personality. At the center of the universe, then, in this action, is the individual self—the self constantly threatened, however, and presenting an obligation. Bellow's hero will protect his personality from the outside or, because he can't live in a nut-shell, insinuate it in and out of chaotic experience, but main-tain it, attempt to maintain it, unbroken.

At the end the assertion is merely another dodge, and the escape is blocked precisely because the inhuman outside *is* within—that, finally, is why "alienation" is impossible. Nor can personality remain untouched. The attempt at self-pro-tection raises severe moral problems. And at the end the person must indeed be broken in order to achieve meaningful life. But the motion of the escape meanwhile irradiates Bel-low's writing. It is the inspiration of his comedy. Because the need is desperate, the assertion of the person is extreme—with *Augie March* and thereafter, though there are hints of the mood before, the assertion is raised to burlesque.

Bellow's personalist hero yelps, quite the gamecock of a new, urban wilderness, quite like his backwoodsman proto-type impelled to brashness by dispossession and inadequacy and the feeling of threatening powers everywhere. He sings himself with quite the same nervy insolence with which Walt Whitman met the world, and like that witty comedian he makes a great gesture of including the whole world in himself but then remains unmarred by it and adopts shifts and eva-sions and contrarieties to remain free of it. And like Walt Whitman, he celebrates himself by the exercise of a free-wheeling, inclusive, cataloguing rhetoric, gripping great bunches of facts in sentences that just manage to balance, racing through various levels of diction, saying with every turn, "Look at me, going everywhere!" It is a gaudy fire-works of a style, in itself a brilliant affirmation of the self, and at the same time it performs the ironic function, by its calculated indiscriminateness, in Bellow and in Walt Whitman too, of discarding everything it picks up. It is therefore the perfect expression of the dynamic, disengaging, mock-heroic hero.

Dahfu accuses Henderson of being a great avoider, and the same accusation may be made against all of Bellow's personalists. Augie is the clearest instance. His "availability" is the flamboyant self-asserting part of him, but it is perfectly and in every engagement countered by his "opposition." At the end he still has all his availability. His great appetite for life and engagement is intact precisely because he has spent it in no experience. At the end he is presented taking what amounts to still another oath of unsusceptibility to all the "big personalities, destiny molders, and heavy-water brains, Machiavellis and wizard evildoers, big-wheels and imposers-upon, absolutists." But the oath is redundant. His unsusceptibility is continuous. Indeed it is a moral failing, and one which Augie is made to realize. The one advice by his many advisers which cuts deep is that he can't be hurt enough by the fate of other people. That is a failing in love and the most strenuous part of Augie's action is in the problem it poses, but it is a failing he never rectifies. To do so would stop him cold.

Augie is a kind of Huck Finn, with what he calls his something adoptional about him, with his participation in a linear series of adventures, his resilience, his mounting good humor. Readers have made the comparison.[9] But he is like Huck too in his reluctance to be civilized. He eludes. He is not to be caught by the shaping influences. He won't be determined. Moreover, he is Huck confined to a city populated by endless duplications of the Duke and the Dauphin, and—no matter that his adventures take him over two continents, he is always in Chicago—without a Territory to light out for, and so he is put to more muscular shifts of duplicity. What the Mississippi and the Territory could do for Huck, Augie must do for himself. His only territory is his personality, which he must keep free. Life is dynamic for Augie, it is process, and the process is that kind of evasion that keeps all events and the person from settling.

A new discipline and another idea of the possibilities of freedom will be needed by the personalist hero who is to avoid evasion and be hurt enough by the fate of other people. Bellow comes to it, but the strong assertion of independent personality secures all of Bellow's lyricism, before and after Augie, and indeed it is not restricted to his protagonists. Radical self-assertion, real assertion of the real, untypical self, is an act of courage in his squeezing world. There is glamour in it which just for itself for the moment transvalues all moral obligations. It commands Bellow's love even for the very Machiavellians he loathes—sometimes, it should be added, with the disastrous result of turning them quaint.

Almost in the very beginning, in 1942, with his second published story, "The Mexican General," [10] there was the first of Bellow's line of resolutely vital knaves. The General is a provincial opportunist who has secured his opportunity with the assassination of Trotsky. He is an arrogant ghoul, well mistressed, a vile entrepreneur at the funeral of the Revolution, and he is made to bear a moral of political corruption. But he is also equipped with Lawrentian innuendoes of personality—he has Indian vigor, he is alive, he has personal force, he is an *Übermensch* just not yet attained to moral transcendence, and the pale moral sophisticate of the story is reduced by him to fascinated helplessness. There is no doubt that the Mexican General is intended as a villain, but, perhaps despite his intentions, Bellow celebrates him.

There will be many like him, with variations in virtue.

Kirby Allbee in *The Victim*, and incidental chieftains, the patriarch Schlossberg, the matriarch Mrs. Harkavy, then Augie's Grandma Lausch and Augie's "first superior man," William Einhorn, and indeed every one of the thirty-odd other Machiavellians in his adventures, then Dr. Tamkin, then King Dahfu with his "strong gift of life" and his extra shadow-casting intensity, and Henderson himself—they are all, if not reincarnations of the General, at least related to him. The descendants inhabit Bellow's shorter pieces as well: plays, stories, monologues, and a curious and festive interview with Joe "Yellow Kid" Weil, an aged oligarch among both the Chicago confidence men and the Chicago intellectuals of Bughouse Square, "an elegant and old-fashioned gentleman" of "round phrases and leisurely speech," a reader of Nietzsche and Herbert Spencer, a masterful man who has refused to be society's obedient slave.[11]

The virtue in the exercise of personality for its own sake is clearly a virtue derived from necessity. It is derived as well from the lessons in necessity inherent in one tradition of Yiddish literature—Bellow has shown a more than passing interest in that literature [12]—the tradition of what has been called *dos kleine menschele*,[13] the little man of the Eastern European ghetto, the *shtetl*, who is forced by the presence of perils everywhere to ingenious ways of personal survival.

One of those ways is in mock-heroism. Yiddish conversation itself, a vessel of the spirit that produced *dos kleine menschele*, is, Bellow himself has said,

> . . . full of the grandest historical, mythological, and religious allusions. The Creation, the Fall, the Flood, Egypt, Alexander, Titus, Napoleon, the Rothschilds, the sages, and the Laws may get into the discussion of an egg, a clothesline, or a pair of pants.[14]

The mock-heroic conversation of Augie and his major successors, it is obvious, is full of the same, sprouting comparative references, to heroes from Jacob to Caesar to John Dillinger to Sir Wilfred Grenfell, to epical events from the Diaspora to the campaigning events of World War II.

This manner of living on terms of familiarity with greatness, Bellow goes on to say, contributed to the ghetto's sense of the ridiculous. But it must have performed a feat of more delicate irony than that, and one to which Bellow would seem to be sensitive. On the one hand, the mock-heroics of the little man renders all conventional heroism absurd, as does that of both Bellow's protagonists and antagonists. But theirs is far from the mock-heroic of tradition, that of Chaucer and Rabelais and Swift. It is not practiced with such broad and easy security. It is, on the other hand, itself real heroism, a mode of strong self-assertion in a community that disallows the self. Given the prison of restrictive circumstances of the *shtetl*, and then those of Bellow's city, it is the one mode by which personal identity can be emphasized at all. Augie's mythical mouthfuls provide rough fun, they burlesque his own bravado and dilute all pretension, but at the same time they call upon Julius Caesar and John Dillinger to witness his daring. There is courage in the insolence of it. The bravado is a thin mask for the bravery. Augie's frisky speech is the power he puts forth to win from all oppressive circumstances a right to exist.

The exercise of personality is everywhere in Bellow's world an act of courage, and the salvation of the self, whether by defiance or evasion, is an honored behavior. The self is where felt reality is, and where meaning may be. Still, the rocks upon which simple exulting personality would founder were discovered at the beginning. Joseph began his journal in defiance of what he called that American asceticism of hardboiledom which does not allow the exhibition of personality, and his whole struggle was for the means by which the self might be preserved in a time of death, but he comes upon the disappointing fact first of his own baseness and then on the necessity of goodness in community. Alone and allowed to test his dreadful freedom, he becomes irritable, self-indulgent, oversensitive, quarrelsome. Perhaps he has not achieved the highest freedom. Freedom should be the condition of dignity. But, meanwhile, he does not know what to do with the freedom he has.

His free self becomes burdensome to him, and he has a continuous lesson in the ultimate achievement of ordinary free selfhood in Vanaker, the lonely, disgusting old man next door, grunting, hacking, thieving, and smelling away his existence. It is when Joseph sees a rat scurrying through some garbage that he resolves to give up his freedom and his self. The self he has held so dear is an "imprisoning self," and the end of his speculation about "ideal constructions" is that the highest of them is that which *unlocks* the imprisoning self. Alienation is not to be made into a doctrine. The other side of freedom is isolation. Alienation is, moreover, morally reprehensible. "What we really want," Joseph discovers, "is to stop living so exclusively and vainly for our own sake, impure and unknowing, turning inward and self-fastened." Joseph's talent is "for being a citizen, or what is today called, most apologetically, a good man," and "goodness," he is forced to know, "is achieved not in a vacuum, but in the company of other men, attended by love."

The ideas of inherent baseness, of human nature sharing the bestiality of nature itself, and of love as an imperative, lurk everywhere for the hero. At some point in his adventuring each of Bellow's heroes finds the beast within. Asa Leventhal must wrestle with his own inhumanity. Augie is rich in spirit and rowdy, and he is unable to stay with his purest feelings. He is confronted by the last of his advisers with a vision of the human soul composed of secrets, lies, and diseases. Tommy Wilhelm is confronted by Tamkin's notion of a corrupting "pretender soul" turning all human beings into murderers. ("Yes, I think so too," says Tommy. "But personally . . . I don't feel like a murderer. I always try to lay off. It's the others who get me.") Henderson sees himself as a bargain basement of deformities, his whole existence proposed in metaphors of beasts. And in one short lyrical instance, in an Easter sermon by one of Bellow's quacky truth-telling rejuvenators, cannibalism is proposed as the law of love and life. "A Sermon by Doctor Pep" begins in a protest against hamburger, for the bad conscience in its disguise of the slain beast, and ends in a protest against the suicide by which a gentle humanity disguises its murders. Men must eat, and murder is the cost of civilization."[15] But that statement is merely ecstatic. Bellow's major heroes, compelled to live beyond the lyrical moment, confront the beast within and the human propensity to murder, but they cannot rest in their perception. They must each of them as well confront the moral conditions of civilization, the cost of which would seem to be precisely the self.

The cement of civilization is love, which is selflessness, and each of Bellow's protagonists is forced, like Augie, to suffer confusion between love and an independent fate. Not only that, he must strain to reconcile those opposites. That is what the struggle for "accommodation" comes to. Joseph strains and fails—or he ends not quite in failure but in a desperate attempt to reacquaint himself with ordinary communal reality. Asa Leventhal, a self-enclosed, self-righteous victim, is assaulted by the imperative of brotherhood, which at the end he cannot accept. But he does reach a large idea of what it is to be exactly human. An old man in the lavatory of a movie theater tells him that Boris Karloff is a law unto himself. One wouldn't be Boris Karloff. To be neither more nor less than human, Asa discovers, is to be "accountable in spite of many weaknesses," and with that discovery he achieves a tentative goodness. Augie, not hurt enough by the fate of other people, particularly fails the severe test of romantic love. The test, his affair with Thea, is most particularly rich in confusion—not only for Augie; Bellow too has groped his way through it. Thea's love is cannibalistic. But it is love nevertheless, a way of discovering other people, and if it is strange to Augie, Augie himself comes to admit that is his own fault.* The struggle for Augie is to make it less strange. And Tommy Wilhelm, and Henderson too, struggle to admit love to their freedom, to be themselves and at the same time to have a place in the human community.

Tommy Wilhelm at the last extremity of his need seizes the day and moves toward the consummation of his heart's ultimate need. But it is only with *Henderson* that a consummation has been achieved, achieved by a Nietzschean idea of heroic self-transcendence based on freedom, an idea that had been hinted in all the previous novels. Despite all circumstances of oppression, despite the violence of nature and the violence of men, despite the cocky, assertive "I," despite all determinisms and despite finitude and death, the individual is free and free to choose. He can become better.

Joseph felt that by some transcendent means human beings

---

* Thea says to him, "But perhaps love would be strange and foreign to you no matter which way it happened, and maybe you just don't want it." Augie, when he is given a moment for reflection, says, "And was it true, as she said, that love would appear strange to me no matter what form it took . . . ? I thought about it and was astonished at how much truth there actually was in this. Why, it was so! . . . And suddenly my heart felt ugly, I was sick of myself."

could distinguish themselves from brute things and he considered that the universal quest was for pure freedom, but the practical means to transcendence was not at hand. In *The Victim* the patriarch Schlossberg suggests as equal possibilities that man is "lousy and cheap" and that he has "greatness and beauty." If those are equal possibilities, then one *can choose*. The means of transcendence is at hand. And what would one choose? "Have dignity, you understand me?" he says. "Choose dignity." But for Asa there are practical difficulties. Augie's Einhorn preaches a doctrine of self-transformation, as does Augie himself, but only in passing. And Tamkin strenuously offers Tommy Wilhelm the possibility of choice. Tommy *can* seize the day and thereby choose life. But he is not yet offered nobility, a word much favored by Bellow and meaning the coalescence of selflessness and selfhood. The individual who would exert his freedom toward such transcendence will need great spiritual capabilities to begin with, and then hard discipline.

Henderson is the man and, in terms of a succession of metamorphoses, he gets such discipline.

By Bellow's own deliberation or by astonishing coincidence, Henderson's career follows with great closeness, with only one initial deviation, that of the spirit in the first parable of *Thus Spake Zarathustra*. Says Zarathustra:

Of three metamorphoses of the spirit I tell you: how the spirit becomes a camel; and the camel, a lion; and the lion, finally, a child.

There is much that is difficult for the spirit, the strong reverent spirit that would bear much: but the difficult and the most difficult are what its strength demands.

What is difficult? asks the spirit that would bear much, and kneels down like a camel wanting to be well loaded.

What is most difficult, O heroes, asks the spirit that would bear much, that I may take it upon myself and exult in my strength? Is it not humbling oneself to wound one's haughtiness? Letting one's folly shine to mock one's wisdom?

. . . Or is it this: feeding on the acorns and grass of knowledge and, for the sake of the truth, suffering hunger in one's soul?

. . . Or is it this: stepping into filthy waters when they are the waters of truth, and not repulsing cold frogs and hot toads?

Or is it this: loving those who despise us and offering a hand to the ghost that would frighten us?

Henderson is not a camel, but he is a strenuous spirit who would bear much and who demands the extremest test of his strength. He engages the Zarathustrian burdens of humility and folly. If he does not feed on acorns and grass, he raises and identifies with pigs that do, and suffers hunger in his soul. He does precisely, among the first of his African tribes, meet the test of frogs in the filthy waters, but without humility, and it is to his sorrow that he repulses them. And he strains to love those who despise and reject him.

Says Zarathustra:

All these most difficult things the spirit that would bear much takes upon itself: like the camel that, burdened, speeds into the desert, thus the spirit speeds into its desert.

In the loneliest desert, however, the second metamorphosis occurs: here the spirit becomes a lion who would conquer his freedom and be master in his own desert. Here he seeks out his last master: he wants to fight him and his last god; for ultimate victory he wants to fight with the great dragon.

Who is the great dragon whom the spirit will no longer call lord and god? "Thou shalt" is the name of the great dragon. But the spirit of the lion says, "I will." "Thou shalt" lies in his way, sparkling like gold, an animal covered with scales; and on every scale shines a golden "thou shalt."

. . . My brothers, why is there a need in the spirit for the lion? Why is not the beast of burden, which renounces and is reverent, enough?

To create new values—that even the lion cannot do; but the creation of freedom for oneself for new creation—that is within the power of the lion. The creation of freedom for oneself and a sacred "No" even to duty—for that, my brothers, the lion is needed. To assume the right to new values—that is the most terrifying assumption for a reverent spirit that would bear much. Verily, to him it is preying, and a matter for a beast of prey. He once loved "thou shalt" as most sacred: now he must find illusion and caprice even in the most sacred, that freedom from his love may become his prey: the lion is needed for such prey.

Henderson speeds from the meek, reverent, cow-worshiping Arnewi in the desert. In the desert he destroys himself, body and soul, in order to become a lion, and in the very process he learns something about the possibilities of self-transformation. He learns, moreover, what it is to contain one's freedom. The lion, Dahfu tells him, is pure Being. It is entirely itself, it is all unobliging will, and, heavy with the clutter of existence, on all sides oppressed, Henderson secures from it a way of confronting the oppressing, death-dealing universe. The lion is for Henderson, and Dahfu, the intensity of the self beyond all reverence, the avatar of freedom, and Henderson, as lion, looks forward to new creation.

Says Zarathustra:

But say, my brothers, what can the child do that even the lion could not do? Why must the preying lion still become a child? The child is innocence and forgetting, a new beginning, a game, a self-propelled wheel, a first movement, a sacred "Yes." For the game of creation, my brothers, a sacred "Yes" is needed: the spirit now wills his own will, and he who had been lost to the world now conquers his own world.

Of three metamorphoses of the spirit I have told you: how the spirit became a camel; and the camel, a lion; and the lion, finally a child.[16]

The last of Henderson's totems is the child he adopts on his plane back to America. The airplane makes a fueling stop and he runs with the child in his arms around the airport in Newfoundland. What Henderson has specifically newly found is his way back, after he had been lost to his ordinary world, but he comes back now in a new movement with a new will to creation: "I guess I felt it was my turn now to move, and so went running—leaping, leaping, pounding, and tingling over the pure white lining of the gray Arctic silence." He is a self-propelled wheel. And he is provided with a sacred "Yes." His service ideal, which had been crushed, has been newly invented, he will enter medical school, and his suicidal violence has been transformed to love.

Thus spake Zarathustra, and it is perhaps of note that Zarathustra at that time sojourned in the town that is called The Motley Cow.

But that is not to suggest anything programmatic about *Henderson*. The novel is not a manual for *Übermenschen*. If the Nietzschean parable is at the center of it, the parable is elaborated, indeed sportively elaborated. *Henderson* is a funny book and it goes off all sorts of ways. Nor is it the summit of a mountain of thought up which Bellow has ben scrabbling all these years. Bellow, too, has been larky and boisterous, full of strong assertions and apothegms which have the finality only of the fullest fiction, which crack on the next turn of events and mood.

And there will be other events.

The novels have unfolded, nevertheless, in a remarkably coherent way and within bounded terms. The issues within which they have worked have been given by these years, given indeed as slogans. "Alienation" and "accommodation," and also "conformity" and "autonomy," complacency and the new luxury, bigness and beatness, the new leisure, the new conservatism, the revival of religion, the nostalgia for radicalism— all these, so quickly wilted by overexposure, have determined the development of Bellow's fiction. That compact of over-journalized slogans after all contains crucial truth about these times. Quite within them, Bellow's novels have all this while been going somewhere—not, of course, toward any summit at all, nor toward any solution to anything. Bellow's domain for investigation finally is nothing less than the bases of all moral behavior, wherein one expects no solutions except by fiat or by sermon. Fiction is only the jittery act of reaching. When the goal is sufficient, as in Bellow's fiction it has been, and when in spite of jitters the reach is serious and long and constant, and one can see that it is reaching, fiction becomes crucial. As in Bellow's case it has.

~III~

RALPH ELLISON

"It is a complex fate to be an American," said Henry James. It is surely a more complex and a more insistent fate to be an American Negro, and not the least complexity would seem to be that neither one's self nor one's society have initial, non-American, private meanings. It is on the one hand, a non-Negro must think, a crustacean kind of fate, because the self must be locked into a definition, Negro-ness, which has nothing to do with the private self one knows. The world outside is, meanwhile, murky, fluid, and hostile. Hence the urgency of accommodation, of breaking through, in order to come to the world. Being a Negro must on the other hand be a matter of conscience. This fate imposes obvious obligations, imposes for reasons of social improvement the duty to assert one's specifically Negro self. Hence the duty to resist assimilation.

And, add another complication, it has been especially in the years of the recent past the clear duty of a Negro writer to explode the mere Negro-ness which everything in his long literary education has made it a matter of conscience for him to accept and prize. The escape from parochialism, the bursting of the special instance, itself has been a recognized stratagem in a long and an inescapable battle. Negro literature is perhaps inseparably a part of American literature [1]—and that is still one more complication—but it is a distinct part and it has its unique imperatives. There are matters that a Negro author must explore and must articulate because others won't, because he knows and others do not, and because he is an instrument of the Negro community. And that would be a simple destiny, but then again it must be only a fragment of the Negro writer's intricate truth. He lives as much in a white world, within a white history and a white literary tradition, and furthermore, like everyone else, he is neither white nor black. For Ralph Ellison and James Baldwin in these few years the road to an accommodation that might realize both society and self has led through a baffling and multiple fiction: that they are Negroes at all. But then the fact that they are Negroes necessarily has determined reality.

Ralph Ellison's *Invisible Man* (1952) is in one of its developments the story of a young Negro equipped with academic talents and oratorical gifts who is set, inevitably, on the road to race leadership. He is a potential Booker T. Washington. He wanders from the road, or is forced from it, and he becomes, not a credit to his race, not a spokesman for it, but a man who realizes that he is invisible. That clarity is one of his tentative triumphs. He has confronted an issue in public, political identity, and he has discovered that the public image erases the possibility of his possessing his personality. His next move, not yet defined, will be, he hopes, toward visibility.

There is an initial dilemma—for everybody, but particularly for a Negro. No doubt Ellison as he wrote confronted himself, confronted a problem in his own visibility, the inevitable determining public image that falls on the Negro author who will sit down to write about what he knows best, the public image that it will take him an act of heroic clarity not to become. If he chooses not to be silent, and if he has conscience, then he will be not the forger of the uncreated conscience of his race, not a prophet—but a spokesman. If he is a spokesman, he does not speak for himself. What he knows best is his own experience, and that is neither universal nor his own. His skin is not everybody's, not even every Negro's, but neither is it a personal matter. It is a political fact that has become an emblem of direct protest, the protest directed against the dominating part of the universe. He is bound by skin, by sensibility, and by conscience to write that sort of novel which, whatever else it might be, will be first of all and in the narrowest sense a political fact.

But in that case he is bound also, as a novelist, to extreme sacrifices. Protest as a literary genre has little flexibility, no subtlety, and circumscribed possibilities. The novel of protest risks sacrifices to its screech and roar of political implication— sacrifices of honesty, profundity, personality, the real complexity of anyone's experience, and great amounts of political reality as well. The protest novel is to the novel what the spokesman is to the man. Protest dissolves flesh. And bound to the dilemma in protest, the Negro novelist is bound to consideration of the extent to which he can possess himself and his experiences beyond their political signification, and he is bound to constant consideration, therefore, of the extent to which he can be a novelist at all.

Ellison in *Invisible Man* achieved a novel by converting just such considerations into his subject. One of the things the novel is about is the thematic possibilities open to the Negro novelist, the seeming inevitability of protest and its crippling constrictions. Ellison's hero discovers that his life is not really available to him. *Invisible Man* is by that much a novel of protest directed against the corruption inherent in protest.

By that much the novel participates in a general rejection, in the years since mid-century, not only of protest but of all social radicalism, of social consciousness itself, and of the notion of man as a static social fact. Protest assumes not only that political action can occur, but that it is on the whole easy, that it can be effected by the rational organization of everyone's basic good will. The protest novel exists to tap a well of altruism and to suggest a channel for it. It assumes, moreover, that man is an animal not only capable but desirous of reason. And these are assumptions that in recent years have come to seem problematic when they have not seemed naive. The years have taught the lesson that man is at least irrational, at best mysterious and protean. Poets perhaps never were the unacknowledged legislators of the world, but no poets have known so clearly as our poets of the dangers of simplification and limitation inherent in the ambition to use literature for legislation. The ambition skips the individual's reality. Indeed, the dangers in protest have been evident to everyone, and anyway a whole decade of proletarian literature not long before our time demonstrated and confirmed its inadequacy, the reduction and the plain sentimental dishonesty it is forced to indulge.

The demonstration has put the Negro novelist, however, to greater cunning. It has forced him to formal inventions as it did no one else. It was a demonstration not only to be denied, but, precisely because the political facts of his life were more pressing, it was one of clearer importance to him than to anyone else. Ellison seems to have spent all the years from his first publication, in 1937, to the publication of *Invisible Man* in 1952, working himself out of and beyond protest. James Baldwin, a younger man, all but began his career in a denunciation of protest,[2] and the corrupting simplicity of protest has been an apparent theme in his fiction.

A narrow protest dehumanizes everyone. But more than others, and obviously, the Negro, in and out of literature, runs the risk of being sociologized into an American dilemma, of being reduced to "a little question," as Ellison has said, "of civil rights." [3] The Negro in America quite without the confirmation of protest literature may find himself all but inseparable from the "Negro problem." More than others, the Negro runs the risk of anonymity, invisibility, of disappearance into stereotypes, those either of overt prejudice or of overt liberalism. "Of traditional attitudes," Baldwin writes, "there are only two—For or Against—and I, personally, find it difficult to say which attitude has caused me the most pain," [4] and he expatriated himself for a while, Baldwin has said, because of the fury of the color problem here, precisely because "I wanted to prevent myself from becoming *merely* a Negro; or, even, merely a Negro writer." [5]

More than others, because the traditions have been made and because the political necessity is pressing, the Negro novelist runs the risk of protest literature, of collapsing his tricksy humanity into a social plea or a social warning. The traditions of protest for the Negro can be seen to be located ultimately in just three marketable ghosts: in Uncle Tom, in the Negro who is white, and in Bigger Thomas, with little choice between them. And not only must the Negro novelist by participating in stereotypes frustrate the truth of the Negro's individual humanity, after which nothing about politics or any Negro can be learned, but he risks converting the stereotype into his own personal reality. When he accepts the stereotype of protest as his truth, then his reality has collapsed into sociology, and he has become his own propaganda.

The obligations to protest, then, are for the Negro writer more imperative than they are for anyone else and its dangers are more dangerous to him, and in fact it didn't need the demonstration of a decade of proletarian literature to make them evident. No doubt Ellison and Baldwin have been nurtured by the general sophistication of recent years about the nature of protest. By the same measure there is no doubt that they have won a greater critical regard than any other American Negro authors have known, with the possible exception of Richard Wright, at least in part because they have participated in a general knowledge.[6] But the effort to push beyond the forms of propaganda has always been urgent for the Negro author. The effort became conscientious and avowed just as soon as Negro literature became aware of itself. All serious Negro novelists and poets, including, one may say, the protest novelists themselves, have shared for several decades in the attempt to free Negro literature from propaganda, to give it room in a wider reality. Even *Native Son,* although it ends in creating a new stereotype, the Negro-as-a-proletarian-grotesque, contributed to the revolt against protest by trying the Negro problem both in terms invented by American naturalism and in terms of a Marxist analysis, terms which were nonracial.

The effort to burst through protest indeed goes back to and is a great part of the Negro Renaissance of the 1920s. The Negro philosopher Alain Locke, more than a generation ago, proposed in its very manifesto, if not the whole scheme, anyway much of the reason for the anti-protest in *Invisible Man,* and he anticipated even the novel's principal metaphor:

[The Negro's] has been a stock figure perpetuated as an historical fiction partly in innocent sentimentalism, partly in deliberate reactionism. The Negro himself has contributed his share to this through a sort of protective social mimicry, forced upon him by the adverse circumstances of dependence. So for generations in the mind of America, the

Negro has been more of a formula than a human being—
a something to be argued about, condemned or defended,
to be "kept down," or "in his place," or "helped up," to be
worried with or worried over, harassed or patronized, a
social bogey or a social burden. The thinking Negro even
has been induced to share this same general attitude, to
focus his attention on controversial issues, to see himself
in the distorted perspective of a social problem. *His shadow,
so to speak, has been more real to him than his personality.*
Through having had to appeal from the unjust stereotypes
of his oppressors and traducers to those of his liberators,
friends and benefactors he has had to subscribe to the traditional positions from which his case has been viewed. Little
true social or self-understanding has or could come from
such a situation.[7]

Ellison in his direct attempt to dissipate the shadow that
obscures personality, and Baldwin in his effort to burst the
stereotypes that imprison personality come at the end of a
clear progress in Negro literature. They inherit an issue already explicitly formulated. They inherit, moreover, several
decades of deliberate experimentation in the forms beyond
protest. Behind them are the inventions of the folk-conscious
participants in the Harlem School of the 1920s, men like
Claude McKay and Countee Cullen and Langston Hughes,
who had worked to counter the stereotype with a fresh apprehension of the indigenous Negro culture. They inherit a
literary history including the experiments of the writers of
the 1930s who under the influence of the Communist Party
converted race themes to class warfare. Their history includes
writers like Willard Motley and Ann Petry, who in the 1940s
attempted to escape the stereotype by writing all-white novels;
and in effect it includes writers of the early 1950s, like Dorothy

West and Owen Dodson and Gwendolyn Brooks, who strategically avoided all the violences of interracial conflict.[8]

And that is to say that Ellison and Baldwin, while of course they have been doing everybody's business, have written first of all out of a determined, distinctive Negro literary problem. And it is to say also, liberal right-thinking to the contrary and the differences in their talents to the contrary, that inevitably they have a great deal in common.

But then—further complication—in fact the dilemma of protest has not been for them quite what it was for writers before them. Ellison and Baldwin have variously succeeded in making out of the necessity of anti-protest a literature of universal implication, and the break they have been able to make from the restrictions of the "little question of civil rights" is also consequent upon their history as Negroes. Even as the Negro plight has become a militant Negro movement —even as James Baldwin has more and more conspicuously become a spokesman for it—the Negro writer has been relatively freer to avoid the hard themes of protest. Ironically, the Negro movement that came to life during the Kennedy administration secured its vitality not in response to new persecutions, but from new melioration; and for the Negro writer who would not be a journalist the Negro cause, while certainly it did not disappear, did become more subtle. A Negro writer, Arthur P. Davis, could say in 1959, "It is obvious to even the most rabid critic that racial conditions in America are far better than they have ever been before." And Negro literature, he could say, has undergone a consequent transformation.[9]

Apparently it has made some difference to Negro writers that Negro militance has followed upon, and indeed been born of, such events since the war as integration in the armed forces, enactments of FEPC laws, rulings against restrictive covenants in housing, against the white primary, against segregation in interstate travel, against segregation in the schools. However limited these and other achievements, still it is obvious that the Negro's situation has improved. If these are still token victories, still they put major victories in sight, and by that much the demand made upon the Negro writer to protest is withdrawn. Moreover, the hard themes of protest have been transferred out of literature. It has made some difference to Negro writers that in the years since the war many of the old battles have been fought, finally, in legislatures and in the courts, or in the streets. The struggle for equality is perhaps ultimately a cultural rather than a political matter, but immediately it is a political matter.

A Negro protest literature continues to be written. And because integration contains a threat to the cultural distinctiveness of Negroes, a new attempt has been recorded to save and to define the African heritage, an attempt supported by the emergence of a native African literature. But what seems characteristic of major Negro literature since mid-century is an urgency on the part of writers to be more than merely Negro.

This has been a time not necessarily of such good feeling as might dissolve the writer's obligation to his racial citizenship. It has not been a time either when the Negro writer has had to struggle to consider himself primarily a writer—that effort had been achieved in the 1920s and 1930s. The time has seemed to urge upon him, rather, a necessity to discover his nonracial identity within the circumstances of race.

Robert Penn Warren in 1957, in response to a question by Ralph Ellison, could say, "The Negro who is now writing protest *qua* protest strikes me as anachronistic," [10] and he would seem to have had evidence. Richard Wright, who had long before abandoned overt protest, had in 1953 in *The Outsider* turned from a racial to an existential sense of personality. The sense of Negro identity as racial but more than racial is what has seemed to give coherence to a decade of *Phylon*, the most prominent Negro literary quarterly. The same sense moved a historian of Negro literature in the early fifties to write history out of the idea that "understanding of life is far more significant than self-consciousness of race." [11] "The releasing formula," Margaret Just Butcher wrote in 1956, "is to realize that all human beings are, basically and inevitably, human, and that even special racial complexities and overtones are only interesting variants. . . . This inner tyranny must be conquered now that the outer tyranny of prejudice and intellectual ostracism is being relaxed." [12] J. Saunders Redding, perhaps the most prominent of Negro critics, in 1951 in his *On Being a Negro in America* could say: "I hope this piece will stand as the epilogue to whatever contribution I have made to the 'literature of race.' I want to get on to other things." [13] And a decade later he would discover that Negro writers have obligations *prior* to Negro-ness: "The human condition, the discovery of self. Community. Identity. Surely this must be achieved before it can be seen that a particular identity has a relation to a common identity, commonly described as human." [14]

It is the feeling that other things can now, or soon, be got on to that is dominant and that distinguishes Negro literature in these years, and it is within this feeling that Ellison and Baldwin have worked. The sense of self within the human condition, the qualities of identity and community, and the motions between identity and community are just what they came forward to write about. And it happens that what they have written about constitutes exactly a special and interesting variant of that motion from alienation to accommodation that has occupied these years generally—the more interesting a motion in their case because their alienation has a longer and a more complicated character, and because accommodation is the less available.

Nevertheless, it was from the special Negro circumstances that Ellison and Baldwin emerged, and the fact has given their fiction special resonances.

The experience that was to be the content of their work is not everyone's experience, and their themes therefore have taken special forms. The community the nature of which they had first to discover was the Negro community, which in all of its institutions, the family, the church, education, political organization, in the South and in the North, and always, had suppressed the individual.[15] And the other community to be discovered, America, had, both South and North, always at the very least frustrated the Negro's independence. The American past was in the American present, a fact become even more obvious now as the climate of integration allowed one to see it. The identity which the Negro writer had to find and assert still wore a black face, to accept which meant, integration or no, acceptance of the stigmata of persecution, and of historical and theological determinations of identity in the black and in the white communities that had nothing to do with the person. Those are discoveries that Ellison and Baldwin make. And accommodation of the realized person to the realized community has been, finally, not only not so easy for them; in fact, in any ordinary forms of being the imagination might conceive, it has been impossible. When Ellison and Baldwin actually become *merely* accommodationist, as at moments they do, they belie their own evidences, they sound like politicians, and they falter. Their work has found its validity in tentative resolutions. Their heroes seek a place in the world in personal fantasies of vengeance, or in a grotesque symbolism of satanic identity, or in accommodations, in the case of James Baldwin, by a painful dialogue between self-assertion and denial of the self.

Their work has found its valid resolutions in rage, in the bitterness passing into a howl of self-pity that has been Baldwin's particular contribution to the business of recent years, and in Ellison's violence and hints of madness. No matter in what impulse to get beyond politics and protest and special-pleading and the paranoia of the ghetto they have made their discoveries—"this hatred itself," said Baldwin, "becomes an exhausting and self-destructive pose";[16] "I wasn't, and am not," Ellison said, "concerned with injustice, but with art" [17]— the result of their discoveries has been nevertheless in their best work a fury. They have not ended in writing simply a more complicated sort of protest fiction. Ellison's invisible man ends by saying, "Who knows but that, on the lower frequencies, I speak for you?" and in an obvious way he does speak for everyone—for everyone, anyway, in America. He explores large questions of freedom and necessity and personality and responsibility, and he explores particularly, as does Baldwin, the nature of the American identity in its struggle with America. But he is a Negro, like Baldwin's heroes even when Baldwin's heroes are white, and he speaks in a particular way, at the mercy of and with the advantages of the extremity of his need.

1. The Initiate

Ralph Ellison's invisible man speaks first of all for himself, a Negro whose career, because he is a Negro, has been a search for a primary, existential sense of himself. The existential question, as a critic says, "lies waiting around the corner for

any introspective person, but it straddles the main highway
for a thoughtful Negro." [18] And despite the statement of faith
with which *Invisible Man* ends, that the hero can accomplish
visibility, this invisible man speaks in the conviction of utter
failure.

In fact, the only way in which he might exist is in an
enormous act of vengeance, a mechanics which Bigger Thomas
had discovered before him. But the world is nothing so simple
for him as it was for Bigger. Simple murder won't do, and
anyway he sees the contradiction in vengeance. He accomplishes revenge and existence only at a remove, in a nightmare underground. He is removed into nightmare not because
it may be that in the ordinary ways of being, men are inevitably determined, nor because there may be no such thing
as the existential self, nor because the gratuitous act may be
really gratuitous and without sense except in dreams. That
would be certainly to open the universal theme. And he is
condemned not because of cowardice or lack of maturity—
despite the fact Ellison has once commented on his hero's
"refusal to run the risk of his own humanity, which involves
guilt." [19] He is not a coward and he is very little guilty. And
he is thrust into a nightmare not, despite the fact that Ellison
has said it, because the frustration of identity is peculiarly the
American theme. He is condemned first of all because he is
black. The novel is glued to the fact.

Invisible Man is in its gross facts little more an autobiographical novel than any other, but not only could it not have
been written by a white man, its first condition is the Negro
as a Negro, Ellison's own long personal discipline and frustration in the public issue. The novel leads to a crisis of metaphysical discovery in the life of a Negro who has not only
been born into but has accepted the public issue as his identity,
who has practiced his identity then in the only way open to

him, by articulating the grievances of his people, by defining himself therefore more and more exclusively as a public issue, until his image is shattered in a public, political confusion. The first condition of the novel is that the hero is an *exemplary* Negro. He incorporates the Negro's experience at its extreme. He has been incorporated into race leadership and its politics, its simplisms, its outright lies, its goading militance, its obsessive sense of injustice, its sacrifices of people, its self-renewing urgency, its bafflement, its blindness, and its yearning, and he has therefore been deprived of himself, and it is that that accounts for the pressure and the rage of his discovery.

His journeys in their larger movements parallel Ellison's. Like his hero, Ellison came from the South, went to a Southern Negro university, came North then and, like almost all other Negro intellectuals of a certain age, rode out the waves of left-wing doctrine, and took the uniform of race leadership. And like his hero, Ellison suffered violent disillusion—*Invisible Man* is the chief evidence of it.

The larger biographical coincidences are not important except that they confirm, what is anyway obvious, that the book is authentic, that Ellison has been there. It is important, however, that Ellison had put behind him some years of error and discovery, recorded in perhaps too much journalism, before he began to write *Invisible Man*. *Invisible Man* is a novel of extraordinary weight, precisely as it bears the history of Ellison's own strenuous adventuring in the definition, as it were, of himself. It happens, indeed, that there is not much in his years of production of essays, reviews, and stories that is important for its own sake. To the contrary, there is nothing in it with the exception of a single story, with the addition of perhaps one other, that might have predicted *Invisible Man*. The naïveté demanded by race leadership lies heavily on

Ellison's early work. Much of it is wracked by contradictions reflecting the shifts of political doctrine. Not a little of it is embarrassing. But then it is exactly the confusion prior to the novel that accounts for the novel. This production, embarrassments and all, most closely defines the first concerns and the sensibility out of which the novel came, and then it turns out to make a discernible progress of realizations which is the hidden career of the novel's hero.

Invisible Man begins far back, in the hopeful simplisms from which a whole generation is still recovering. Ellison is to be found in 1940, in *The New Masses*, saying of a white novelist: "Len Zinberg indicates how far a writer, whose approach to Negro life is uncolored [*sic*] by condescension, stereotoyped ideas, and other faults growing out of race prejudice, is able to go with a Marxist understanding of the economic basis of Negro personality. That, plus a Marxist sense of humanity, carries the writer a long way. . . ." [20] He is to be discovered, in the same year, making common cause of the Negro's cause and agitation for an embargo on aid to Finland.[21] And *Invisible Man* is to be traced to Ellison's engagement in 1940 with the political activity that was called the Third National Negro Congress:

> Returning to convention headquarters, we find the delegates pouring in. There is a steady roar of voices. We look about for acquaintances.
>
> "Look! What's that guy's name?" I look up; a short man with a high forehead and glasses squeezes past.
>
> "That's John P. Davis."
>
> "*Davis*, the national secretary?"
>
> "Sure."
>
> "But I've seen his pictures. I thought he was a big guy."
>
> "He's big, all right," someone says. "He told off Dies."

"Thought that was *Ben* Davis."

"Yeah, but this one told him too."

A tall man in a cattle man's hat has been listening: "Now wasn't that something?" he says, "*Both* of 'em got him told. All my life I been wanting to see some of our Negro leaders go down there to Congress and let them know how we felt about things. Didn't think I would live to see it, but it happened. And that's why I'm here this morning!" [22]

The folksiness in this engagement is merely literary and by that much it is, obviously, a device of deliberate propaganda. What is astonishing and significant is the fact that Ellison must at times have carried on his political discourse with himself at the level this reporting indicates—that, and much more of the same in some ten years of writing, says something of the journey he had to make. [23]

It was not a political apprehension of the Negro's plight, but a reading in 1935 of "The Waste Land" that, Ellison has said, turned him to writing. "Eliot said something to my sensibilities that I couldn't find in Negro poets who wrote of experiences I myself had gone through." And again, ". . . I wondered why I had never read anything of equal intensity and sensibility by an American Negro writer." [24] What that something was that spoke to him, it seems clear, was not Eliot's particular despair of secularism, nor of modern purposelessness, nor his counterposing mythical method, but much more simply his panorama of frustration, frustration made the first condition of life, together with the hint of an apocalyptic thunder, expressed through a montage of ironies. Ellison's concern with the age, metaphysics, and myth came much later. It was with the voice of thunder, by direct sponsorship of Richard Wright and thundering against specific frustrations that were the first conditions of Negro life, that Ellison entered publication. First, in 1937, he appeared in Wright's magazine, *New Challenge*—with a review of E. Waters Turpin's *These Low Grounds*—and then in 1938 and regularly from 1939 through 1942 he appeared in *The New Masses,* and then through 1943 in *The Negro Quarterly.*[25]

And it was, as of course it would have had to be, with some responsiveness to left-wing politics that he spoke. It was to the Communist Party that the Negro intellectual in those pressing years was most likely to be attracted. Richard Wright provided an example. Moreover, there weren't practical political alternatives. There was the black nationalism, noble but unrealistic, that had flared in Marcus Garvey's "Back to Africa" movement of the 1920s and that sputtered still. There was the much less extreme but nevertheless claustral nationalism of such groups as the NAACP, and then the National Negro Congress, which in any event was soon overrun by the Communist Party. There was then a conservative strategy of assimilation, the emblem of which was Roosevelt's "Black Cabinet," which looked like betrayal. The Communist Party, meanwhile, had made manifest, spectacularly, as other parties had not, its concern for the welfare of Negroes. It agitated. And beyond the daily activity of agitation, there had been in 1930–1934 its League of Struggle for Negro Rights, presided over by Langston Hughes. Then there had been its long and conspicuous defense of the Scottsboro boys. In the national elections of 1932 and 1936 it had run a Negro as its vice-presidential candidate. The Communist Party seemed, as the New Deal and the NAACP did not, to be engaged, active, and adequately radical. It was doing something. Moreover, the Communist Party covered all ideological bets by encouraging Negro nationalism within an assimilationist program.

Negro nationalism was joined to a broader program of protest and subsumed in the scientism of Marxism. Beyond that,
the Party had decided that American Negroes constituted a
nation, that there was to be manufactured within the American nation a Negro Soviet Republic. There is no telling, and
it does not matter, how seriously anyone took that policy. Its
real function was in salvaging racial identity and racial pride
from a dogma of class warfare and at the same time in unit-
ing Negroes and whites in a common revolution.

Ellison moved toward left-wing politics, and there can be
no doubt that he profited from his political engagement. At
the very least, he had opportunities to write—to write journalism, anyway, and get done with it. Much of the production
of these years, of reviews, essays, occasional fiction, is dedicated, as of course it would be, to shocked outrage at obvious
injustices. If politics gave Ellison opportunity to learn that an
oracular outrage soon becomes stale and static, it did him
some service. It taught him by that much the nature of
protest. At its best, the production of these years does go
far enough into its occasions to achieve some power. A story
of 1940, "The Birthmark," moves swiftly beyond the fact of a
lynching to a violent apprehension of the guilt, the historical
determinations, the fear, and the corrupt sexuality that have
their issue in the crime.[26] But it, too, is marred by the smudge
of left-wing politics that is on so much else of this production,
by faith in enlightened organization. In the story the victim's
sister interrupts her grief to say to her surviving brother,
"They asked us last month to sign a piece of paper saying we
wanted things like this to stop and you was afraid."

At its worst, Ellison's outrage is smothered in recommenda-
tions, and in implausible jargon. His review for *The Negro
Quarterly* of William Attaway's *Blood on the Forge*, a novel

about three Southern Negroes who move into disaster as they
move into the industrial North, observes: "The impersonal
brutality of the mill strikes upon their folk personalities," [27]
and Ellison goes on at length to accuse Attaway of unnatural
gloom in his refusal to admit that trade unionism would
have redeemed his characters. Attaway was the principal
novelist of the principal event in American Negro history
after Emancipation, the so-called Great Migration at the time
of World War I from the farm to the factory, and because
Attaway had found no advantage in proletarianism over peasantry, Ellison was under some obligation to attack him.
Again, a dramatic essay on life in Harlem, for *The New
Masses*, is fastened to an interview with a Mrs. Jackson, whose
son Wilbur is in the army, whose eldest daughter can't get a
job, whose youngest boy is a heller, and whose nephew William has been killed in service with the Merchant Marine.
Mrs. Jackson tells us, *more majorum*, that William's union
has helped out a great deal. "We used to get after William for
being with white folks so much, but these sure have shown
themselves to be real friends." [28] And there is much more,
on a riot here, an eviction or a lynching there, recruiting talk
on the necessity of a discrimination of white folks, on trade
unionism, on humanitarianism in the Soviet Union, and
through it all Ellison's manifest consciousness of spokesmanship.

Ellison was young in these years. No doubt *Invisible Man*
is a reflection on himself out of sudden maturity. But this
work needs no apology. Ellison had a necessary day of spokesmanship which ended in fruitful disillusion. Moreover, like
Richard Wright and Langston Hughes before him, he had
access to schooling in literary techniques. And beyond that,
because he was a Negro spokesman, his Negro-ness was both

confirmed and made problematical, a *question* of identity and not an answer.

American leftists did after all break down racial barriers, and they created social situations in which a Negro writer might have commerce with other writers who possessed an idea of the necessity of literature. In a polemic for *The New Masses* in these years in behalf of social realism, Ellison interrupts himself to say: "It is no accident that the two most advanced American Negro writers, Hughes and Wright, have been men who have *experienced freedom of* association with advanced white writers . . ." [29] and indeed it isn't an accident, and in saying so, clearly Ellison was reflecting on his own current experiences. Clearly in these years Ellison moved in a *literary* world. He was doing much reading in criticism and fiction which was not devoted to the question of civil rights. He was reading the Russians. He was reading Joyce. He would seem, from some of his later essays, to have been perhaps overly impressed by some literary critics, notably Kenneth Burke and William Empson.* Malraux became important to him. Hemingway especially became a rich problem for him. Hemingway was a realist who was only on incidental occasions a polemicist, and for many years, beginning abruptly in 1940 and continuing right through his later essays, implicitly and explicitly, Ellison has struggled with Hemingway's rhetoric and with Hemingway's idea of craft. Hemingway had discovered for literature the patterns of modern American speech, but not the sinuous, metaphorical, often violent, flamboyant speech of Negroes. Heming-

---

* Ellison says of *Invisible Man:* "The three parts represent the narrator's movement from, using Kenneth Burke's terms, purpose to passion to perception." The formula surely will fit almost any work of fictive narrative, and therefore is the less useful, but it happens that it doesn't fit *Invisible Man.* For an example of Ellison's uses of William Empson, see "Richard Wright's Blues," p. 205.

way's rhetoric of understatement was compelling, but it rested
on common assumptions which whites did not share with
Negroes, and furthermore it was inadequate to public issues.
Hemingway's account of the act of writing was authentic,
but he had given to the mere act of writing priority over
public morality.[30]

Disengagement from public morality, Ellison was later to
say, was the failing of all the Lost Generation writers. Fiction
is by nature social and engaged. And it is one of the important
facts of *Invisible Man* that it has deliberate social extension.
But in discovering in these years what Hemingway did not
offer him, and again in discovering that, as he has said,
Malraux "was the artist-revolutionary rather than a politician
when he wrote *Man's Fate,* and the book lives not because of a
political position embraced at the time, but because of its
larger concern with the tragic struggle of humanity," he discovered a way out of propaganda, and out of the simplicities
of spokesmanship.

Moreover, from a perch of ideology he could investigate the
identity of the Negro for whom he was, putatively, the spokesman. The political progress of the production of these years
of Ellison's association with Marxist politics is from a dogma
of class warfare to a more and more emphatic, critical Negro
nationalism. In 1940 he was impressed by Len Zinberg's
"Marxist understanding of the economic basis of Negro personality." In 1943 in a review of another white novel on
Negro life, Bucklin Moon's *The Darker Brother,* Ellison was
saying that the author missed the human meaning of Negro
experience because he was white, because there is a great
"psychological distance" between Negroes and whites and
any attempt to communicate over that distance must be "a
conscious study in comparative humanity."[31]

In the same year an editorial statement in *The Negro Quar-*

terly—Ellison was managing editor of the journal and the statement seems to be his—first honors those Negroes who regard the war as a white man's war and who therefore reject it, and then urges "an attitude of critical participation, based upon a sharp sense of the Negro people's group personality." [32] Misunderstandings between Negroes and whites, the statement says, are inevitable at this time in history. And it goes on to urge Negro leaders and spokesmen to come to terms with their own group. The specific way of coming to terms is, moreover, in "learning the meaning of the myths and symbols which abound among the Negro masses."

> For without this knowledge, leadership, no matter how correct its program, will fail. Much in Negro life remains a mystery; perhaps the zoot suit conceals profound political meaning; perhaps the symmetrical frenzy of the Lindy-hop conceals clues to great potential power—if only Negro leaders would solve this riddle. . . . The problem is psycho logical; it will be solved only by a Negro leadership that is aware of the psychological attitudes and incipient forms of action which the black masses reveal in their emotion-charged myths, symbols and war-time folklore.

The lumpy Marxist vocabulary is still there, and the anxiety of public obligation, but clearly by this time Ellison's ideas were become more complex and his field of inquiry so problematic that it could not be comprehended by the "Marxist understanding."

The statement makes of folklore a political strategy, but what is important is that there is in it an assertion that a Negro folk character exists and that much of it is mysterious and not economically determined. It is an assertion that in fact

in years just prior Ellison had alternately made and denied.*
For a Negro there was every good reason to deny the folk
character. There were sufficient grounds in the facts of the
degraded and constricted conditions of Negro life, in the fact
that American social pressure has always been against separatism and most particularly, most bafflingly, against the
separatism of the Negro, and not least of all in the fact that
by the 1940s a long history had accumulated of exploitation
of Negro culture for the amusement of whites. The acceptance of Negro culture was self-destructive. To accept it was to
take a role in a darky entertainment. Not the least of Ellison's
reasons for rejecting it seems to have been in the fact that he
was repelled—so a variety of his statements from these years
testify—by the exoticism and by the voguishness of the literature of the Harlem School, a literature that had been invented
in a white man's novel, Carl Van Vechten's *Nigger Heaven*.[33]
Negro culture had become so much a complex of stereotypes,
accepted by whites and Negroes, that in a way it did not exist.
Or if it did exist, to accept it was a personal betrayal and
also a political betrayal of Negroes.

Ellison was able now even to deny Negro culture, to seek
an identity outside it (indeed outside American culture)
precisely while he was a spokesman for a variety of Negro
nationalism, and at the same time he could discover, not Negro
life—which presumably he knew very well—but the literature
of it and the formulations that other Negroes were putting on

---

* So Ellison says of Langston Hughes, that he became "more the
conscious artist. His work followed the logical development of the
national-folk sources of his art." "Stormy Weather," p. 20. But two
years later, in a review of Attaway's *Blood on the Forge*, he could
say: "Certainly . . . few folk values withstood the impact of the industrial era. . . ." "Transition," *The Negro Quarterly*, I (Spring
1942), 91.

Negro life. Ideologically, he was against the Negro Renaissance. "This movement was marked by the 'discovery' of the
Negro by wealthy whites, who in attempting to fill the vacuum
of their lives made the 1920s an era of fads." The Negro
Renaissance was also timid and it was middle class. But as a
Negro and as a writer, Ellison was in the same moment
educated in the assertion that the Negro Renaissance made
of the fact and the dignity of a unique Negro culture. Richard
Wright and Langston Hughes spoke to him not only as
ideologues, but as Negroes who were finding their way to a
folk consciousness quite outside political doctrine.

It could not, of course, have been only an education in other
Negroes' efforts to define anew a folk culture that led Ellison
to assert that it existed and therefore to accept it, and then
to make the effort his own. With the coming of the war,
the left itself had less and less identity, purpose, or vigor to
offer anybody. The evidence of his editorial statement in
The Negro Quarterly, confirmed by the evidence of *Invisible
Man,* suggests that Ellison became disinfatuated with all
efforts of white liberalism. If so, he could have been left with
no political alternative other than a more emphatic Negro
nationalism. Moreover, critics whom Ellison must in these
years have been coming upon, at least at second hand, critics
like Van Wyck Brooks and Constance Rourke and, in England, Maud Bodkin, not to speak of Ezra Pound and T. S.
Eliot, had for many years been defining as a general problem
the apprehension in literature of myth, nationality, and folklore. The exploration of folk culture secured a general intellectual effort.

And it secured an effort not only at the highest. With the
coming of the war it became, as evidenced, say, by the vast
popularity of such an author as Louis Adamic, an item of
popular political morality. If America fabricated a popular

image of itself during the war, it was a refined version of the melting pot, a melting pot in which all the pieces got cooked but retained their individual flavors. And that had something to do with the democratic response to Hitler's racial policy. The Negro problem for Negroes, specifically, became complicated beyond the fact of economic exploitation. It was not a white man's war, quite obviously, despite the continued facts of economic exploitation and some new facts of segregation. American Negroes were involved with America, and not only because of mobilization. The war must have forced on Ellison an immediate problem of identity that Marxism had obscured, a problem in the Negro-ness and in the American-ness of American Negroes.

In any event, just as Ellison reached some pinnacle of spokesmanship, as an editorial member of *The New Masses* and then as the managing editor of *The Negro Quarterly,* he seems to have become less interested in racial injustice. He made his last contribution to *The New Masses* in 1942, and *The Negro Quarterly* collapsed with its fourth issue in 1943. Ellison's production after 1943, of reviews, essays, and short fiction was concerned almost exclusively with finding a new definition of Negro culture, with the problem of acceptance of a Negro folk identity, and with the nature of the relationship of Negroes to America.

The mythical mystery in the zoot suit and the Lindy hop is a matter touched upon, and then no more than touched upon, only in *Invisible Man.* It is one of the faults of *Invisible Man* that it only mentions a distinct culture in Harlem, in which half the novel takes places, where it should discover a drama of culture. But meanwhile in these years Ellison was directed, apparently by the knowledge of his own youth in a semirural area of Oklahoma, and probably by his aversion to the sensationalism of Harlem literature, to a version of pastoral in which Negro folk patterns might be discovered.

It was a direction in which he had moved before. A story in *The New Masses* in 1941, "Mister Toussan," [34] had begun in his mind, it would seem, as a tribute to Toussaint L'Ouverture, a revolutionary's salute to a fellow revolutionary. But as the story came out the presence of Toussaint is the least notable item in it. The story invents two Negro boys, Riley and Buster, who have been robbing the cherry trees of a white neighbor. They have been shooed off with a shotgun, and as they sit and loll now on Riley's porch, watching the mockingbirds freely attacking the orchard, Riley is reminded of a school lesson and he recites his interpretation of the story of Mister Toussan.

There is in the story an obvious strategy in the making of a folk hero for the masses, and the story is, by that much, heavy-handed. There is in Riley's telling and in Buster's enthusiastic response much pitiful compensating, and the story is, by that much, sentimental. Much is made in the story of the freedom of the mockingbirds—Riley's mother, in the background, sings, "I got wings," the point being that she just thinks she has; the boys watch a pigeon smoothly escape from an automobile; they speculate that if they had wings they would fly a zillion miles away, maybe to Chicago, "or anywhere else colored is free"—and the story is to that extent merely protestant. But in fact its sentiments and its political implications are quite overwhelmed by its manner, and its manner becomes its subject. The point Ellison finally makes about Riley and Buster is that they act and, especially, talk like Negroes. The dialect is made with love. It has its own music, and it sounds authentic. The point in Riley and Buster's speculation on flight is finally that it takes the form of a Negro wishing game. The point of the Toussaint story is at the end that it is a chant, with alternate recitation and response:

"He shot into 'em . . ."
". . . Shot into them boats . . ."
"Jesus!! . . ."
"With his great big cannons . . ."
". . . Yeah! . . ."
". . . Made a-brass! . . ."
". . . Brass . . ."
". . . An' his big black cannon balls started killin' them peckerwoods . . ."
"'. . . Lawd, Lawd . . ."
". . . Boy, till them peckerwoods hollered *Please, Please, Mister Toussan, we'll be good!*"

And the whole story is fitted into the pattern of a Negro slave tale, provided with a rhyming prologue typical, a note says, to slave stories:

> Once upon a time
> The goose drink wine
> Monkey chew tobacco
> And he spit white lime.

and ending with another purely formal rhyme:

> Iron is iron,
> And tin is tin,
> And that's the way
> The story ends.

The chief fault of the story is that the manner and the purported subject have little to do with each other. He had trouble, Ellison has said, in learning to adapt myth and ritual to his work, and this is one of the places where the trouble shows. But Riley and Buster were effective agents of his learning. He used them two years later for a more deliberate exploration of Negro folk character, in a story called "That I Had the Wings," [35] and this time he did grab at least some of his issues out of the folk material—and the folk material led him, it happens, to a profounder desperation.

There is still much obvious symbolism of birds and flight— a symbolism repeated in a number of other stories and in *Invisible Man*. It is Riley's wanting to be able to fly that, as the title suggests, gives the story its occasion. Riley has the previous day fallen from the church steeple. This day he tries to teach some chicks to fly by fastening them to parachutes and dropping them from the roof of the barn. Chicks don't fly and these particular chicks are murdered in the noble attempt Riley forces on them. But in this story the political sentiment and the appliqué of folk character, the chanting, the rhyming, the musical conversation, the mythicizing of folk heroes—in this case, Louis Armstrong—the comic, formalized fantasies of rebellion ("Amazin grace, how sweet the sound. A bullfrog slapped his granma down")—all these are made to create a pattern of Negro initiation and inevitable failure.

Once again Riley's mother—this time she has become "Aunt Kate"—is in the kitchen singing a spiritual, and the conflict of the story is not in Riley's opposition to an abstract white world, but in his opposition to her and all she, "born way back in slavery times," represents. He is a part of her. The songs he sings, the rhymes he uses, are parodies of hers. And at the same time her songs, her religion, her slave-mindedness, her repressive concern that he learn his place—all these are emasculating. He turns around to answer her when he should have been catching the chicks and when he himself had almost learned the secret of flight, and that is when his ironic initiation occurs. The chicks are killed. The old rooster in the yard charges Riley and wounds him.

If I jus hadn't looked at her, he thought. His eyes swam. And so great was his anguish he did not hear the swift rush of feathers nor see the brilliant flash of outspread wings as Ole Bill charged. The blow staggered him and, looking down, he saw with tear-filled eyes the bright red stream against the brown where the spur had torn his leg.

"We almost had 'em flying," said Riley. "We almost. . . ."

When he becomes finally involved with his own history, with his Negro-ness, his possibilities snap closed. He is symbolically castrated.

A parallel initiation by a not-so-symbolic castration is the real climax of *Invisible Man,* and a genital wound, a circumcision, is in another and much later, much more elaborate Riley and Buster story, once again made the condition of initiation. In that story, "A Coupla Scalped Indians," [86] published in 1956, Riley is again involved with an elderly Negress, now the local witch. She entices and she terrifies, and she embodies the black past, but now he is pushed one step beyond his failure to a new, just chastened, promise of possibility. Riley's terror is at the climax dissipated and he takes the road again to manhood when he hears a band, the sound of horns, in the distance.

The symbolic horns don't really meet the symbolic witch, and on a symbolic level the story doesn't really work, but then if it did, presumably Ellison's career would be finished. He would have solved the Negro problem.

His exploration in the 1940s of Negro folklore and ritual brought him right back to the Negro problem, and to a perception of it to which Marxism was irrelevant. He came to, among other facts, the sociological fact of the matriarchic

nature of the Negro family, to what in his essay of 1945,
"Richard Wright's Blues," he called the "pre-individual"
values of the Negro community, the all-obliterating racial
consciousness, the presentness in Negro life of the history of
slavery, the repression and violence in Negro life. And all
his discoveries seem to have brought him to a question of
identity of which initiation was one metaphor—and invisibility was another. It is not only by whites that the Negro
is not allowed an independent manhood, and is not seen.
De-individualization is in the mechanics of Negro life itself,
and therefore folk expressions of Negro life, like jazz and
the blues, are apt to be rebellious, an ironic and a much
qualified assertion of the right to exist for one's own sake.

It is out of the discoveries of these years, immediately, that
Invisible Man came. The novel is all the dilemma of these
years—and its quick solution on the last page is just a grace
note and it is faked—of a man who can accept neither a black
nor a white identity, of a Negro who is lost between disin-
fatuations both with white liberalism and Negro denials, lost
between the Negro nation and America.

The war, it would seem, had everything to do with shaping
just that last aspect of the dilemma. The war seems to have led
Ellison to his discovery of America, and to the idea he was
to elaborate in *Invisible Man* and in some later essays, of the
American democratic tradition as a distinct and informing
idea and the proper idea of the American novelist. And the
war seems to have led him to the nineteenth-century American novelists who, he has said, gave him the method and
the spirit of moral assertion with which he wrote *Invisible
Man*.

. . . I felt that, except for the work of William Faulkner,
something vital had gone out of American prose after Mark

Twain. I came to believe that the writers of that period
took a much greater responsibility for the condition of
democracy, that they still possessed the frontiersman's awareness that the country, while great with promise, was still
unknown and mysterious, and I came to believe as well
that they truly believed in democracy and that, indeed, their
works were imaginative projections of the conflicts within
the human heart which arose when the sacred principles of
the Constitution and the Bill of Rights clashed with the
practical exigencies of human greed and fear, hate and
love.[37]

But the *idea* in American democracy was not, after all,
something Ellison was certain of. In 1946, after he had begun
Invisible Man, he was agreeing with Malraux that American
writing is nonintellectual, that its "creators possess 'neither the
relative historical culture, nor the love of ideas (a prerogative
of professors in the United States)' of comparable Europeans." [38] It was not until 1957, long after he had found his
way through the novel, that he took his agreement back. The
background of ideas in the American novel, he now discovered
in an essay, was not apparent simply because it was, in the
Declaration of Independence and the Bill of Rights, so explicitly formulated. "What the observer (a Frenchman) missed
was that the major ideas of our society were so alive in the
minds of every reader that they could be stated implicitly in
the contours of the [novel's] form." [39] And Ellison may change
his mind again, but what is meanwhile important is his agreement as a Negro with the *American* tradition.

The war abroad, Ellison has said, forced many Negroes to
face their feelings for their country for the first time, regardless
of second-class citizenship, and they discovered that, willy-nilly,
they were Americans and that America was the country they

loved. In saying so, he was speaking, obviously enough, for himself. The war and his own travels in the Merchant Marine do seem to have forced him to confront his feelings, but then his love for America, too, was something he could after all not so easily accept, precisely because his public engagement was deep.

The issue is put nicely by a pair of stories he published in 1944 which cast votes either way. A story called "In a Strange Country" [40] leads its hero, an American Negro sailor in the Merchant Marine, to a town in Wales. As he leaves the ship, he is set upon by a gang of white American sailors, and he is rescued and befriended by some local Welshmen. For these strangers, he sees obliquely through his swollen, blackened eye, incredibly, color does not exist. But that perception contains its irony. They regard him as a black *Yank*. He is moved through a troubled vision to the reflection that the beating he has just received is part of a family quarrel, which Welshmen finally cannot understand—that America is his only country, that he *is* a black *Yank*. And at the meeting of a Welsh singing society he discovers himself, quite beyond both bitterness and volition, suddenly singing "The Star-Spangled Banner."

> It was like the voice of another, over whom he had no control. His eye throbbed. A wave of guilt shook him, followed by a burst of relief. For the first time in your whole life, he thought with dreamlike wonder, the words are not ironic.

The affirmation is clear and easy enough, perhaps too easy. In the same year, and it would seem with the same breath, a story called "Flying Home" [41] takes its hero, a Negro flyer on a training mission, on a quite opposite voyage. The flyer crashes into an Alabama cotton field. The occasion of the story was all political and journalistic. A Negro air school had been established at Tuskegee during the war, apparently as a sop to civil libertarians. Its pilots never got out of training. The school became a sufficient issue for Judge Hastie to resign from the War Department in protest over it, and it was an issue about which Ellison had spoken.[42] The story is written in the mood of protest, but its significance is that its protest becomes a broad comment on the inevitability for a Negro of racial over national identity in America. Its very title, taken from a jazz piece by Benny Goodman and Lionel Hampton, suggests as much.

The flyer, an overt symbolism in the story suggests, is an older Riley, still struggling to fly above his condition, and because he is a Northern (as it were, second-generation) and an educated Negro, one of that small elite chosen for the school, and because he is in flight training, and because he can in fact fly very well, he has almost beaten the terrific odds. His crash teaches him his conceit. As he waits for a rescue plane from the base, he is met by an old Negro field hand who is friendly to him, and whose friendship and whose assumption of fellowship repel him. The flyer is repelled not because he is arrogant and falsely sophisticated—the story is not merely about his comeuppance. The old Negro really is obnoxious, the slave from whom he has in great measure delivered himself. It is part of the old Negro's tarnishing slavishness that he compares the flyer to the ugly black buzzards, called Jim Crows, that also fly over the Southern landscape. The field hand is himself a slave because his own wings have been clipped, because he has assented to his master's version of himself, because he has finally enslaved himself and with him all other Negroes. The flyer's allegiance cannot be to this old black ignorant man. His domain for self-assertion can be only among those who can appreciate him, which is to say with his white officers (though his relationship to them is admittedly complicated), someday with the national enemy "who would recognize his manhood and skill in terms of hate. . . ."

But then he is met by a white man who is neither the national enemy, nor an agent, like the white officers, of the national compromise, but a Southern plantation owner who is brutal, violent, American, and overwhelming, and who orders him put in a strait jacket. He has always been in a strait jacket. And at that point the old Negro's stretch of friendship becomes his salvation and his only knowledge. He is rescued by him. In a little ornamental action, then, he watches a buzzard "glide into the sun and glow like a bird of flaming gold." That is gratuitous and it falsifies. The rescue is not so golden. But the moral is absolute. Living between whites and blacks, he is black.

Because, despite the flaming gold, the moral is won hard, "Flying Home" is a powerful story. But then its moral is no more satisfactory than the other. The exclusive alternatives of national and racial identity are still equally impossible. And that fact points further to the fact that rest for Ellison's distressed hero can be only outside those public alternatives, outside, that is to say, ordinary, public realities. That will be the implicit resolution of *Invisible Man*. Its hero takes up residence in the irrational. And it is the explicit resolution of just one story prior to the novel, a very short story of 1944 called "King of the Bingo Game," [43] which puts together a great deal of Ellison's knowledge, which fakes nothing, and which bursts all public categories.

It, too, begins in a mood of protest, much like that of the portraits of Harlem Ellison had been writing a few years before, and like that of many other proletarian vignettes of unemployment. Its anonymous Negro hero sits in a movie theater, waiting again for the bingo game. He is out of a job and can't get a job because he has no birth certificate. His wife is going to die because he has no money to get her a doctor. Beyond those conventions of 1930s protest literature, he is assaulted by a theater full of odors of peanuts and wine, by rustlings and gurglings, and by all the human imperatives he can't meet, and, moreover, by flickering shadows on the screen. By stealing five bingo cards, he has stolen a chance against the bingo wheel, but it is his sense as he sits here that the wheel and all fate is fixed, and fixed against him. The movie is fixed. He has seen it three times running, now. The girl in the picture never gets undressed. Yesterday after the movie he had seen a bedbug on a woman's neck, something seemingly extraordinary, but when he had felt in his pocket he had found the same hole, the same goose pimples, the same old scars. Nothing gets out of hand. Nevertheless, when the game begins again now, he sweats to keep up with his five cards and to keep just ahead of his hopelessness. And he does win, and he stumbles forward into the light, screaming, "Bingo!"

He has won $36.90, but he has stumbled into a worse nightmare. He is, he is told, one of the "chosen people," and his further reward is that he will be allowed to press the button that will spin the wheel, and if the wheel comes to rest at double-zero, he will win the jackpot. He presses the button, and then he continues to press it, he can't let go, and he realizes suddenly that so long as he presses the button, he has mastered the wheel. He has discovered what no one, none of the Negroes out in the audience who are yelling and catcalling now, who are embarrassed for him because he is a Negro, has ever known. Desperate and exulting under the whirl of lights, he grips the button harder, and he finds that it sends back an answering shock of power. It crosses his mind at the same moment that he has forgotten his name, but no matter, he has been reborn, he is The-man-who-pressed-the-button-who-held-

the-prize-who-was-the-King-of-Bingo. "This is God!" The cur-
tain is rung down on him. The saucy young white man who
is the master of ceremonies struggles with him, and then two
policemen try to hold him. The button is finally taken from
him. Without surprise he watches the wheel come to rest at
double-zero. He has learned the secret. He is very happy. He
will receive what all winners received. But he does not see a
short bowlegged man step up behind him and set himself for
a blow. He feels only the pain exploding in his skull. He has
time for just a last thought that his luck had run out on the
stage.

There is in this last movement of the story, as there is in all
Ellison's stories of about this time, a sudden eclipse of point
of view, a sudden shift of perspective, which elsewhere, because
it becomes a heavy mannerism of pity, becomes annoying. But
it is here precisely right. The story is finally about a man in
a world of flickering, mocking perspectives, in a movie theater,
who earns a sudden, sneaking blow from behind. His madness
at the bingo wheel has something to do with that of Malraux's
Baron Clappique at the roulette table. There can be little doubt
that Ellison was thinking of it. The Baron, too, discovers
Fortuna in the wheel and, more particularly, he finds that
through the wheel's agency he is for the first time embracing
his own destiny, actually possessing himself, and the wheel
ironically therefore is a kind of suicide for him. It takes him
outside the reality of ordinary determinations. But the madness of Ellison's hero here has larger dimensions. His world
is in the first place not a mechanical, determined one. The
only naturalistic element in it is the fact that he is unemployed,
and that is the least part of it. His world is a movie theater,
a cave of muffled noises and shadowy images, presentiments of
reality. The hero's stumbling lunge forward to the source of
power is a Platonic pursuit of the source of all phenomena,

and if he does not achieve it, that is because that way is too arduous and too confusing for any man. He goes mad and, for his hubris, he is struck down. His apprehension of the source of creation can only be a brief ecstasy, after which he is re-settled in confusion.

The story has larger dimensions than anything the "Negro question" proposes, but it contains just the vision that Ellison, who had made an inevitable career of the Negro question, would seem inevitably to have come to. The exclusive in-escapable realities were black and white, but by the time he wrote this story, they were neither of them his reality, but rather flickering, undependable shadows, as in a movie, end-lessly infatuating, promising, and at the end always frustrating, finally neither to be embraced nor hated. The story would seem to be a brief gloss on his entire career, beginning with the itch of protest against obvious injustice, proceeding to a confusion that is not ethical but metaphysical. His hero at this pitch might find a place in a world only by finding an-other world. That the quest in this story is Platonic is perhaps an accident. Ellison's mind does not seem really to work in that mystical way. But the madness, the hero's journey out of the world, is certainly not an accident. It is just the end to which the hero of *Invisible Man,* after many more intricate wanderings in a fixed world, or in a world which seems fixed, will be forced to come.

2. *The Invisible Man*

Out of the world and apart from ordinary defined experi-ence is just where, in fact, the hero of the novel always finds himself. The large action of *Invisible Man* is all a circular

voyage, consisting of four prominent adventures. It begins
with a ritual of the hero's initiation, a test of his bravery,
of his knowledge of caste, and of his sexuality, and it ends
in failure, with the hero castrated, presented with proofs of
his cowardice and ignorance, in a condition prior to his initiation. He is at the end back in the underworld from which
he had tried to emerge, with this difference only, that he has
illuminated his underworld and he now knows where he is.

That is the great irony the novel deliberately plays on itself
—the world moves, the hero tells us in almost the first words
of the Prologue, not like an arrow, nor in a spiral, but like
a boomerang; his end, he says, is in his beginning. And it
should be said immediately, the novel's great fault is in the
fact that its end *is* its beginning. The novel is a furious
picaresque which plunges the hero forward through a series
of violences. Moreover, it is *all* an initiation rite. The hero
moves from childhood to the age of manhood, and from the
South to the North, and he is one of those heroes who move
from the provinces to the capital, to the center of power, from
innocence to experience. He moves, moreover, through what
seems at all points a linear exploration of the "Negro problem," through ideologies by which it might be approached,
and beyond that, through what one of the symbolic structures
of the novel suggests is an exploration of some one hundred
years of American history. But for all that multiplicity of
parallel actions, the novel has no real progress except that at
each stage it clarifies and reinforces the hero's dilemma.

"'Ah,' I can hear you say," the hero says in almost the last
words of the Epilogue,

"so it was all a build-up to bore us with his buggy jiving.
He only wanted us to listen to him rave!" But only partially
true: Being invisible and without substance, a disembodied

voice, as it were, what else could I do? What else but try
to tell you what was really happening when your eyes were
looking through?

But the witness is not here being responsive to the witness
against him. This appeal is a last-ditch attempt to rescue the
book from what must have seemed to Ellison its strategic error.
The amount of clarity the novel finally comes to is enormous,
and so much clarity is shocking, but still it is a clarity without
any further effect. The novel doesn't finally go anywhere.

It is a fault that apparently led Ellison to the desperate,
empty, unreasonable, and programmatic optimism of the
last few pages of the novel: ". . . we [Negroes] were to affirm
the principle on which the country was built. . . ." We "were
linked to all others in the loud, clamoring semi-visible
world. . . ." ". . . I've overstayed my hibernation, since there's a
possibility that even an invisible man has a socially responsible
role to play." One asks this hero how he is to come out and
be socially responsible? Upon what ground in reality can he
affirm *any* positive principle? Just what is he going to do?
Everything in the novel has clarified this point: that the
bizarre accident that has led him to take up residence in an
abandoned coal cellar is no accident at all, that the underworld
is his inevitable home, that given the social facts of America,
both invisibility and what he now calls his "hibernation" are
his permanent condition. And really his only extension into
the upper world can be in negative acts and fantasies of vengeance—which do indeed make up another ending to the
novel.

And it is just another consequence of its circularity that
Invisible Man has many endings. The novel sets out to gain
clarity but no new discovery. Its ending is in its beginning.
Therefore, with every gain in illumination, the novel con-

cludes. There is a constant increase of wattage, but what is to be seen remains the same. And then the consequence of that fact is that—except in the Prologue and the Epilogue to the novel, where the hero speaks in time present and out of all his experience—the hero is fitted with a perceptiveness that is far inferior to Ellison's. Or, if not always, that becomes a fault. He is sometimes an *ingénu,* sometimes a naive Gulliver when gullibility should be impossible, sometimes, suddenly, the author. There is a constant struggle between the two, Ellison straining not to let his protagonist know too much because that will give the book away, and sometimes failing. And finally the consequence of this latter fact is that a great deal of the novel is in a great density of symbols and puns. They don't, as the danger is, clog the action. They do contain the material. But they don't always contribute to the material. Because the hero can't know too much, because every discovery risks being the last discovery, because Ellison knows very well what each of his hero's experiences comes to, much of the hero's experience is converted into tantalizing hieroglyphics. The puns, which should be devices of compression, mount on each other and, like the major episodes of the novel, they tend each of them to tell the same and the whole story.

But then if at the end Ellison cops a plea—"what else could I do? What else but try to tell you what was really happening when your eyes were looking through?"—his plea is in every way valid. The novel's task is just the perception of obvious, repeated facts which no one sees. The task itself must be constantly emphasized and repeated in a great variety of ironic symbols, because that is a dramatic necessity in the nature of the task. The repetition is the proof that the task is authentic. The hero is first a high-school boy in a Southern town, then a college student at a Negro university, then, briefly, a laborer in a Northern factory, then a leader in what in the novel is called the Brotherhood, and finally an underground man. That is his whole story, all of it devoted to one struggle which is perpetual and obsessive because all his experience does really come to the same thing, an unremitting and fruitless attempt to achieve visibility. The book is filled by a lifetime of events, all of them leading back to the same meaning.

So in the Prologue, speaking of his invisibility in his coal cellar, the hero says he needs light because without it he is not only invisible but formless, and it is part of the joke he intends that he is, what someone calls him later, a nigger in a coal pile, that black can't be seen in the dark. The obvious is not obvious. The need is for illumination. And a series of leaders with whom the hero becomes engaged and who promise perception turn out to be blind. A Negro minister at his college, the Reverend Homer (Blind Homer) A. Barbee, preaches a sermon of hope, faith, and endurance, and falls flat on his face. Brother Jack, the local leader of the Brotherhood, sees salvation in the dialectic of historical necessity and can't see a thing because he has a glass eye, just because he has given his eye to the Brotherhood's vision. The Founder of the hero's Negro college, a great leader of his people and a thin disguise for the hero's first hero, Booker T. Washington, is presented to him first in an ambiguous statue in which the Founder is either lifting a veil from the face of a slave or lowering it.

And the task the novel sets for itself, perception of the obvious that is not seen, is reiterated in constant talk and punning, which jumps out everywhere, on eyes, vision, and visions.[44] The hero is troubled by a burning eye within. His one current friend, in the Prologue, time present, is "a junk man I know, a man of vision," who has supplied him with wire and sockets with which to illuminate his underground— the double joke in that being that electricity is light and

power and therefore vision, and that a "junk man" is a narcotics peddler, one who has visions to sell. A moment later in
a marijuana sleep the hero has his first, this time surreal,
vision of the facts of Negro experience. And there is more
around every corner. All the novel's purpose is reiterated constantly, in fact, as its basic metaphor is elaborated: the hero
is invisible because no one sees him, and it is the function of
every episode to confirm the fact that this black man is condemned to a hopeless struggle to be seen.

The hero's end, then, is in his beginning. Quite literally.
The novel happens between the Prologue and the Epilogue
and those episodes constitute a single dramatic action: the
hero, now, in his cellar, is doing sums in his career, writing
his memoirs. And except for its burst of optimism, the
Epilogue goes nowhere that the Prologue hasn't already been.*
The novel, apparently, owes much to *Notes from the Underground* and not least an ending that it does not clearly earn.
Moreover, between the Prologue and the Epilogue, the novel
moves in a series of circles—concentric planes of meaning,
each traveling right back to its beginning, each mode of adventure confirming the circularity of the hero's voyaging. Each
adventure is itself a repetition of each of the others and all
the hero's experiences come to the same thing, but from a
variety of ways of experiencing. His adventures are of a
political order, and then they also have personal significances
for him, having to do with his search for a personal identity,
and then they are historical, marking a journey through a
history of America since Emancipation which comes out where
it entered, and finally they are adventures in a metaphysics,
and each plane of adventuring rounds back to where it began.

It all began, the hero says, with his grandfather, an odd old

---

* Ellison says that he wrote the Prologue after he had finished the
action proper of the novel.

guy. He has been told he takes after him. On his deathbed his grandfather had passed on advice which, the hero says, has become a curse.

> "Son, after I'm gone I want you to keep up the good fight. I never told you, but our life is a war and I have been a traitor all my born days, a spy in the enemy's country ever since I give up my gun back in the Reconstruction. Live with your head in the lion's mouth. I want you to overcome 'em with yesses, undermine 'em with grins, agree 'em to death and destruction, let 'em swoller you till they vomit or bust wide open."

By the end of the novel the hero comes to see in his grandfather's "Yes" a greater affirmation than anything in the novel suggests his grandfather meant. He discovers in it assent to the great principles on which the country was built. But in any event, between the beginning and the ending, his grandfather's riddle defines his every gambit. The grandfather's incantatory phrases contain, Ellison has said, "a rejection of a current code and a denial become metaphysical." [45] The hero is set earnestly to wish his way out of the curse, and the curse composes his being, his actions, and his purpose. He comes to each adventure saying Yes and he learns, or in every adventure but the last he almost learns, at the same time to say No. In the last adventure he goes underground, and it is one of the many puns brought together in that development that his "underground" is a post of constant subversion.

Between, then, his grandfather's curse in the beginning and his acceptance of it in the Epilogue, the novel moves the hero through adventures in the typical ways Negroes and whites manage, or don't manage, to live together in America. He is moved in each case to the point where all relationships disappear in an explosion, from the way of the caste system of a

Southern town to that of the subtler caste system of the
Negro college created and endowed by whites, the caste inherent in latter-day abolition, to that of the factory in the industrial North, to that of the dogmatic brotherliness of the
Brotherhood, finally to the ultimate extension of all these
ways: the race riot with which the action proper of the novel
ends. And the issue of each of these adventures is a race riot
of one dimension or another, and that is the point of them
all. An earnest, yea-saying young man reluctant to be a
saboteur explores the typical relationships between Negroes
and whites and finds them charged with incipient violence,
needing but the slightest accident to set them off. The hero
moves from one episode to another because in every one an
accident happens.

The accident is always just a slight and unavoidable lapse
from the propriety he struggles to maintain. In the first
episode he delivers his high-school valedictory address. It is
a speech on the proper subject—humility is the secret and
the essence of progress for the Negro—addressed to the Southern town's most prominent white citizens, who are drunk at
this moment and who pay no attention to him. Benumbed by
the noise, the smoke, and the reek of the stag dinner for
which he is a part of the entertainment, he speaks the words
"social equality" for "social responsibility," and by his slip he
springs from the crowd a moment of sudden, terrifying silence.
In this moment of his triumph, he is crowded suddenly back
into the dark, the dark from which, by his academic prowess
and his show of humility, he has thought to escape. Humility
is not a technique of progress, but the means of his subjuga-
tion, and he dare not *not* be humble. That is something his
grandfather had known.

At college, next, with all proper respect he chauffeurs a
visiting Northern trustee, Mr. Norton. He takes Mr. Norton

to a place Mr. Norton wants to visit, the cabin of a local sharecropper, and discovers himself in a double accident. The sharecropper tells a story of incest and Mr. Norton suffers a heart attack. Still properly deferential, the hero takes Mr. Norton to a local saloon, which unfortunately this day is entertaining the Negro veterans from the local madhouse, and he deposits him into the middle of a riot. The adventure ends with his being expelled from college because, so the college president tells him, he has actually obeyed the wishes of a white man and not merely seemed to. Then in the North, as a laborer in a paint factory, he stumbles into a union meeting and, earnest to please everyone, he finds that because he is a Negro, he is a scab, and as such a catalyst to violence. Then as a favored recruit in the Brotherhood, he takes a single step on his own authority: he organizes a public funeral for a Brother shot by the police, which results in the riot in Harlem that is his last adventure. It is his one lucky accident that in that riot he tumbles into an open manhole, leading to his coal cellar.

The lesson in his accidents is, of course, the instability in all typical relationships between Negroes and whites in America, and the impossibility for a Negro of propriety enough. There is always a boomerang somewhere. Beyond that, these accidents function to reveal to the hero that he is not a person in his relations with whites, but a role, and furthermore they serve to reveal to him the kind of role he plays. It is always the same. The end of the novel is finally his ironic acceptance of his role along with his acceptance of his grandfather's curse.

His whole fate is present, though the hero is not allowed to know it, in that first adventure the climax of which is his dreadful slip of the tongue. A great part of the novel, indeed, is in that initial episode. What is revealed here is what is going to be revealed to the hero, in different circumstances,

but with not much modification, in his every subsequent adventure.

In fact, in this first adventure he is clearly threatened but
not actually punished for his slip of the tongue. The townsmen allow him to continue his speech, on the condition that
he never forget his place. But it is his place, precisely, that
the episode fixes. The scene of the speech which the hero
supposes to be his valediction is itself a race riot. With some
of his schoolmates, he has been made to participate in a prior
entertainment for this town smoker. He and his friends are
to stage a battle royal.

> We were a small tight group, clustered together, our bare
> upper bodies touching and shining with anticipatory sweat;
> while up front the big shots were becoming increasingly
> excited over something we still could not see. Suddenly I
> heard the school superintendent, who had told me to come,
> yell, "Bring up the shines, gentlemen! Bring up the little
> shines!"

They are herded before a magnificent, stark-naked blonde,
and threatened if they look and threatened by the crowd if
they don't. They are held there, made to suffer sexual embarrassment becoming sexual torture, and made to participate
then vicariously in the lurching obscenities of the town's
ranking citizens. They are goaded, threatened, tantalized,
tickled, promised money, beaten, degraded and insulted,
worked to the hysteria which is that of their audience, and
then thrown blindfold into their battle royal where, in blind
passion, they punch and kick at each other while the white
mob howls around them. After the battle, at the end of their
strength, they are forced to another frenzy by being made to
scramble for coins on an electrified rug.

It is to this crapulous mob, in this coliseum, that the hero then talks about "social equality." The episode is a sustained orgy. It not only mocks the hero's earnest dogma of pacific humility, and it not only baptizes him in the terror that, he will find, lurks in all adventures of Negroes among American whites. There is no telling what craziness and what brutish violence lie at any next step. More than that, the episode concentrates, brilliantly, and it exposes at the pitch of a ritualistic frenzy the interior facts of caste, not only its mechanism of economic exploitation (the hero tries to make a deal with one of his schoolmates and is rebuffed, division has been effectively imposed upon them), but all its deeper exploitation of the Negro as a ritualistic scapegoat.

The hero is not only discriminated against. The politics of this system goes much deeper. In fact, he is coddled by that white man, the school superintendent, who has most immediate authority over him—the school superintendent presents him for his speech with a pat on the back, a brief case, and a scholarship. He and his schoolmates are not without honor. These whites use them in ways curiously like love. It is the function of this caste system to suppress a great deal more than the Negro, and it is the lesson of this episode that these Negroes incarnate for these whites everything that they suppress. The Negroes are made by them into the bacchants they themselves dare not be. They are made agents of, and at the same time sacrifices to, the forbidden, everything that is dark, their irrational craving for cruelty, their greed and their sex and their itch for self-destruction, the swoon of the id. These Negroes become for them, then, underground men, irrational, sinful, Satanic, the embodiment of the urgent dark, the pressing power of blackness. And beyond that, they act out for them the whole violent struggle for civilization, by first becoming the dark powers and then by exorcising themselves in violent self-punishment. And then again, in a way to triple the irony, in the same moment the Negroes justify the usage that has in the first place made them scapegoats by performing the whole of this ritual for money.

The battle royal is an extraordinarily compressed piece of work, and its one fault is that it is both more intensely maintained and more exhaustive than anything else in the novel, and so the hero's adventures hereafter become more or less adequate echoes of it. But in any event it does contain, both in its significances and in its form, the most of the hero's career. The same chaos of appetites and guilt that is the real, hidden nature of Negro and white relations is exploded at the hero in each of his subsequent accidents.

That same chaos is what is revealed in the double accident of the Mr. Norton episode. The sharecropper, upon command, *lures* Mr. Norton to a heart attack. His story of incest has a truth of blood in it—his name is "Trueblood"—a truth that Mr. Norton, a New England gentleman and a latter-day, declined Calvinist, cannot in any other way accept. He is fascinated, as it were, into a heart attack which is the equivalent of the townsmen's orgiastic smoker. Trueblood plays out the amoral role assigned to the Negro boys of the battle royal. He does what Norton cannot do. His incest has been with his daughter, and Norton, too, has a daughter. " 'You did and are unharmed!' " Norton shouts. " 'You have looked upon chaos and are not destroyed!' " He acts out a scapegoat ritual with Trueblood and then he gives Trueblood money. Trueblood has done him some service. And the saloon episode contains the same implications, only now reversed: the Negroes use Norton for their purposes of vengeance. When he enters, the madmen go mad, and overwhelm him with the madness of blood.

As the hero moves north, madness, confusion, violence, the

bursting of the irrational, are always the last and the purest expressions of the relationships between black and white. He has been warned by Southern Negroes—by one of the crazy veterans, and then by his college president. His advisers have told him that he is invisible, and they have echoed his grandfather's advice. His proper life is a war, at least a guerrilla action. In the North of industry and labor unionism, then, he finds that black is a disturbing secret of the white social fabric, a secret which has been tucked almost out of sight by a stated ideal of liberty, a secret which to his peril he unwittingly springs. He becomes a laborer in a paint factory called Liberty Paints whose pride is its Optic White, a paint that will cover just about anything. The paint is so very white, he discovers, because it is made with a dash of black dope. But it must be the right dope, and when he mixes into it a little other dope that looks and smells the same, the paint turns gray. The action is of course the hieroglyphic of the episode. He is not the right dope. He is an innocent who cannot quite meet the precarious propriety established in the industrial North between black and white. His boss tells him that he doesn't belong in a paint plant. He does not know his tucked-away place.

And he lets loose a riot. In his simple need for a job he stumbles on the complicated fact that industry uses Negroes as scabs. The plant has typically been hiring Negroes in order to undersell its union labor, and so the hero is caught in a contest between labor and capital which has become another contest between white and black. The conflict in this episode is between the local union and the plant's representative Uncle Tom, the right dope. The hero is an innocent who in his innocence will choose neither side. He is therefore a traitor to both sides, and so he brings about an explosion. The

plant's Uncle Tom, threatened by this traitor and in an in-
sane need to preserve his place, traps the hero in the boiler
room and throws the switches that will blow it up.

It is a Negro who throws the switches, but the explosion is,
for all that, the race riot that is always the hero's lesson. ". . . I
seemed to run swiftly up an incline and shot forward with
sudden acceleration into a wet blast of black emptiness that
was somehow a bath of whiteness." He knows the same old
confusion. That it is a Negro who tries to destroy him—he has
just a moment before been feeling an inflation of racial
pride—is another harsh irony. The Negro's warfare has that
other front. Moveover, industrial unionism isn't the solution
Ellison had once told William Attaway that it was. It is another episode in the constant racial war.

Then the Brotherhood, with its doctrinaire idealism that it
wears as a mask, is still another. The hero wanders into it
because at this time in history it is present, because he and
the Brotherhood have use for one another. The hero has
verbal powers for sale, and the Brotherhood offers him not
only a job but a platform, leadership and spokesmanship.
The Brotherhood, moreover, is obvious about its brotherliness. But then the Brotherhood is not brotherly at all. It
uses the hero in order to manipulate Negroes to its own ends
of sabotage and disruption.

It should be said that the Brotherhood Ellison invents is just
as mysteriously malignant as the Communist Party that was
being invented in the late 1940s by Louis Budenz and Whit-
taker Chambers, and it is somewhat less credible. So one-eyed
Brother Jack—who has lost his other eye in unspecified social-
istic activity—will break uncontrollably into an unspecified
foreign language, and one sees specters of bearded bolsheviks
with bombs. Whatever else the Brotherhood is, it is secretive,
un-American, and it is grotesque. But then this is not another

of those stories of the late 1940s of the god that failed. It is little concerned with that political event. And the melodrama is, after all, right. The Brotherhood is the ultimate of the hero's social experiences, the climax of his maturity and of his trek north. It is the society that is completely rational, scientific, the final expression of the historical dialectic, and it is the society in which the irrationality of race warfare should disappear. It is, as it were, the Enlightenment itself, but then the hero finds when he is in it that it has a disturbing ambience, that the lights flicker, that there are ominous rustlings and furtive sounds. And when the explosion that completes his engagement with it comes, what is revealed is neither the Red menace nor the fate of a dogma, but that this last hope of a society *too* is an unstable composition of guilt and patronage and perverted sexuality, that it is as unknowledgeable about the Negro as any other society, and that it *too* exploits him, and for reasons that are irrational.

As he joins the Brotherhood, the hero glimpses for the first time "the possibility of being more than a member of a race." But the joke is on him. It is precisely a Negro that the Brotherhood wants him to be. It fixes his place. Brother Jack, in their first meeting, objects that "you fellows always talk in terms of race!" but another member feels it would be better if the hero were a little blacker. At a Brotherhood party he is asked to sing a spiritual—"*all* colored people sing." He is made to lecture on the Woman Question—the Brotherhood in effect offers him white women—and his first convert tells him that he is "so—so primitive!" "Why," he asks himself,

> did they have to mix their women into everything? Between us and everything we wanted to change in the world they placed a woman: socially, politically, economically. Why, goddamit, why did they insist upon confusing the class

struggle with the ass struggle, debasing both us and them—
all human motives?

And the answer, implicit here as it was in the battle royal
of his youth, is in that deep exploitation that makes him a
ritualistic outlaw. The wife of a Brotherhood leader calls him
a "buck" and begs him to rape her. He is the house Dionysus.

What the Brotherhood would have him be is presented to
him in the crazy, bitter self-destruction of another Negro
Brother, Tod Clifton. The hero discovers him on Forty-second
Street selling tissue-and-cardboard dancing Black Sambo dolls.

> . . . he's Sambo, the dancing, Sambo, the prancing, Sambo,
> the entrancing, Sambo Boogie Woogie paper doll. And all
> for twenty-five cents, the quarter part of a dollar. . . .

The doll grins and grins. It throws itself about "with the
fierce defiance of someone performing a degrading act in
public, dancing as though it received a perverse pleasure from
its motions." It is "an obscene flouncing of everything human!" It is a darky entertainer, a cardboard satyr on an invisible string, and though the hero doesn't know it, it is
presented to him by Tod as a portrait of the hero as the
Brotherhood's Negro.

The hero doesn't realize until later that the doll has a grin
on both sides of its cardboard head, and that has something to
do with his grandfather's curse and with his coming descent
into the underworld. But meanwhile the doll comments on the
brotherliness of the Brotherhood, and the racial content of this
perfectly rational society. Brother Tod himself has an obscure history in the movement. He had once beaten up a
white Brother, in error it is said. Through the movement the
hero comes upon the factions of Negro politics and particularly upon a fanatic nationalist who calls himself Ras the

Exhorter, who calls the hero a traitor. Somewhere inside, the
hero knows that Ras is right, that in this enlightened, this
light, white society, black men and white men aren't brothers.
There is division that isn't healed by the scientism of the historical dialectic, and more than that, the Brotherhood has set
him against his brothers: ". . . black men fighting in the street
because of the white enslaver?" says Ras. "Is that sanity? Is
that consciousness, scientific understahnding?" In fact it would
seem to be, and so the hero's home, it will turn out, is outside this rational world of scientific understanding. The Negro
in the movement who is the most successful brother is an
opportunistic Uncle Tom, Brother Wrestrum, who in a passion to deny Negro-ness becomes the white man's Negro, does
the Brotherhood's dirty work, and becomes its rest room. The
Brotherhood's chief theoretician is white Brother Hambro
who would be a brother to Ham, the ancestor of Negroes, but
he equably tells the hero that the Negro members will have
to be sacrificed to a higher plan. "Brother Jack," the hero
comes to know, is the equivalent of "Marse Jack."

He comes to realize, before he goes underground, that the
historical dialectic is "a crummy lie they kept us dominated
by," and that he is not included in it. He resolves, precisely,
to yes the movement to death—but not before it has made him
the unwitting instrument of a riot in Harlem that is the
battle royal all over again. Brother Tod is shot on Forty-Second Street by a white policeman—Tod's *Tod* is the hero's own
and Tod precedes him into the underworld. The hero, acting
as the spokesman he has become, on his own authority organizes a public funeral for him. He brings Harlem to a fever
of generalized protest, and then he finds that the Brotherhood,
far from leading that protest to practical action, condemns him
as a racist.

But he has started something. The fever in Harlem climbs

to a confused, bloody riot. The riot is on the one hand a revel: "And I saw a crowd of men running up pulling a Borden's milk wagon, on top of which, surrounded by a row of railroad flares, a huge woman in a gingham pinafore sat drinking beer from a barrel which sat before her." And it is on the other hand an orgy of self-destruction. As he runs in the mob, the hero finds that there is a spontaneous organization and leadership in it—a man named Dupre efficiently leads a small body of Negroes in burning down a tenement— but its inevitable conclusion will be in its massacre by white policemen. And the chief politics of this mob is that it engages Negro against Negro. The hero is pitched against Ras, who with this opportunity has mounted a black horse, taken the costume of an Abyssinian chieftain, and become Ras the Destroyer, urging the crowd to what can only be suicide. It will be a suicide for which the Brotherhood is responsible, the hero now realizes, because at the crucial moment it abandoned leadership. Ras hurls a spear at him. The night of the battle royal the hero had tried to point out to his principal opponent in the ring that they were beating each other for *them,* but his opponent wouldn't make a deal, and now with reinforced clarity the hero shouts at Ras and the crowd:

"They want a race riot and I am against it. The more of us who are killed, the better they like—. . . . It's true, I was betrayed by those who I thought were our friends—but they counted on this man, too. They needed this *destroyer* to do their work. They deserted you so that in your despair you'd follow this man to your destruction. Can't you see it? They want you guilty of your own murder, your own sacrifice! . . . They want the streets to flow with blood; your blood, black blood and white blood, so that they can turn your death and sorrow and defeat into propaganda. It's simple, you've known it a long time. It goes, 'Use a nigger to catch a nigger.' . . . Don't you see it? Isn't it clear . . . ?

But the Negroes in the crowd don't see it, it isn't clear, and they move to—lynch him!

The hero runs, pursued by the Destroyer's destroyers, and a moment later, having eluded them, in this nightmare he is then pursued by a couple of white men armed with baseball bats, until he plunges in a fortunate fall through an open manhole into his coal cellar. The cellar will be his home and, finally, it will be his political position. He is neither a Southern humiliationist, nor Booker T. Washington (he couldn't make his peace with millionaires), nor a black trade unionist, nor a radical assimilationist. Nor, though an undercurrent to his last adventure suggests that the position is strongly attractive to him, can he be a Negro nationalist.

The speeches of Ras are, it happens, far more eloquent than any made by the hero. It is clear that Ellison found it easier to be eloquent in Ras's behalf.* His hero, who, we are told, strangely moves crowds by the secret power in his speeches, doesn't really orate very well. Ras on his black charger does have excitement and nobility about him. But Ras, and the nationalism he represents, *are* suicidal, and they are vulnerable to exploitation. Moreover, they aren't compatible with the reality of American life for Negroes. Just prior to his fall, the hero overhears a discussion between two Negroes on the

* Clearly Ras was written in anger. Ellison says: "In 1950 my wife and I were staying at a vacation spot where we met some white liberals who thought the best way to be friendly was to tell us what it was like to be Negro. I got mad at hearing this from people who otherwise seemed very intelligent. I had already sketched Ras but the passion of his statement came out after I went upstairs that night feeling that we needed to have this thing out once and for all and get it done with; then we could go on living like people and individuals." *Paris Review* interview, p. 69.

street about Ras. Ras, they think, is exotic, crazy, and funny. "And man, that crazy sonofabitch up there on that hoss looking like death eating a sandwich. . . . Crazy, man. Everybody else trying to git some loot and him and his boys out for blood! . . . and that hoss shot up the street leaping like Heigho, the goddam Silver!"

The hero is then, at the end, back where he began, before all his political experiments failed him, without doctrine. None of these political positions he has tried has met the reality of American life for Negroes. They have all, to the contrary, been only different ways in which the complicated exploitation of the Negro takes place. And the hero, after he has outfitted his coal cellar, commits himself only to the role he has always had. He will be a something hidden and deeply disturbing in American life, constantly felt and never seen. Committing himself to the role, he has become a thief—he steals light and power from Monopolated Light and Power—and a saboteur.

It is just the same negative resolution that confirms him as an invisible man, because all his adventures at the same time as they have had political significances, have been a search as well for personal identity. More than for others, because as a Negro he is more than others a political fact, as his politics ends up negative, he is negative, invisible. All of his voyages are from point zero to an adequate politics. All of them bring him back to his beginning. In the same movement they each take him from invisibility toward anticipated visibility and then back to zero. At the end, having been frustrated in every promise of visibility typically offered a Negro in America, he ominously accepts the identity that has been given him, one that is negative but that is an identity none the less.

He is invisible first of all because nobody, neither white nor black, sees him, but only the roles they project onto him. "I am invisible," the hero says, "understand, simply because people refuse to see me." At best, and least confusingly, he is at various times for some Negroes an overtly public race leader. But then his invisibility is not only in the fact that others do not recognize his individual humanity. It is also, he is to learn, essential. All his life, the hero says at the very beginning of his memoir, he had been looking for himself.

> It took me a long time and much painful boomeranging of my expectations to achieve a realization everyone else appears to have been born with: That I am nobody but myself. But first I had to discover that I am an invisible man!

And it is the process of boomeranging that proves that he is essentially invisible. Each of his adventures is an attempt at self-definition as they each present a seemingly fixed version of the world's reality, within which he might have a place. He tries in each version of reality to make a place for himself. And then his every version explodes into chaos and he is exploded out of it.

Each version ends in death. That is another meaning of his descent into the underground. But then that death has still other implications. It is most particularly as a Negro that he makes this negation the symbol of his life, and if his boomeranging experiences have carried him back to himself, that ur-self is composed of the race and the tradition with which he was born. His individual humanity—though other Negroes in the novel don't recognize the fact, and if they did he would be turned into something else—is general and exemplary. Each of his adventures, seen in another way, has been an effort at accommodation, or assimilation, or simply compromise, and each therefore has been to some extent an effort at denial of race. Whether he will be the humble darky of the Southern provinces, or a co-operative idealist, like Booker T. Washington, or try to steer himself between the two sides as they have got into an industrial war, or try to include himself with whites in the historical dialectic that is bigger than everyone, he obscures his real self. And each catastrophe strips him of all identity but the fact that he is a Negro.

The night after the initiation rite of his high-school valedictory, the hero has a dream. In the dream his grandfather bids him open his new brief case, in which the school superintendent had tucked away his new scholarship. But he finds just envelope contained in envelope in an endless series, and then finally an engraved document that reads: "To Whom It May Concern. Keep This Nigger-Boy Running." After his double accident with Mr. Norton, he contemplates being expelled from college, his eyes fill with tears and he thinks, "Here within this quiet greenness I possessed the only identity I had ever known, and I was losing it," but when Dr. Bledsoe does expel him, he addresses him as "Nigger," and he tells him some of the grim facts of his real identity. At the paint factory, after he is blasted by the old Negro foreman into another expression of the war between black and white, the hero finds himself in the glistening white factory hospital. He has been in a coma, and he wakes now inside a peculiar glass box. He has forgotten his name and address, and the narrative then carries him through some symbols of rebirth. The doctors have performed on him, he overhears them say, the equivalent of a prefrontal lobotomy, and he does feel a new remoteness and the welling within him of an alien personality. But he is left with a core of basic memory, basic identity that is in the deepest facts, the folk facts, of Negro culture. A doctor flashes a card at him inside his box, reading "WHO WAS YOUR MOTHER?" and he can't remember, but he thinks to himself, "I don't play the dozens." * In the next instant he does, at the doctor's prodding, remember Buckeye the Rabbit. "It was annoying that he had hit upon an old identity. . . ." And when the doctor puts before him "BR'ER RABBIT" he does play the dozens: "He was your mother's back-door man."

And as in a series of tremors, later, he is shifted out of the Brotherhood, he discovers not only that Brotherhood exploits him as a Negro, but he discovers facts of Negro experience, his experience, which Brotherhood does not contain and for which the historical dialectic does not account. As the Brotherhood is his ultimate adventure in self-definition, it most elaborately prepares his descent back to himself. In his initial meeting with Brother Jack, he is told that his past, his "old agrarian self," is dead. "*History* has been born in your brain." He is given a new name by the Brotherhood, to honor and protect this birth. When he addresses his first mass meeting, he declares that he has found his true family, people, country, and he glimpses the possibility of being more than a member of a race. But throughout his engagement with Brotherhood, at every inconvenient moment, he has a persistent consciousness of a self within him that is racial and that is not dead, that this new identity does not incorporate, that it costs him always a greater effort to suppress. The "malicious, arguing part," he calls it when he first becomes aware of it, "the dissenting voice, my grandfather part; the cynical, disbelieving part— the traitor self that always threatened internal discord."

---

* "The Dozens" is a game particularly common among Negro children which creates a pattern of mutual insult out of an exchange of slurs on the cleanliness, odor, legitimacy, fidelity, and heterosexuality of the opponents' immediate family. See Stanley Edgar Hyman, "American Negro Literature and the Folk Tradition," the first part of an exchange on "The Negro Writer in America," *Partisan Review,* XXV (Spring 1958), 205; reprinted in *The Promised End* (Cleveland and New York: The World Publishing Company, 1963), pp. 295–315.

He is not one of the Brothers. His own history is active in him, and it is not theirs. His history is, to the contrary, that of the Brotherhood's enemy, Ras the Exhorter—"Brothers are the same color," says Ras, and he knows where the hero comes from. "You from down South! You from Trinidad! You from Barbados! Jamaica, South Africa, and the white mahn's foot in your ass all the way to the hip." Tod tells the hero, prophetically, that it is "on the inside" that Ras is strong and dangerous, and he tells him that " 'sometimes a man *has* to plunge outside history.' " Tod himself then leaps into the irrationality outside history and thereby presents the hero with a desperate question:

> But he knew that only in the Brotherhood could we make ourselves known, could we avoid being empty Sambo dolls. . . . I'd . . . hold on desperately to Brotherhood with all my strength. For to break away would be to plunge. . . . to plunge! . . . Why did he choose to plunge into nothingness, into the void of faceless faces, of soundless voices, lying outside history?

That the cloak of the Brotherhood's scientific historicism that he has been wearing as an identity does not fit him, he begins now at the level of full consciousness to recognize. Shortly after Tod precedes him into death, he comes upon a trio of Negro zoot-suiters—boys, he is forced to reflect, outside the history that Brother Jack understood, who might be anything, perhaps even the true leaders, and the only way he has to account for them is to reflect that history and therefore the true metaphysics is not rational.

> What if history was a gambler, instead of a force in a laboratory experiment, and the boys his ace in the hole? What if history was not a reasonable citizen, but a madman full of

paranoid guile and these boys his agents, his big surprise!
. . . For they were outside, in the dark with Sambo, the
dancing paper doll; taking it on the lambo with my fallen
brother. . . .

When he returns to Harlem, he realizes that it is not the
Harlem that the Brotherhood has defined. When Negroes
come to Tod's funeral, it is for no reason accounted for by
the Brotherhood's theoretical dialectic, and on this occasion
he does not preach it. Bortherhood does not determine his
response, either.

The climax to his engagement with Brotherhood and history, and to all his attempts at self-definition, is his own acci-
dental plunge into the void—which is Negro-ness. Before he
falls into his underground, he falls, through some bizarre
circumstances, into the Harlem underworld—into, as it were,
the underlying Negro experience. It is where he has all along
been heading, or, alternatively, where he has always been.
Through all his adventures he has felt a tug to simple racial
identity. He is moved repeatedly by its folk expression in the
blues. He is embarrassed once when a white short-order cook
offers him pork chops and grits, and then his embarrassment
embarrasses him. He eats a hot yam on the street and feels
a sudden freedom. "I am what I am," he says.

Moreover, through all his adventures he has been meeting
monitory Negroes and collecting portentous tokens that point
to this plunge. There had been his grandfather. Then Trueblood. The mad veteran of the Golden Day had told him that
he is "invisible, a walking personification of the Negative,"
and had told him some other things, to play the game but
not to believe in it, that he is hidden, if he will but know it,
right out in the open, and that the world is possibility. Dr.
Bledsoe had told him how *he* only *seemed* to yes the white

millionaires. The Uncle Tom of the paint plant was a Tom but he lived in the boiler room, mysteriously, underground, and he controlled the whole works. And there had been Brother Tod to point the way.

And as the hero adventures, he collects odd, ambiguously meaningful things in the brief case the school superintendent had once given him. There is first the dream message, "Keep This Nigger-Boy Running." In a Harlem rooming house he acquires an antique toy bank, a piece of early Americana, a cast-iron figure of a very black, red-lipped, wide-mouthed, white-eyed, grinning Negro, bearing the legend FEED ME. In the Brotherhood he meets an elderly Negro who had spent a lifetime on a chain gang for once having said no to a man who wanted to take something from him, and he accepts from him a link of the leg chain he finally broke. And later he stuffs into his brief case one of Tod's Sambo dolls.

All of his advisers and all these mementos have the same veiled, complicated advice for him: of a something unique in Negro life, of something in Negro life hidden, mysterious, and willfully obscured, a something kinetic and not fixed. Negro life contains the necessity for hiding, duplicity, treachery, for adopting shifting roles while the real reality goes on beneath. And the perfect metaphor for all the advice he has received is invisibility.

Invisibility is the lesson in his penultimate fall into the Harlem underworld, into, as it were, the heart of darkness. Pursued, ironically, by Ras's black legions, the hero puts on a pair of dark glasses and a wide-brimmed hat, and in that disguise he makes a discovery of identity. He has lost the identity he has thought he has had. Ras's legions don't recognize him. But he has unwittingly put on the uniform of a man named Rinehart, for whom he is everywhere mistaken. Rinehart, by that accident, becomes the last of his tutors, and

the significant thing about Rinehart is that he has no positive
identity, only a shifting appearance.

Everybody knows Rinehart, and, since he is so easily mistaken, it would seem that he is known to nobody. B. P. Rinehart—the B. for Bliss, the P. for Proteus[46]—is a numbers
runner and he is a lay minister. As a runner he would seem to
be a nigger boy who has kept running but who has made a
function of it, who somehow has come to own the track. As
a minister, he is a priest precisely of the Invisible. One of his
handbills reads:

> BEHOLD THE SEEN UNSEEN
> BEHOLD THE INVISIBLE
> YE WHO ARE WEARY COME HOME!

He is also, the hero discovers, a gambler, and a briber, the
envy of one class of Negroes, the terror of another, a fabulous
figure, a lover who has recorded fabulous achievements, and
he is, someone says, a "confidencing sonofabitch"—with clear
antecedence in Melville's Confidence Man.[47] He is a master
of disguises and a master of chaos. He is beyond ethics—he
has "a smooth tongue, a heartless heart and [is] ready to do
anything"—and he is outside social determinations, and therefore he is a bringer of bliss. Therefore he is also threatening.
He is a grinning, yessing mask, the person behind which is
invisible and might be anything or nothing. It is Rinehart
who finally teaches the hero his new metaphysics of irrationality. When the hero puts on Rinehart's dark glasses, he is
struck by the fluidity of the forms he sees through the lenses.
He reflects, when he knows more, that Rinehart's world is
possibility. "The world in which we lived," he now sees, "was
without boundaries. A vast seething, hot world of fluidity, and
Rine the rascal was at home."

When he reaches his Epilogue, the hero abruptly dismisses

Rinehart as a personal possibility, apparently because Rinehart is antisocial. Rinehart is another of the victims of Ellison's abrupt affirmativeness. But even so, at the end he sets it down as one of the hero's ironic lessons that his world is possibility—and it would appear to be the case that Ellison, at this desperate point turned to optimism, refuses to see that Rinehart has made the world-as-possibility identical with the world-as-chaos. Rinehart is, in fact, the novel's most convincing end. The hero's progress has throughout been repeated lessons in the fact that the world, so far as he is concerned, is not fixed. It provides him with a nonidentity. After much boomeranging, he discovers that he is essentially invisible, and Rinehart is the incarnation of the invisible.

Rinehart is the culmination, too, of the historical process the hero has been in all his adventures tracing. Rinehart is the underground, the secret of Harlem, the complicated city. He is a master of its latest inventions: he drives a Cadillac and at his religious meetings he uses an electric guitar. The secret he incarnates is chaos, an ancient secret, but he has learned to manipulate it. By accepting its lessons, he has given a final formulation to the history of Negroes in America, and so he has mastered his and the Negro's history.

That history, accomplished in the novel by still another system of ironies, is on the one hand a backward progress by the Negro in America from freedom, or the promise of freedom, to chaos. Perhaps at the bottom of the joke is Booker T. Washington's *Up from Slavery*. Specifically, it is a history that goes from Emancipation, to Reconstruction, with a glance backward to the heyday of enlightened Abolition, to the present, and in each phase the hero sets out to explore the promise of freedom only to find that all principles have turned irrational. On the other hand, the history he discovers is of the implication of the Negro in America. In the Prologue, in his

marijuana dream, his sense of time subtilized by the marijuana, the hero sees and hears various levels of Negro history.
First he hears the shout of a backwoods minister preaching
the text, "the 'Blackness of Blackness' "—a text to announce,
here as in Jude, the Lord's accursed, "who were before of old
ordained to this condemnation."

That is the far beginning, and it is another name for the
absolute truth that, when at the end he descends into the underground, the hero will accept and turn into his positive
identity. But now he tears himself away from the preacher's
voice to listen to the tale of an old slave, a woman who has
borne sons to her white master. So he enters history. The
woman's story is "all mixed up." She hates and loves her
master, who is the father of her sons. She loves more the
freedom that her master promised but never gave, but then
freedom, she knows, is in love, in attachment, and she hates
her master and has poisoned him. Her sons know no such
confusion. They simply hate. But it is the confusion after
the promise of freedom that the hero learns and will learn,
and the intense involvement of the slave with the master.

He accounts for his own life, as he begins the telling of
his own adventures, by remarking that he was in the cards
eighty-five years ago, the time his grandparents were told
that they were free and believed it. But then his grandfather
had not after all believed in his freedom, nor had he seen his
life in terms of it. Rather, he had defined his life in terms
of a war. The war is what it would seem Emancipation eman-
cipated, and not the forces of progress. That is a historical
judgment that the hero, at a remove, in his first adventure
proves. When he comes to deliver his valedictory address, he
is at his own age of emancipation, looking forward to a
progress of manhood in a reasonable, good-willed, defined
community. He assumes a liberal community of effort to

overcome the confused past. But then the promise of freedom serves only as a preliminary to the battle royal. He is initiated by Emancipation, as was his grandfather, into war.

He presses forward nevertheless, though beset by discord, to a reasonable solution to the Negro problem, to, as it were, the Reconstruction phase of his racial career. At college he associates himself with those Negroes, and particularly Dr. Bledsoe, who wear vestments of power donated by Northern millionaires. And in Mr. Norton he meets postwar Northern liberalism itself:

> A face pink like St. Nicholas', topped with a shock of silk white hair. An easy, informal manner, even with me. A Bostonian, smoker of cigars, teller of polite Negro stories, shrewd banker, skilled scientist, director, philanthropist, forty years a bearer of the white man's burden, and for sixty a symbol of the Great Tradition.

That is, a composite Brahmin. Norton is a late member from Concord, ridden by secret depravity and by investment capitalism—he looks on the college as an investment—and he has degenerated into patricianism. Norton says to the hero, "Through you and your fellow students I become, let us say, three hundred teachers, seven hundred trained mechanics, eight hundred skilled farmers, and so on. That way I can observe in terms of living personalities to what extent my money, time and my hopes have been fruitfully invested." He finds his significant ancestry in Ralph Waldo Emerson, but his Emersonianism has evaporated into fleecy liberal platitudes. And he particularly suggests Charles Eliot Norton, that true believer in a democracy under the moral guidance of the privileged. Charles Eliot Norton once founded a night school in Cambridge and he once raised money to build a model apartment house in Boston for poor families. Mr. Norton, guided by what must be the same impulse, is one of the founders and a trustee of the hero's college.

The hero gratefully assents to Mr. Norton's promise of moral guidance up from slavery into responsible freedom, and finds then that Mr. Norton is a source not of freedom but of confusion. That confusion is itself equipped with some historical sources. The descent by Mr. Norton on Trueblood is the equivalent of a visit to antiquity, to slavery. Trueblood, a remote peasant, lives in a cabin built during slavery times, and Norton finds it astonishing that it has endured. Trueblood finishes his story of incest with the words: "I sings me some blues that night ain't never been sang before," and there is a suggestion in his words that he is the first singer, the Caedmon, of his race. And when Norton uses Trueblood as the scapegoat of his own guilts, all unconsciously, he is as unconsciously finding his way back to the historical source of his philanthropy, and thereby saying something about post-bellum Boston liberalism. His philanthropy contains, much as did slavery, a profound and hidden economics of exploitation.

Mr. Norton hopefully enters the saloon called the Golden Day, and he is shocked. The episode condenses numbers of bitter ironies. *The Golden Day,* Lewis Mumford's book describing the efflorescence of American culture in the years 1830–1860, stands at once for the inspiration of Mr. Norton's liberalism and its end, and it is another irony that the period described by Mumford's phrase is that as well of the efflorescence of slavery. The golden day is filled with the spirit of Abolition, and the clients of the Golden Day saloon are men risen far beyond slavery. They are teachers, scientists, lawyers, physicians, the end products of the progressive liberalism that set them free, and they are all crazy. They provide a mirror to the golden day. On the one hand, they are not and have never been free. They are black. On the other hand, they bring a truer enlightenment to the liberalism of the golden day. They provide the fact beneath the platitudes, of the constant and confused war between white and black. One of the mad veterans of the Golden Day, a surgeon, tells the hero that Mr. Norton is not only a trustee, but one of the first trustees, a "trustee of consciousness," which is assent enough to his historical role, but then he tells Mr. Norton that while he is for some of the Negroes there the great white father, he is "to others the lyncher of souls," and "for all, you are confusion come even into the Golden Day." That is the point of this historical engagement of the hero. The golden day, with its bright promise, had stumbled in a confusion which by the agency of a later, ennervated liberalism, has become confounded.

His reconstruction in the South having failed, having in fact collapsed into riot, the hero participates next in that next epochal event of his racial history, the Great Migration —a migration from the South to the North, the traditional road of freedom, from the country to the city, from agrarianism to industry. The Great Migration is to be another promise of progress in freedom which is not redeemed. Its end, too, is chaos bared, because it is just the same promise as that which was implicit in the liberalism of the golden day. Now that liberalism is even more distant from its source, and it has been progressively emasculated.

Fresh from his engagement with Mr. Norton, the hero comes to New York and falls upon the mercies of a young Mr. Emerson, the son of a Mr. Emerson, who has himself now become a rich New York businessman. Young, psychoanalyzed Mr. Emerson, a reader of *Totem and Taboo,* some of whose best friends are Negroes, offers the hero conspicuous kindness. He knows something about tyranny too. He considers himself his father's prisoner. He offers himself up as Huck Finn to the hero's Nigger Jim (a gesture which makes full sense, it happens, only when it is assumed that young Emerson knows about Leslie Fiedler's discovery of a homosexual theme in *Huckleberry Finn*).[48] And young Emerson invites the hero to a party at the Club Calamus—another pale progeny, apparently, of the Golden Day.

When the hero enters industry, his paint factory, it is, as is historically appropriate, by using "Emerson's name without his permission." (Though there would seem as well to be a private joke in the event. Ralph Ellison's middle name is Waldo.) Come to industry, he discovers that the promise in the Great Migration was just a device of industrial capitalism, that he is an unwitting and certainly an unwilling weapon wielded against labor unionism, and he discovers that his coming to terms with this technological society will be nothing if not violent. The industrial war is, so far as he is concerned, just another, though a more complicated, version of the same war. The Great Migration leads him back to chaos. Specifically, the factory explosion sends him to the hospital, into, perhaps, the systematic persecutions that after World War I followed the Great Migration. It is the hospital's intent to put the hero in a glass box and render him docile. He is submitted to the equivalent of a lobotomy, which is in its turn the equivalent of another operation waggishly suggested by one of the doctors—castration. The point of the operation, a doctor explains, is that "society will suffer no traumata on his account."

The operation does not secure the intended results, and the hero is plunged then into the final one of the great events of his racial career, the Great Depression. He discovers his whereabouts by coming on what may be taken as the Great Depression's most conspicuously typical event, a tenement

eviction. It is an event that provides him with another punning metaphor for his history, "dispossession," and it provides
him at the same time, as is historically appropriate, with a
seeming opportunity. The event is his introduction to the
promising radical politics that could flourish because of such
events—he makes a speech to the crowd and is on the spot
recruited by the Brotherhood. There is seeming opportunity
in the Brotherhood, of course, because it seems brotherly, because it is active, because it seems to make the Negro's cause
its own. Beyond that, it imposes on the hero a version of his
racial history that unites him with the majority, thereby elimi-
nating the war that he has borne in his secret consciousness.
The evictees for whom the hero has just spoken are, Brother
Jack tell him, "agrarian types" who are being "ground up by
industrial conditions," and so, all Brotherhood doctrine would
seem to say, the race war is subsumed by and solved by the
class war.

To wage the class war instead is not only the way toward
freedom, but it is freedom itself. Like other Negro intellectuals during the Great Depression, the hero accepts this unique
promise provided by the Great Depression. There is an alternative only in the futile nationalism of Marcus Garvey, for
whom, in the novel, Ras the Exhorter-Destroyer stands. But
then the Communist Party did not secure its promise, and so
neither does the Brotherhood. It abruptly withdraws its concerns for Harlem—and the hero comes on the fact that the
race and the class wars are not identical. Furthermore, he
discovers that he is bound to maintain the race war within
the ranks of the Brotherhood. Brother Jack is one-eyed and
cannot see him. The hero, after his first revelation of Jack's
duplicity, looks around a corner of his mind and sees "Jack
and Norton and Emerson emerge into one single white figure." The Brotherhood's version of history is arbitrary and

does not include his history. And therefore the hero is forced
back to the version of reality that at bottom he knows—which
is, it turns out, Rinehart's, and which is in the image of chaos.

Rinehart is what this history comes to, and he is its hero.
He is the climax of the progress up from slavery. Chaos is his
freedom. He moves easily in it. He secures his living from it,
and if he has been condemned to it, he takes from it also the
implements of his revenge. He has made chaos a base of
political action. He is a thief, a rascal, an underground man
engaged in the subversion of society. Like Melville's hero, he
undermines confidence, and thereby the very foundation of
society.

The hero's last adventure, in the Epilogue, in his hole in
the ground, serves to confirm and to deepen Rinehart, and
Rinehart, the underworld man, is the last of a series of puns
for the "underground" which now, in a last shift, is to become
actual. The hero's progress has been a series of boomeranging
reversals, and he returns now to the most final reversal of all.
In every instance when he has thought he has been moving
upward, he has been moving down. Especially as he has
neared his last adventure there has been a play of punning foreshadowings about him all unwary. He attends the
Brotherhood's social events at an apartment house named the
Chthonian. He attempts to secure secret information about the
Brotherhood from a girl named Sybil—as Aeneas consulted
the sibyl before he entered the underworld. From the beginning his grandfather had spoken to him from the grave. The
technically accommodated Negro of the paint plant had been
an underground man. The Brotherhood itself is a secret,
underground organization. The hero's progress has all along
been a descent.

He has gone out into life repeatedly, he has been frustrated
repeatedly, and at the end he descends into death. That is

one implication of his drop into his underground. He has looked for definition, and found chaos. He has made a series of voyages into the world which is a white world, and he ends in the pit of darkness. He has sought rationality, and he ends in the heart of the irrational. He has looked for tranquillity, and he ends in hell. There are all these suggestions brought together in his fall. His search for an adequate politics, for a technique of accommodation, his search for a personal identity, his adventuring through his own racial history, have all led him to this complete negation. The hero in his hole in the ground is back to where he began.

But his descent into the underground is the climax to still another set of implications in his adventures, and his return now to his beginnings is a full and stable resolution to all his adventures. With this final reversal, his reverses have come to an end because, like Rinehart before him, he now accepts reversal as the positive law of his being. It is his metaphysics. He is an invisible man in a world without form—but that, his underground adventure, like the Rinehart episode, goes to prove, is something. He does have an identity and a place, only they are contrary. There is a paradox in the fact that the hero's place in the world is underneath the ground, out of the world, but then the paradox is twisted again when the hero converts his hole in the ground into a home. His coal cellar, Ellison has himself pointed out, is not a sewer, but a source of heat and light and power. The hero converts all his losses to assertion. In fact he has found his politics and his person, and he has made sense out of his history, and so in his fall there is finally an ascension—which Ellison ultimately blurs by his promise that the hero will someday rise to do good among men.

His adventures have gone to prove to the hero, simply, that he is black, and, not so simply, that blackness is equivalent to the reverse of things. Now he asserts his blackness, accepting and using all its qualities and associations. The "Blackness of Blackness," the text offered by the preacher of the Prologue, has been, in effect, the text he has had to learn. In the Prologue he had said that he had to illuminate the blackness of his invisibility. Blackness is the cause of his persecution, of the deprivation of his individual humanity, of his apartness. But blackness is also the dark secrets in his persecution, all the totems and taboos that have been thrust upon him. His adventures in light and dark, in what amounts to the Manicheism of the American racial situation, have provided him with the lesson that he is Satan, whose residence should be in the underground, or as he incorporates lawlessness and irrationality he is Dionysus, or he is the darkness just behind consciousness. He is that which is hidden and deceptive and destructive, that which in nature is alien to man, invisible but present, the shadow upon the world. And he is the very principle of the boomerang which scatters all progress, all history, and all the enlightened ethics of civilization.

He embraces the *blackness* of blackness and thereby becomes an underground man—like Dostoevski's hero, an incarnation of that which is just beneath the surface of things, that is treacherous, irresponsible, and mad.* He embraces that fate to which he was "before of old ordained," and thereby

---

* As important a source of the hero's underground adventure would seem to be a novella by Richard Wright, "The Man Who Lived Underground," *Cross Section,* Edwin Seaver, ed. (New York: L. B. Fischer, 1944), pp. 58–102. In Wright's novella, too, a Negro protagonist stumbles into an abandoned underground room which he converts to a home. Ellison's hero illuminates his cellar with 1,369 lights and he plans to have in it five radio-phonographs. Wright's hero papers the walls of his cellar with one-hundred-dollar bills, hangs the walls with gold watches and rings, and strews the floor with diamonds. Like Ellison's hero, he arranges for light by stealing electricity. Like Ellison's hero, he finds his freedom underground.

inherits that "power of blackness" which Melville said "derives its force from its appeals to that Calvinistic sense of Innate Depravity and Original Sin, from whose visitations, in some shape or other, no deeply thinking mind is always and wholly free."

The invisible man's end is in the embrace of his diabolism—diabolism is his politics, his identity, his history, and his metaphysics. And his future is to be Satan's—treason, violence, revenge. These are the normal activities now of his underground life. Most of the time he walks softly, he says in the Prologue, so as not to awaken the sleeping ones. He restricts himself to the subversion of Monopolated Light & Power. And he dines on his favorite dessert of vanilla ice cream and sloe gin—white, presumably, seeping blood. But once, with little direct provocation, he had beaten and almost killed a white man. An invisible man tries to make himself felt.

And the true end of the invisible man's proper adventures is in a dream of gigantic vengeance. Fallen into his coal cellar, he dreams of Jack and Emerson and Bledsoe and Norton and Ras and the school superintendent. They demand that he return to them, and when he refuses, they castrate him—they do, that is to say, what they have done. They throw his bloody parts over a bridge, but now his sex catches there, beneath the apex of the curving arch of the bridge, and drips blood into the red water. The hero laughs and tells his torturers that it is their own sun hanging there, and their moon and their world, and that dripping upon the water is all the history they are ever going to make. And then the great bridge itself gathers itself together and slowly moves off, "striding like a robot, an iron man, whose iron legs clanged doomfully as it moved." The hero, full of sorrow and pain, shouts that it must be stopped, but that terrifying figure is his own metamorphosis. And the great dark threat in it is his resolution.

After that all messages would seem to measure Ellison's desperate reluctances. But the hero is turned, in any event, at the very end, to a staccato of abrupt affirmations—of democracy (". . . we, most of all, had to affirm the principle, the plan in whose name we had been brutalized and sacrificed"), of love (". . . in spite of all I find that I love. . . . I *have* to love"), of the mind, of social responsibility, and of the immediate prospect of his emergence. It must be said that Ellison is to be seen at the very last moment trying to take back the book he has written, or at the very least muffling all its severities, and that is unfortunate. But then it should be said as well that lacking some such attempt, there will be nothing more for Ellison ever to say.

The constant technical flaw in *Invisible Man* is that it so frequently comes to an end, and Ellison is put at every point to a greater muscularity to make the next scene more intense, more thoroughly revealing of what has already been largely revealed. It is the concomitant of that flaw that *Invisible Man* is a death-driven novel. Its movement is to confirm again and again that the hero doesn't exist, and Ellison's difficulty, to put it another way, is to resurrect the hero for each subsequent adventure. The novel's series of ironic negations is, after all, a series of negatives. It can and does reach its last possibility. Ellison will be left with only stale repetitions of the act of dying unless he can in fact assert social responsibility and mind and love—and, because the "Negro problem" is entirely an American problem, democracy. That is the only way he can keep possibility open.

That is to say that the end of *Invisible Man* is the beginning of another novel, one that will draw the complicated positive engagement of the hero in this life, specifically this American life. It is the huge achievement of *Invisible Man,* meanwhile, that it has got a vastness of experience as Negroes

particularly must know it—there can be very little that it has
left out—into a single meaning. The novel creates a negative
metaphor, invisibility, that is fully analytic and fully inclusive,
that does hold together for a moment the long experience of
chaos that has met Ellison's vision.

∾ IV ∾

JAMES BALDWIN

A Question of Identity

The invisibility of the Negro in America has in fact been James Baldwin's underlying metaphor also, and when he has been most responsive to his materials he has made of invisibility, the failure of identity, a lyric of frustration and loss. What is most revealing for the case Baldwin comes to represent, however, is that the fury in his frustration and the pathos in his loss have led him, in a progress of three novels and far too many personal essays, ever further from the clarity with which he began. What promised to be a dramatic recognition of the actual conditions of invisibility in his first novel, *Go Tell It on the Mountain* (1953), became a rhetoric of privileged alienation. As a Negro, Baldwin was society's victim. As a victim, he was alienated. As an alienatee, he presented himself with vast moral authority. In the space of a few years the rhetoric and the authority have done him less and less service, and he has been left to fall back on an iteration of the word "love." Love in its demonstration has become, finally, a fantasy of innocence.

The plight in invisibility has remained a plight for Baldwin, despite his uses of it as an instrument of moral authority and despite the fury in his words. His heroes are victims, caught between despair and spite, their spitefulness directed sometimes against the very sympathy which as victims they earn. They are heroes who cannot make themselves felt in the world, heroes for whom society almost provides but then doesn't quite provide a clear, felt identity. The story Baldwin tells repeatedly, in his novels, his stories, his writing for the theater, and in his essays, is of the attempt of a heroic innocent to achieve what Baldwin usually calls "identity"—"identity" is by all measure his favorite word, but on occasion the word is "manhood" or "maturity"—and the thwarting, then, of this hero by his society. The hero is prevented from entering the world. He does not achieve the definition provided by a place in the world. If sometimes in a final movement he does locate himself in a peripheral place and in a special expression of the self, in the expatriate community of Paris, perhaps, or the world of jazz, more often he finds himself shunted into one or another expression of neurosis—religious mania in *Go Tell It on the Mountain* and in Baldwin's play *The Amen Corner*,[1] homosexuality elsewhere, a nightmare violence such as that in the first movement of *Another Country* (1962). And the hero's fulfillment stands, then, ironically and bitterly, for the quantity of his pain.

The hero's plight in Baldwin's fiction and semi-fiction has many equivalences. To be a Negro in Harlem is, it turns out, the same thing really as to be an American Negro abroad. That, in turn, is the same thing as to be an upper-middle-class Negro in Atlanta, Georgia, or it is the same thing as to be a Northern Negro visiting in Atlanta. Given a slight shift of circumstances, to be an American Negro at all is the same thing as to be an American, and then to be an American is the same thing as to be sexually ambivalent. The adventures of Baldwin's different heroes have a sameness. An occasional essay in 1959 on school integration in Atlanta, "Nobody Knows My Name," * discovers its principal interest in those middle-class Negroes of Atlanta who, because of their inherited position, cannot fully find themselves in either camp, white or black. There is the story, it would seem, that Baldwin is best equipped to see. And their condition is different only in what may be called accident from what would seem to be its opposite case, that of the hero of Baldwin's "white" novel, *Giovanni's Room* (1956), whose inherited condition is simply that he is an American. As an American, the novel argues, he cannot love, and therefore he cannot give himself to either camp of lovers, heterosexuals' or homosexuals'. In both instances the protagonists are born to a fatal ambivalence of position which confers on them a kind of invisibility. They suffer the same manifest nonexistence in society. And their story, once again, is not essentially different from that of the American Negro in Paris who is the subject of a number of Baldwin's essays, whose American-ness separates him from Europeans while his color does not allow him to be an American. He is separated by his nationality, moreover, from other colored persons, the North Africans in Paris, and he is separated by the motives of his expatriation from other American Negroes in Paris. The "American Negro in Paris," Baldwin indeed says in one of these essays, "Encounter on the Seine," "is very nearly the invisible man."

And it is the loneliness in invisibility that is the affective

---

* The case of Southern Negro educators is another case in point. They too, because their position is between the black and white communities, solicit Baldwin's special interest, and his sorrow. See "The Hard Kind of Courage," *Harper's Magazine,* CCXVII (October 1958), 62, and "They Can't Turn Back," *Mademoiselle,* LI (August 1960), 351. Still another such case is the ambiguity of the position of Negro leaders in Harlem. See "The Harlem Ghetto," *Notes of a Native Son.*

basis of this constant story. Baldwin's heroes are projected as
having an original, unique identity, which society does not
so much corrupt as obscure. "Nobody Knows My Name"
might stand as the title for everything that Baldwin has
written—as in fact it does stand as the title for his second
collection of essays. The yearning of all his heroes, in their
many circumstances, is for recognition, and they find themselves enmeshed in society's misunderstandings. In Ellison's
use of the metaphor, invisibility became the hero's essential
identity—Rinehart, the underground man, and the Invisible
Man are citizens of the invisible world which is the other
side of this phenomenal world. Invisibility in Baldwin's use
of it is the cloak of unseeing which society forces upon the
hero, which hides his unchanged identity, and which im-
prisons him therefore in anonymity.

The matter is not entirely a simple one. Identity, Baldwin is to be found saying often enough, is something to
be *attained* or *achieved,* especially in America, most especially
by a Negro, and that is to imply that "identity" is dynamic
and progressive. The Negro's past, he says, is an "endless
struggle *to achieve* and reveal and confirm a human identity." [2]
And Baldwin says: "The necessity of Americans *to achieve*
an identity is a historical and a present personal fact. . . ." [3]
Commenting on someone's incidental observation that the
trouble with Norman Mailer is that he is white, he says:

> What my friend meant was that to become a Negro man,
> let alone a Negro artist, *one had to make onself up as one
> went along.* This had to be done in the not-at-all meta-
> phorical teeth of the world's determination to destroy you.
> . . . This is not the way this truth presents itself to white
> men, who believe the world is theirs and who, albeit un-
> consciously, expect the world to help them in the achieve-

ment of their identity. But the world does not do this—
for anyone. . . .[4]

Identity, that is to say, is created in experience and in the
consequent yielding of innocence. Or identity is merely maturity.* And in his fiction, which of course depends on some
forward movement, Baldwin's hero struggles against the invisibility that has been thrust upon him and he thereby does
make an effort to define himself.

But the *achievement* of identity isn't the story Baldwin
actually tells. The identity to be achieved, it always turns out,
even when the effort is announced as successful, is that identity that the hero has always had. It is his birthright, which
society had obscured from him. In a number of essays, for
instance, Baldwin has discussed his own expatriation to Paris
in the years just after the war, and the point of all these
essays is that expatriation, while it confirmed his invisibility,
gave him opportunity, not to discover, but to recover himself.
So he says, "From the vantage point of Europe [the American
student] discovers his own country." In an atmosphere, Baldwin says, in which the racial matter was relaxed, he found
again both his American-ness and his Negro-ness. The
American Negro discovers that his birthright is distinct from
that of the African.

> I left America because I doubted my ability to survive the
> fury of the color problem here. . . . In my necessity to find
> the terms on which my experience could be related to that
> of others, Negroes and whites, writers and non-writers, I
> proved, to my astonishment, to be as American as any
> Texas G.I.[5]

* The opposite of maturity, anyway, is non-identity. American students abroad present the din of a mob's "cacophony of affirmation"
because the individuals among them lack "individual maturity." "A
Question of Identity," *Notes of a Native Son*, p. 131.

In other personal essays more or less concerned with identity, Baldwin's chief occupation is actually his own childhood. "Identity" is something that one once had, or at least almost had, in the past, in childhood. And indeed, the child who has not yet quite defined himself but who has not yet either been lost is, an inventory would prove, Baldwin's favorite subject.

The hero who is dispossessed of his place, robbed of his identity in the world, and who is therefore lonely, is everywhere in Baldwin's writing, where it is his story Baldwin sets out to tell and, more significantly, where it isn't. The hero of an occasional interview with Ingmar Bergman becomes, expressly, Baldwin himself. ". . . I amused myself, on the ride back into town, by projecting a movie . . . and it then occurred to me that my bitterness might be turned to good account if I should dare to envision the tragic hero for whom I was searching—as myself. All art is a kind of confession. . . ." [6] And the vision to which the piece comes is, only not quite so expressly, of that hero who is lost in a society that does not confer definition. Bergman, in Stockholm, had his father, his past, and therefore a perception of moral authority on which to draw. Baldwin's New York is a place where youngsters were "searching desperately for the limits which would tell them who they were. . . ." There is something to impress loneliness even in the melancholy past tense in which the observation is cast. Again, an essay, "Faulkner and Desegregation" begins: "Any real change implies the breakup of the world as one has always known it, the loss of all that gave one an identity, the end of safety," [7] and manages at a stroke to insert Faulkner into a drama of loneliness. Baldwin's response to the position Faulkner took on desegregation is, of course, indignation, but the device of Baldwin's indignation is—as it is elsewhere for Norman Mailer, then for the whole United States delegation to the United Nations, for white Americans generally and for Negroes generally—pity that one should be so lonely, so outside the world.

The recovery of identity is the theme, and the drama is in the hero's loneliness and the injustice of his having to strive for identity in the world that would make him invisible. The recovery of identity, it is suggested, will be the means of his accommodation in the world. But it has been Baldwin's difficulty as a novelist, briefly, that with the discovery of loneliness—enunciated sometimes as a wail, sometimes as a sigh, sometimes with a graceful bitterness, occasionally in radical obscenities—he has tended to end his explorations. There is no doubt that his hero suffers authentic affliction, an affliction that takes ingenious, complicated forms—and that, too, is something that Baldwin knows very well. "Complication" and its cognates, when he is describing his lack of identity, are words constantly at his lips. But still it is not the complicated affliction, despite his knowledge of it, not what it is to *be* an invisible man, but how and how much it hurts, the pity of it, that engages Baldwin.

Pity with some sarcasm in it has been the mode of his indignation, and pity without sarcasm has been the usual mode of the honor he pays to his heroes. Pity is his note, available both to his heroes and to his villains, who do occupy an identical position. They are all outside the world. They are pitiful because, being outside the world, they are unable to attain any normal social connection with it. That is the despair of invisibility. They are without parental love, if it is a child's story that Baldwin is telling, or they are without romantic love, if it is that kind of story. Or they are expatriates and therefore without community. Or, as in the case

Baldwin made out of Faulkner, they may be trapped in the archaic past and therefore disbarred from the social connection of current politics.

That is to say nothing, of course, about the truth of Baldwin's perceptions, in his fiction or his essays, but to say something only about their pattern and their circumscription. It is one story that Baldwin tells, even in his many fictions which are presented in the form of essays. And it is clear enough that the story is his own. The matter is in fact the more clear in Baldwin's many informal essays. Whatever their ostensible subject, what is most prominent in them is the pronoun "I." And the pity in Baldwin's response, either without or with its trill of sarcasm, is finally, without exception, pity for himself.

To discover that his sorrow is self-centered is not, of course, to discover Baldwin in a breach of etiquette. A writer of fiction does write out of himself, and self-pity might be the means of his perception. All art is a kind of confession. The pity, when it is intensive, may be a device of analysis, the way into the detail of a particular reality.

Baldwin's uses of his pity for himself have been largely extensive and repetitive, and one of the results of *his* self-pity would seem to be that as a novelist he has made a specialty of the informal essay. One looks to the essays for the motives of the fiction. The essays are indeed always dramatic—they are passionate, a sentience moves through them. They do include real experience—Baldwin's own, but slightly transformed by their subjects. And they are "personal," in the sense not of coziness, but in the fact that they create a person. They are quite as much concerned with the style—the identity, precisely—of the man speaking as they are with their various topics. They have that feeling of an intimate involvement. They are themselves, that is to say, *almost* fiction.

But then they aren't fiction. One expects of serious fiction a thoroughness and a probing that Baldwin's essays have not, a progress of events, a moving through contradiction and complication. The pity Baldwin brings in his essays to what is at bottom always his own plight does not move. It is already completely formulated, and it is not analytic but appreciative. It stops short. Fiction pure would demand that he go on, into himself, that he participate in himself. And the informal essay permits him the pity without real involvement. It permits him to shift ground and in many various ways to repeat himself without going on to an end. The essays present him with many applications of an insight he has already had into his own nature and situation, and excuse him from the imaginative pursuit of it.

The essays don't have the seriousness of fiction. It happens, and by the same measure, that they don't have the seriousness of essays either, even though the insight on which they are built has every validity. The single insight does apply equally to Baldwin's own experience as a Negro and an American, and to what was the position of William Faulkner, and to that of expatriates in Paris, and, in fact, to everyone everywhere. Raised to its metaphysical dimensions, it is that insight into man's perpetual condition which tells of man's loneliness on this isthmus of a middle state. It is the insight which Baldwin latterly, with a flourish, has come to call the tragic sense of life. There is in it not only a truth, but a cliché which becomes a significant truth only when one gets down to cases. And Baldwin's difficulty as an essayist, briefly, is that he tends to arouse expectations of cases which he doesn't satisfy. If, by writing essays, he evades the demands of fiction, by writing essays as fiction he evades the demand of thorough ideas.

In the essays, he creates character, a series of images of

himself. That is the chief function of his rhetoric, and the dramatic rhetoric not infrequently substitutes for substantial argument. Baldwin establishes an attitude toward issues, or he establishes a person in the act of confronting them, but on the one hand the person is not pursued and then on the other hand the issues themselves are left often unconfronted. There is a person in these essays always, one feels, about to make himself clear, about to say something that will be, because he is so involved, really illuminating—and then there is a rhetorical flourish and what "ideas" are produced, especially given the advertised engagement, are only flat or hopelessly vast.

An essay on the Negro Muslims concludes, for instance:

> Any effort, from here on out, to keep the Negro in his "place" can only have the most extreme and unlucky repercussions. This being so, it would seem to me that the most intelligent effort we can now make is to give up this doomed endeavor and study how we can most quickly end this division in our house. The Negroes who rioted in the U.N. are but a very small echo of the black discontent now abroad in the world. If we are not able, and quickly, to face and begin to eliminate the sources of this discontent in our own country, we will never be able to do it on the great stage of the world.[8]

Now this is all very strong, very stern, and it has lofty solemnity. Moreover, it is true. But in fact it doesn't quite come to the point of discourse. It is at best newsy—there is a new, more militant black discontent abroad in the world—but then that is at best stale news. The threat in the advice is of the evaporating sort, carefully modulated into pathos, and the advice in it is an instrument which frustrates talk about the issues—just how will we go about ending "this division in our house"? The essay sends the issues off, as it were, to committee. What the statement finally presents is *merely* drama. The statement creates a hero, Baldwin himself, who is being ominous and militant but good-willed, too, and who is telling us for the last time. The hero is not so militant, it should be said, as the Muslim rioters who are Baldwin's subject—one might speculate on Baldwin's use here and in a number of other essays of "we." * By taking the Muslims' case really as his own, he might not only make a political statement but he would commit a political act. There would be an idea in it, if not a reasonable one. He stops short of that, as he does in his later, more elaborate discussion of the Muslims in "Letter from a Region in My Mind." Both essays exist after all only to supply a hero with an attitude, to supply Baldwin with the dramatic component of an idea.

When Baldwin speaks on the current politics of the Negro's situation in America, what is ultimately accomplished is a prophetic posture, a hero threatening an apocalypse which is itself lacking in particulars. "Any honest examination of the national life," Baldwin says, "proves how far we are from the standard of human freedom with which we began. . . . If we are not capable of this examination, we may yet become one

---

* It was the assumption of *"our* forebears" that "the black man, to become truly human and acceptable, must first become like *us."* "Many Thousands Gone," *Notes of a Native Son,* p. 45. "It is only too clear that even with the most malevolent will in the world Negroes can never manage to achieve one-tenth of the harm which *we* fear. No, it has everything to do with *ourselves* and this is one of the reasons that for all these generations *we* have disguised this problem. . . ." "In Search of a Majority," *Nobody Knows My Name,* pp. 134–35. "What it comes to is that if *we,* who can scarcely be considered a white nation, persist in thinking of ourselves as one, we condemn ourselves . . . to sterility and decay. . . . *He* [the Negro] is *the* key figure in *his* country. . . ." "Letter from a Region in My Mind," *The Fire Next Time,* pp. 107–08. Italics mine.

of the most distinguished and monumental failures in the history of nations." He says:

> When a race riot occurs in Atlanta, it will not spread merely to Birmingham. . . . (Birmingham is a doomed city.) The trouble will spread to every metropolitan center in the nation which has a significant Negro population. And this is not only because the ties between Northern and Southern Negroes are still very close. It is because the nation, the entire nation, has spent a hundred years avoiding the question of the place of the black man in it.[9]

He says: ". . . the white man's world, intellectually, morally, and spiritually, has the meaningless ring of a hollow drum and the odor of slow death."[10] It is all true, of course. But the process by which the truth was to be dramatized, given a human voice and a human action, has somehow become more important than the truth. Where it should be, there is the author full of large eloquence.

In other moods Baldwin seizes subjects in order to project, it may be, a role of besieged integrity,* or perhaps of terribly calm paternity—the need of the young for an image of authority provides Baldwin with a frequent parenthesis.

---

* "I don't like people who like me because I'm a Negro; neither do I like people who find in the same accident grounds for contempt. . . . I consider that I have many responsibilities, but none greater than this: to last, as Hemingway says, and get my work done. I want to be an honest man and a good writer." "Autobiographical Notes," *Notes of a Native Son,* p. 9. On the writer's accomplishment of fame, Baldwin writes: "It is the point at which many artists lose their minds, or commit suicide, or throw themselves into good works, or try to enter politics. For all of this is happening not only in the wilderness of the soul, but in the real world which accomplishes its seductions not by offering you opportunities to be wicked but by offering opportunities to be good, to be active and effective, to be admired and central and apparently loved." "The Black Boy Looks at the White Boy," pp. 224–25.

Or the role may be one of a lonely outsider who is really an insider. So he pauses, for instance, in his essay on Norman Mailer, to say: ". . . the things that most white people imagine that they can salvage from the storm of life are really, in sum, their innocence. It was this commodity precisely which I had to get rid of at once"; and then he says again, in reply to Mailer's speculations on the nature of power, "Well, I know how power works, it has worked on me, and if I didn't know how power worked, I would be dead." [11] The least observation to be made is that this essay on Mailer is about Baldwin. Baldwin calls it "The Black Boy Looks at the White Boy," but in fact both boys look for the most part at Baldwin. And the statement might be the beginning of a deep narrative of what it is to be a Negro in the United States, or it might be the credentials of a discursive idea, but the idea is not engaged, and the statement after all is only an affective parenthesis, another flickering view of the author in still another stance bespeaking loneliness and the unloved.

The affectation of ideas is bombast, and Baldwin's difficulty as an essayist has been that he has allowed bombast to do his work. But then nothing proves so clearly as this disappearance of ideas the nature of the frustrations he has known as a novelist. The essays are almost without exception the statements of a spokesman, of a Negro addressing whites. Spokesmanship is at least their first intention. Baldwin *reports* as, naturally, a qualified insider, on such matters as school integration in the South, anti-Semitism in Harlem, the Negro response to American politicians, white and black. Spokesmanship, even for one who is committed to it, must entail a first uncomfortable assumption that one is speaking for a community, and that is an assumption that Baldwin particularly must find difficult. He has at least once, in passing, in a review, said as much: ". . . popular belief to the contrary, it is not enough to have been born a Negro to understand the history of Negroes in America." [12] And Baldwin, whether or not his representation is accepted,* must find the assumption of spokesmanship distressing because he is not committed to it, because his vision is personal. His subject is himself. And it is the evidence of his best work, in fiction and essays, that a spokesman is just what he does not want to be. Something like this reluctance must be behind the final equivocation of his essays that should be polemical, the strange use of a first-person plural that dissociates him from Negroes, the final failure to give his indignation the form and the force of argument.

Moreover, not only the lie, but the personal danger in spokesmanship, is something that Baldwin knows very well. He all but began his literary career, in an essay, "Everybody's Protest Novel," [13] with a speculation on its dangers. The essay uses *Uncle Tom's Cabin* to define the hypocritical simplicities of protest literature. Mrs. Stowe's passions were sentimental, sociological, and theological, Baldwin says in effect, and she was therefore divorced by each of her passions from the complications of real human experience and real human beings. What she intended as salvation actually dehumanized. The great and subtle danger of her novel lies, however, not in its hot misguided liberalism, but in the acceptance by its victims of the terms of its dehumanization. For Baldwin, who was writing his own first novel as he wrote the essay, and

* That not all Negro spokesmen regard Baldwin as the spokesman for Negroes is the burden of the review by Henry F. Winslow in the NAACP's journal, *The Crisis,* of his first collection of essays, *Notes of a Native Son:* ". . . for all the high sound he is capable of giving the half truths presented they melt down to very little." Baldwin is marked by "peculiarity rather than profundity." "The content of Mr. Baldwin's essays proves him to be the victim of limited inquiry. . . ." "They Speak of Brotherhood," *The Crisis,* LXIII (June-July 1956), 376.

clearly trying to define that novel, the seditious historical effect of *Uncle Tom's Cabin* was *Native Son*. "Bigger is Uncle Tom's descendant, flesh of his flesh, so exactly opposite a portrait that, when the books are placed together, it seems that the contemporary Negro novelist and the dead New England woman are locked together in a deadly, timeless battle. . . ." As a protest novel, *Native Son* accepts all of Mrs. Stowe's categorizing of tricksy, unique human identity, and it therefore creates a hero who "admits the possibility of his being sub-human" and who battles his world according to the criteria of an imposed black-white theology that has nothing to do with his humanity. "The failure of the protest novel lies in its rejection of life . . . in its insistence that it is [the human being's] categorization alone which is real and which cannot be transcended." And it follows therefore that the honest novelist will choose the uncategorized, individual human life.

This is really an easy enough, and in recent years it has been for everyone an obvious enough, thing to say. For Negro writers it has been obvious for a somewhat longer time, but harder. "What is today parroted," Baldwin says in the same essay, "as [the novelist's] Responsibility . . . is, when he believes it, his corruption and our loss," and it is clear that for Baldwin social responsibility was at the beginning of his career a clear and pressing problem. Because he was a Negro it must have been there waiting for him when he sat down to write. The fulfillment of such responsibility in any overt way, by protest or by spokesmanship, snuffs out all the complexity and the paradox of the individual human personality. Social responsibility is, too, the cloak of invisibility.

Then it would be the job of the novelist to be deliberately unmindful of his responsibility, to dive into the individual human personality, into the only one, presumably, the depths of which he can know, namely his own. The business of the novelist Baldwin in fact says, again in the same essay, is "revelation" of "the disquieting complexity of ourselves," "this web of ambiguity, paradox, this hunger, danger, darkness. . . ." And that elegant prescription is indeed implicit everywhere in Baldwin's writings. It is his advice to himself when he talks, as he does everywhere, of identity. And this conception of his task is not merely a choosing of the "psychological" or, perhaps, the "existential" novel over the "social" novel. For Baldwin certainly it has to do with the possibility of his writing honestly at all. That is a problem to which as a Negro writer he is simply born.

But for a Negro writer of talent and conscience there is no avoiding the burdens of spokesmanship, and it is not only a matter of conscience and of the obvious social necessities. Indeed, it would seem that for Baldwin the very attempt to avoid spokesmanship led him to it, and if he is not very good at it, that betrays not a failure of rigor or courage but a crisis of honesty. It is the fact that in all of his fictions, including his one "white" novel, writing honestly and in pursuit of the complex personal truth, he has found himself come around to the point where there is nothing else to do but howl his frustration, or turn to essays and write spokesman-like protest. "It is quite impossible," Baldwin says in another early essay, "to write a worthwhile novel about a Jew or a Gentile or a Homosexual, for people refuse, unhappily, to function in so neat and one-dimensional a fashion." [14] One can't, obviously, by the same token, write a novel about a Negro. But one can't either, Baldwin seems to have discovered repeatedly, write a story about a Negro and deny that he is a Negro, deny that what Ralph Ellison called the "little question of civil rights," what Alain Locke called the Negro's "shadow," do constitute much of the reality of the person.*

That dilemma gives way to another. This Negro-ness as a personal reality may really be a kind of invisibility. The fact that he is a Negro, that his life is in great part the effect of a long history and a ramifying system of persecution, prevents what Baldwin calls identity. And so at the point of discovering Negro-ness, at the point where his heroes are about to discover it, Baldwin must turn to speak publicly as a Negro, to some immediately social purpose, therefore as a spokesman, to the distortion or abandonment of the personal identity. And then if he doesn't speak convincingly as a spokesman, it is because that personal identity, and not social salvation, was the goal.

The goal was the same, of course, for Ralph Ellison. A sense of the self was to be made compatible with a sense of society. In *Invisible Man* it is the pattern of frustrations that would seem to prevent identity that, ironically, creates it. The

---

* There is some evidence that Baldwin wishes that one could, for the purpose of fiction at least, disregard the Negro-ness of the Negro. That is one implication from the fact that he has written a "white" novel, *Giovanni's Room*—a novel which is neither a case-study nor an entertainment after the manner of the Negro writer Frank Yerby, but intended clearly as an exploration and revelation of the person. More important, it is an implication of his not infrequent statement which is to the effect that Negroes are just like everybody else, or anyway like all other Americans. "One may say that the Negro in America does not really exist except in the darkness of our minds." "Many Thousands Gone," pp. 24-25. ". . . I proved, to my astonishment, to be as American as any Texas G.I." "The Discovery of What It Means to Be an American," p. 4. One would, of course, deny neither statement. The statements are, when one is talking immediate politics, truisms. Baldwin has in another breath, moreover, and more frequently, said the opposite. But to say at all that the Negro as a Negro doesn't really exist is, for a Negro, not only a startling bit of Olympianism, but a denial that Negro-ness is any part of his own specific disquieting complexity.

hero's invisibility becomes essential and positive. In Baldwin's fiction, the search for identity is, however, everywhere engaged in, and nowhere actually achieved, although there are instances when Baldwin would want us to believe it is achieved. His heroes are forever on their way to being something, or to being somebodies, when they find themselves suddenly in a labyrinthine confusion, identity denied them. And because identity isn't achieved—isn't, that is to say, identified—Baldwin's drama is finally the way identity is frustrated. His hero's climactic action, it follows, is suffering, and pity is Baldwin's comment.

But then something is attained, if only because in order to conceive that identity is the goal, Baldwin must contain in his drama some notion of what it would look like were it to be had. And what it would look like has as much to do with the fact that it cannot be attained as anything in the obvious public situation of the Negro. What is Baldwin's idea of identity is something that fiction in fact can't accomplish. It seems not only, in the case of his Negro heroes, to have nothing to do with Negro-ness, with color, but to be unrelated to any hair, bone, flesh, cartilage, circumstances, or experience. Its one identifiable, but not necessarily constant, component is sex. It is libido, or it is Soul, a small, pure, passionate flame. It is something always in the past. It is the sort of thing that life as seen in fiction must snuff out. Fiction is a gathering of experience in the world, and experience is what corrupts Baldwin's identity, and is its natural enemy.

Baldwin's idea of identity is after all, to use his own word, "theological"—and after all it would seem to make some difference, despite his intentions and his removal, that he was, as he has said, "practically born in the church." [15] Richard Wright's Bigger Thomas suffers, Baldwin says, by his acceptance of the raging puritanical theology that moved

Harriet Beecher Stowe—black is evil. But it is Baldwin himself who accepts what is a preliminary idea behind Mrs.
Stowe's puritanism, that to be in the world at all is to be
depraved. In the same essay Baldwin advises that "our humanity is our burden, our life; we need not battle for it;
we need only to do what is infinitely more difficult—that is,
accept it"—but that, the accepting of our humanity, is just
what he makes it impossible for his heroes to do. The advice is not for Baldwin, what it might seem, merely a lofty
glibness. It proposes the riddle within which his own fiction
moves. Our humanity, if that means an involvement with
our actions, is that which pollutes the pure expression of pure
passion, and purity is what finally Baldwin seems to mean
by identity.

A passion so pure that it is beyond all metaphors would
seem to be Baldwin's idea ultimately of identity and reality.
But only ultimately. In various places in his work—although
not, it happens, in any chronological sequence of change—
identity wears various guises, which look like identifications,
the name that nobody knows. But then either the guises are
not sustained, and what appeared to be identity is revealed
to be only an attitude or a passing polemical opportunism, or
the mask slips, or the mask fails because it is obviously not
a face.

The Negro's and Baldwin's basic identity may reside, for
instance, in the fact that Negroes are Americans. Americanism
is one of Baldwin's guises. "Negroes are Americans," he says,
"and their destiny is the country's destiny." [16] The Negro "is
not a visitor to the West, but a citizen there, an American;
as American as the Americans who despise him, the Americans who fear him, the Americans who love him. . . ." [17] The
Negro "has been formed by this nation, for better or for
worse, and does not belong to any other—not to Africa, and

certainly not to Islam." * In Europe the American Negro begins to realize his relationship to white Americans. "Now he is bone of their bone, flesh of their flesh; they have loved and hated and obsessed and feared each other and his blood is in their soil." [18] These are of course statements of political implication, existing in a context where black nationalism, the quantity of the American Negro's alienation from America, is the question. But they also say what they say, that the American Negro is to be identified as American.

And that consideration might be for Baldwin the beginning of another, harder, more experiential idea of what identity is, but in fact it is only the beginning of an infinite regress because identity, Baldwin is to be found saying just as frequently, is just what Americans themselves don't have. The Negro identity may be that he is an American, but the American identity is nothing, or nothing yet that one can put one's finger on.

America's history, her aspirations, her peculiar triumphs, her even more peculiar defeats, and her position in the world—yesterday and today—are all so profoundly and stubbornly unique that the very word "America" remains a new, almost completely undefined and extremely controversial proper noun. No one in the world seems to know exactly what it describes, not even we motley millions who call ourselves Americans.

---

* "Letter from a Region in My Mind," p. 95. It happens that Baldwin is to be discovered just a few pages prior to this statement recommending Muslim separatism. The Muslim ambition (so like that of the Communist Party through the 1930s and 1940s) to form a separate Negro nation within the boundaries of the United States is not necessarily, Baldwin says, fantastic. Moreover, such separatism "would seem to be [the Negro's] only hope of not perishing in the American backwater. . . ." P. 88.

The key words in the passage promise to be "almost" and "exactly"—if America is *almost* undefined and no one knows *exactly* what the name means, then one will expect that the author, especially as he is writing an essay called "The Discovery of What It Means to Be an American," will clarify the matter *somewhat*. But the passage says quite as much about what it is to be an American as the essay is going to say. America lacks definition. And elsewhere Baldwin speaks of the alienation of Americans from their own past and their inability therefore to know who they are,[19] and he speaks elsewhere again of the American "confusion" and the American "incoherence."[20] And then all arguments disappear when Baldwin speculates that it is lack of identity that makes Negroes American: "The necessity of Americans to achieve an identity is a historical and a present personal fact and this is the connection between you and me."[21]

Just what it is that Americans, as such, don't have and that would fill them with identity, Baldwin suggests most particularly in *Giovanni's Room*. It seems to be sex. But prior to and beyond that discovery there are other guises of identity. In the single most searching, least equivocating essay Baldwin has written, the Negro's identity emerges from the calderon of Western experience as Satanic. The essay, called "Stranger in the Village," begins with the event of Baldwin's brief residence in a tiny Swiss village where no black man before him had ever set foot, and from that pure case develops the drama of the Negro's basic estrangement in the West. It goes on to his citizenship in America, to make the point that the American racial drama is changing the culture of the West, but meanwhile, in the Swiss village and prior to the alteration of our culture, the Negro is given identity by Christian myth. The cathedral at Chartres says something to the villagers, or would say something to them if they could hear it, Baldwin says, that it does not say to him, but on the other hand it speaks to him as it cannot to them.

> Perhaps they are struck by the power of the spires, the glory of the windows; but they have known God, after all, longer than I have known him, and in a different way, and I am terrified by the slippery bottomless well to be found in the crypt, down which heretics were hurled to death, and by the obscene, inescapable gargoyles jutting out of the stone and seeming to say that God and the devil can never be divorced. I doubt that the villagers think of the devil when they face a cathedral because they have never been identified with the devil. But I must accept the status which myth, if nothing else, gives me in the West before I can hope to change the myth.

And this as a speculation on identity, even temporary identity, is full of imaginative promise. It suggests a coherence of psychological and social insight—exactly, that of an underground man. But then it is only half an imaginative statement, a parenthesis in an essay which demands a development of a different kind of truth. Baldwin doesn't indulge or sustain it. It is only a face for a moment put on identity to make it frightening, much like the image that, Baldwin says elsewhere, Richard Wright created in Bigger Thomas. Bigger asserts his "identity" by making manifest the brutal American image of the Negro.[22] But Bigger isn't, Baldwin goes on in that essay to say, the Negro's identity—and neither, it is by the same token to be seen, is the devil—but only one of his roles, and it is a role which, Baldwin says, being all responsive hatred, marks the surrender of the Negro's identity.

The fact that he is forced to contain roles, at an extremity that role proposed by Bigger or the devil and ordinarily a role in a routine of daily cunning in his relations with whites, suggests at times what would seem for Baldwin to be at least a condition of the Negro's identity. The Negro ordinarily, Baldwin says again and again, is forced to consider whites much more intensely than they consider him, and he is forced to strategies in his dealings with them. "This is, indeed, one of the causes of the bottomless anger of black men: that they have been forced to learn far more about whites than whites have ever found it necessary to learn about them." [23] And he says, "since white men represent in the black man's world so heavy a weight, white men have for black men a reality which is far from being reciprocal. . . ." [24] The consequences of that fact, as Baldwin develops them sporadically in various places, are that the Negro invests much of his life in outwitting white people, and that the Negro bears toward white people an attitude which is designed to rob them of their naïveté. And it is an associated fact that Negroes are almost always acting.

This very virtuosity, one would think, might establish for Baldwin the grounds of the identity he seeks. The image of his hero might be located anywhere on an arc from the Confidence Man, or, for that matter, Rinehart, to Tyll Eulenspiegel. In fact the hero as trickster does occupy an occasional place in his fiction, which is always about identity. The hero of "Previous Condition of Servitude," Baldwin's earliest published story, tells a white friend, first, that it was part of his earliest education to learn how to act with policemen— "I let my jaw drop and I let my eyes get big. I didn't give him any smart answers, none of the crap about my rights" —and then:

There are times and places when a Negro can use his color like a shield. He can trade on the subterranean Anglo-Saxon guilt and get what he wants that way; or some of what he wants. He can trade on his nuisance value, his value as forbidden fruit; he can use it like a knife, he can twist it and get his vengeance that way.[25]

And in a story twelve years later, called "This Morning, This Evening, So Soon," the Negro hero sits again with a white friend and tells him again that a Negro must know how to act with policemen and he makes again, in effect, the consequent generalization.[26] He is, of course, the same hero.

It is significant that despite twelve years and changed circumstances he is the same hero, that the same episode and the same observations are repeated and not developed. This trickery by which Baldwin says his hero lives is a shocking thing, but not so shocking apparently that it really becomes part of him. It doesn't change his life. He is still free to see it. It doesn't contribute to his identity, but in fact it is another of the special circumstances that prevents identity. His heroes don't *want* to be tricksters, and despite the fact that they say they practice tricks, they don't act like tricksters. They want to manifest *themselves*. The young man of "Previous Condition of Servitude" continues:

> I knew these things long before I realized that I knew them and in the beginning I used them, not knowing what I was doing. Then when I began to see it, I felt betrayed. I felt beaten as a person. I had no honest place to stand.

The middling-young man of "This Morning, This Evening, So Soon" comes to the end of his observations on trickery by saying, "I always feel that I don't exist there [in America], except in someone else's—usually dirty—mind." Trickery doesn't create a trickster. It robs the hero of himself. It is not even an activity, but a plight, a falsification which frustrates the something within.

The something within is something prior to all the pressures of large social determination and to a man's action in the large world. This humanity which cannot be categorized might then take its shape from more intimate pressures, those of the family and of ancestry, from the pressures of the Negro neighborhood and of the folk tradition. The Negro family, it turns out in Baldwin's fiction, is another conspiracy to prevent identity, but meanwhile those fictions—as distinct from the personal essays—in which Baldwin most obviously commits himself personally, do take the family and the Negro environment for their setting. The folk tradition is in his fiction, too, and it promises another condition of identity.

The expression of identity might be in the music of Negro folk tradition. An essay, which is for the most part about *Native Son,* begins: "It is only in his music, which Americans are able to admire because a protective sentimentality limits their understanding of it, that the Negro in America has been able to tell his story,"[27] and as an aid to the telling of his version of it, Baldwin has used Negro musical motifs here and there throughout his work. His titles are almost as often as not fragments of spirituals and blues: "Many Thousands Gone," "Nobody Knows My Name," "This Morning, This Evening, So Soon," "Come Out the Wilderness," *The Fire Next Time. Go Tell It on the Mountain* uses the spiritual of the title and uses fragments from a number of other spirituals as a binding device. There is at least by such reference a presence of Negro music in Baldwin's work. The music contributes a tone, and that tone at the very least reinforces the yearning that anyway is in much of the work. The music projects a style, which may contain an identity. Negro music has specific character, and by appealing to it Baldwin does manage to borrow something, at the very least a useful ornamentation.

But then if there is within the tone and the style and the character of Negro music a deep secret of identity, something literal and certain but something which Americans are unable really to understand, Baldwin does not reveal it. His one most thorough use of the music of Negro tradition is in his story called "Sonny's Blues." [28] The story is largely an attempt to translate the blues into the terms of fiction. It fails to do that, perhaps for the sufficient reason that music doesn't translate, but it does seem to arrive at a statement of the Negro motives that may issue in the blues. Sonny's brother, a respectable Negro and a schoolteacher, tells the story. He has fallen out of touch with Sonny, who is not respectable, and through the story he is to come to understand and to regain his brother. Sonny is a young Negro caught on the one hand between the degradations, the slumminess of Harlem, and on the other hand the bourgeois, white ambitions of the relatives among whom he finds himself. Sonny's problem is precisely the burden of his racial identity: he must keep himself from drowning in the degradations and sorrows of Negro life, but something within him demands also that he be "with it," meaning, within the bounds of the story, that he not be white, that he acknowledge his racial community. The Negro community has offered him first heroin, a temporary escape from the feeling of degradation and slumminess. But he has discovered that the same environment contains a music, jazz, and through jazz he is to be provided with the means of reconciliation. The function of Sonny's blues is that it allows him fully to know his racial identity. At the end of the story his brother listens to Sonny's piano, and thinks:

He had made it his: that long line, of which we knew only Mama and Daddy. And he was giving it back, as everything must be given back, so that, passing through death, it can live forever. I saw my mother's face again, and felt, for the first time, how the stones of the road she had walked on must have bruised her feet. I saw the moonlit road where my father's brother died. . . . And I was yet aware that this was only a moment, that the world waited outside, as hungry as a tiger, and that trouble stretched above us, longer than the day.

The story of the Negro that the music tells is of ancient sorrows somehow borne, that may be borne still in a world that still confers suffering. That is what Negro-ness is.* Or that is what it might be. But then the significance of this lyrical statement really is in the fact that nothing in the story serves to make it true. The music is another of Baldwin's promises of identity that is not paid. It is signficant that it is Sonny's brother, the schoolteacher, the would-be white man, and not Sonny, who tells this story and who translates the message of the blues. Sonny's brother is the man most in need of reconciliation and most in need of the blues. And it happens that what he observes about the music is quite super-fluous to anything he has in the story learned about it, just as what he hears in Sonny's playing is less important dramatically than the fact that he hears it and responds. Sonny is from the beginning full of unspecified Negro-ness, and that is the difference between the brothers. The protagonist comes, we are to believe, to some implicit understanding of Sonny's

* That this is not distinctly the *Negro* tradition is a fact which Baldwin himself has realized. He elsewhere uses the meaning that this passage comes to, to define tradition itself, any tradition. "For a tradition expresses, after all, nothing more than the long and painful experience of a people; it comes out of the battle waged to maintain their integrity or, to put it more simply, out of their struggle to survive." "Many Thousands Gone," p. 36. This still leaves open the question of what a people's "integrity" is.

suffering, and then, at the climax, when he hears the music, the magic is worked. The dramatic impact of the story, that is to say, is not in his understanding of anything that is in the music, but in his reconciliation with what his brother in the first place vaguely represents. What he says he understands in the music is unimportant. Any message of reconciliation would have worked as well. And all that the climax really proves by showing it on stage is the wordless communicativeness that is in the music, and the direct and spontaneous communicativeness that is especially the strategy of jazz.

It is directness and spontaneity of expression that in this story of identity is finally referred to, and not any content of tradition. And it is something very much like that that Baldwin discovers when he pursues the folk tradition in other directions, into the South or to Africa. He has made this pursuit infrequently but he has made it sometimes, and with some promising. The essay "Nobody Knows My Name" begins: "Negroes in the North are right when they refer to the South as the Old Country." The Northern Negro "sees, in effect, his ancestors, who, in everything they do and are, proclaim his inescapable identity." The American Negro, Baldwin says elsewhere, has been significantly separated from his African antecedents, but nevertheless they are part of him. "I know . . . that the most crucial time in my own development came when I was forced to recognize that I was a kind of bastard of the West; when I followed the line of my past I did not find myself in Europe but in Africa." [29] "Go back a few centuries," he says again, "and . . . I am in Africa, watching the conquerors arrive." [30] Here, then, in the South or, behind it, in Africa, is a hint of identity. And especially if it is true that experience obscures identity, in this primitve incarnation identity should be apparent.

It is not, as Baldwin presents it, immediately apparent, but it is, precisely, primitive. "The American image of the Negro lives also in the Negro's heart," Baldwin says once,[31] and here, in his discovery of Negroes, as it were, darker than he, he presents some proof of it. The Negro of the Old Country is as he appears in Baldwin's essays, for the most part a militant engaged in the current heightened battle of the South, and so questions of his distinguishing identity are not distinctly raised. But there are hints. On the occasion of what he records as his first visit to the South, in "Nobody Knows My Name," Baldwin observes of the "familiar" landscape: "What passions cannot be unleashed on a dark road in a Southern night! Everything seems so sensual, so languid, and so private." The school integration dispute has nothing to do with education, but it "has to do with political power and it has to do with sex." And in fact the underlying metaphor of the whole of this fictive essay is sexual. Only its overt observations have to do with political power. The distinguishing thing about these Old Country Negroes is that they are living a history that is covertly sexual.

And in one of the few stories that deals at all with the South, "Come Out the Wilderness," [32] there is the same tugging suggestion, that sex *is* the Old Country identity. The heroine, in this case, has just come out of the South to what she thinks of as the gray rigidities and the meaningless abstractions and the cruelty and confusion of Manhattan. She has come, so an explicitly Freudian content of the story suggests, bearing the burden of an explicitly sexual trauma. She is living now with a white man. She is thereby obsessively punishing herself. Her brother once had caught her in a compromising situation and said to her, "You dirty . . . you black and dirty." Black is therefore the color of sex, and in her affair she is exploiting her blackness and her carnality. And both, the story keeps suggesting, are products of her

Southernness. She has relatives in Harlem who have, by moving to Harlem, become respectably and repressively religious. The Northern Negro women among whom she works have a cold sterility about them. She is herself a person of high moral awareness, but as she is Southern she is more black and so her morality is different; she is pure, and it is the mark of her purity that she is sexual.

The South also prevents or corrupts expression, sexual or otherwise. That is a part of the story of *Go Tell It on the Mountain,* and of some of the essays. But the ur-, pre-Northern Negro as the incarnation of uncorrupted identity does occupy some part of Baldwin's imagination. The Southern Negro and, more notably, the African, have preserved a cultural and therefore a psychic wholeness. "The African . . . has endured privation, injustice, medieval cruelty; but the African has not yet endured the utter alienation of himself from his people and his past. His mother did not sing 'Sometimes I Feel Like a Motherless Child'. . . ." [33] And then the mark of this wholeness, again in the case of the African, is undifferentiated sexual energy. Baldwin says it between the lines, but he says it. In an essay, "Encounter on the Seine," about the attitude of American Negroes, which is to say of Baldwin, toward the North African students at the Sorbonne, the drama of the encounter fills momentarily with jungle rhythms. The American Negro faces the African before him, and: "Yet, as he wishes for a moment that he were home again, where at least the terrain is familiar, there begins to race within him, like the despised beat of the tom-tom, echoes of a past which he has not yet been able to utilize, intimations of a responsibility which he has not yet been able to face." Then, in a parenthesis in an epitaph for Richard Wright, Baldwin remarks that when an American Negro "faces an African, he is facing the unspeakably dark, guilty,

erotic past which the Protestant fathers made him bury . . .
but which lives in his personality and haunts the universe
yet." [34] And the conception of the African as dark, as the
darker brother, as mysteriously guilty, as secretly erotic, lurks,
if it does not always come to expression, somewhere in whatever Baldwin says about Africans.

It is with the Southern Negro and the African, who don't
after all occupy him very much, that Baldwin makes his
longest reach toward an identifiable identity. Writing as he
does so exclusively out of himself, they of course wouldn't,
except in a speculative way, occupy him very much, but
that they do at all take a place in his drama of the search
for identity provides the clearest indication of the nature of
the goal. It is not roots that Baldwin seeks, as it is not the
product of any particular response to any particular life. It
is merely something that has been buried. It is something that
will reveal itself when the individual is stripped of particularity. It will therefore be felt, if still not seen, only in moments of ungoverned passion, in pure hating and pure loving
—and it is therefore, in Baldwin's fiction, bound to fail of
achievement. Fiction has the techniques to accomplish the
departure from Eden and the coming of worldliness. Innocence travels toward experience. And worldiness is a drama of
perpetual qualifying, just such a one as Baldwin sometimes
does complain of. So, he says, the Negro in his relations with
white Americans is prohibited "anything so uncomplicated
and satisfactory as pure hatred." [35] On the other hand, the
characters of Baldwin's fiction are prohibited anything so uncomplicated as pure loving. Or when they are not prohibited,
as is the case particularly in some moments of *Another
Country,* the fiction surrenders to rhapsody.

It is the search for purity that is the scheme of Baldwin's
fiction. The "identity" of his heroes is finally without form.

It was Bellow's Augie March who started with the faith that a man's character is his fate, but he ended with the lesson that a man's fate is his character. Augie's moral engagament with the world identifies him. Baldwin's drama is pre-moral. The problem of his heroes is rather the pure transmission of pure impulse. They can neither hate nor love because their world—the world itself—is complicated and imposes limitations. They are therefore lonely in the world, and therefore pitiable. The world closes in on them, and their responsive action is either surrender to themselves, a turning inward, or, in the attempt to burst out of their isolation, they take to bizarre and extreme expression of the impulse within.

The deep problems of accommodation are always just around the corner and waiting for Baldwin's heroes. They constitute the reason for Baldwin's writing. They are not met because Baldwin's heroes end their adventures in a cry of loneliness, or in incredible pathos. But then, despite the fact that Baldwin has heroes of various colors practicing their heroism variously, in narratives that look like essays and in narratives that are fiction, it is not anyone's loneliness which engages Baldwin. He is concerned with his own, and his deepest and most promising work has been in that fiction that has drawn specifically on an identity which, willy-nilly, he does have.

One of Baldwin's difficulties has been a proneness to universalizing formulas. His largest achievement so far has been *Go Tell It on the Mountain,* his first novel, written either before he was violated by such formulas, or written out of a completeness of experience that was not yet dependent for the extension of its significance on a leap to universals. The novel creates in its protagonist an intimate version, not of what it is to be, but what it is to become a Negro in America, what it is to accept the conditions that create that identity.

Its protagonist, an adolescent boy named John Grimes, is at the point of his inheritance. The action of the novel will take him through the day of and the day after his fourteenth birthday. He has just become conscious of his sexuality, and become guilty about it. The time of his initiation into manhood is upon him, and the particular device of his initiation is a ritual of salvation in the Harlem store-front church, The Temple of the Fire Baptized, in which his family worships.

The greater part of *Go Tell It on the Mountain* is a series of flash-backs into the lives that have brought his aunt, his stepfather, and his mother to this moment in this church, and his salvation will be an implicit acceptance of their lives. He will become part of his ancestry and his history. The novel is in that way John's exploration of his history. What the novel therefore in that way creates—though it also operates in another, altogether less fortunate, way—is the Negro's historical condition, and it does so with subtlety, fullness, and thoroughness of apprehension. The triple flash-back allows Baldwin to hold within a single vision the experiences of a long history of the Negro in America. He can incorporate into it slavery and abrupt emancipation, the frustrations and the extremes of the life of the peasantry of the Old Country, the battle within the peasantry, and intimately within the family, for order, continuity, and moral stability. At the same time he contains within the vision the development of a religion that is an instrument at once of ethical prohibition, of promise, hatred, and of emotional deliverance. In the same moment he can contain the Negro experience of the trek to the North, the illusory promises of the North, with its sharper frustrations and its greater desperations.

And Baldwin gives all this history a ritual amplitude in the singing and the tambourines and the praying of the forlorn faithful of The Temple of the Fire Baptized. Moreover, the three persons who provide the flash-backs make a large coherence of their experiences as Negroes: the aunt who has opposed her bitter resolution to the brutalities and the crudenesses, South and North, of Negro life, and reaped for her pains baffled outrage; the stepfather who has baffled his own sense of sinfulness, his own crudeness, his sexuality, his vitality, and his vengefulness as a Negro, into an obsessive religion that makes Satan and Jesus instruments of his own personality; the mother who has been forced by the violences and the sheer confusions of the racial situation to search in her husband's religion for an ultimate kindness.

What Baldwin achieves in these three persons is, precisely, an identity, an engagement in life that has produced unique definition, and by intricately relating these ancestors he presents his protagonist with an actual inheritance—a tradition that is of the folk and is not folksy, that contains the political and the social facts and is neither sentimental nor a documentary of protest nor a social study nor, as would be the danger that Baldwin particularly would run, a history of the spirit crushed by history. These people have one way and another lived and become their lives.

Their lives, heavy with despairs and with dehumanizing bitterness, appear to the protagonist necessarily not as an inheritance, but as a burden, in fact as damnation. They constitute a blackness settling inevitably upon him which he must struggle to resist. He has early decided that he would not be like his father or his fathers, that he would have another life. He does accept his father's family, at the climax of the novel, out of a chaos of motives, in a fit of hysteria and exhaustion taken by him and everyone else at the moment of his salvation. He is made to accept it because he is made to know that the way to the soul's freedom is through damnation and death. The moment is a seizure. He is seized, possessed by the Power, hurled by It to the threshing floor where, an ironic voice within him insists, he will "become like all the other niggers," and he hears in this moment a sound as from the grave of rage and weeping, which he recognizes he has heard all his life. He sees in the grave the "armies of darkness," "the despised and rejected, the wretched and the spat upon, the earth's offscouring." He is of their company, he knows now, and "they would swallow up his soul." Their death is imposed upon him, their dread testimony, and their desolation, and then, having gone through this dark, he has a sight of the light of the Lord and is saved. The light and the dark have kissed in his soul. He will weep again, now that his weeping has begun, and go through the darkness again, but he is free. He is at peace with the faithful and is one of them, and he walks with them in the novel's last scene, in the dawn through the streets of Harlem, where screaming ambulances are carting away last night's death.

In fact, the dark that John goes through is not so substantial as the scheme of the novel hopes for. Much of it is just Biblical reference. John doesn't really know the lives of his aunt, his stepfather, and his mother. Only the reader does. And that is a technical fault. The novel would say that in this crucial moment the history that has all along been implicitly present to John will become actual. But if not all the comment, at least all the materials, of a drama of the making of identity are here. It is a long, full, ordered, and specific experience that is settled upon John. And there can be no doubt that Baldwin draws it from the identity he has.

But then John is encumbered with a weight of other materials which only seem to be part of the same drama, which convert his acceptance into a denial, and they are such materials as will hereafter stop much of Baldwin's fiction short of resolution. It is the fact that everyone in this novel has "identity" except John, whose role is comprehended by his sensitivity. And that is not the effect of the structure of the novel, which demands only that he begin in innocence, but of the fact that he is from his beginning equipped with quite another kind of identity, just that spark of pure passion which Baldwin's later heroes will try vainly to protect. John is not initiated, but victimized, and the novel demands that his identity-as-passion must be snuffed out. It is snuffed out, not by the oncoming of his racial experience, which would be sufficient if the two ever met, but, more appropriately, by the contingencies of a pure Oedipus complex. John is by Baldwin's design first of all a ready victim—he is the smallest boy in his class at school, he has no skill in sports but he has an intellectual bent, and he has no friends. He is initially unlovely and unloved, and therefore fiercely protective of whatever he can find within him, that which Baldwin calls his identity. It is that which his guilt-ridden, vengeance-ridden stepfather—in the principal action in John's story—as fiercely tries to destroy. His intelligence, says Baldwin for John, "was his identity, and part, therefore, of that wickedness for which his father beat him and to which he clung in order to withstand his father."

His intelligence is not his whole identity, as things work out in this novel, but that "wickedness" is, and its expression is not intellectual but sexual. John first feels a shock of guilt about the identity he has opposed to his father on the day that he first masturbates, and it is at this point that his opposition to his father becomes critical. ". . . John's secret heart had flourished in its wickedness until the day his sin first overtook him." The object of his sexuality is, certainly not expressly, but clearly enough, his mother, who loves him, protects and receives him, who remembers his birthday, and whom on occasion he imagines as a young girl. His stepfather, on the other hand, rejects him, is filled with hatred and a clear preference for John's stepbrother. Indeed the primary psychological motivation for John's search for religious salvation is his search for a father who will love and forgive him.*

He doesn't of course find one in the flesh, but he finds an older boy among the church's congregation who has before this shown a willingness to embrace him, to whom now that he is saved he turns for tenderness and a "holy kiss" which becomes "like a seal ineffaceable forever." And if there is any doubt about the direction of this development, a story by Baldwin contemporary with the novel, "The Outing," which uses the same setting and the same characters, is expressly about young John Grimes's initiation into homosexuality.[36]

This progress of John's identity has nothing to do with his initiation into the lives of his fathers except that, ironically, it discredits it. John doesn't become a man. Baldwin does attempt at least once to make some deeper connection between the Oedipal and the racial dramas. In his hysterical vision on the threshing floor John remembers seeing his father naked and wanting the power to castrate him, and he associates this guilt with the sin of Ham, who had looked on the nakedness of his father, Noah, and so been condemned, with the whole Negro race, to perpetual servitude. But this is at best a local cleverness. The story of John's thwarted capabilities for love doesn't engage his racial drama. John is a victim not because he must accept an oppression of Negro experience—that would make him *somebody*—but he is a

---

* "Then he would no longer be the son of his father, but the son of the Heavenly Father, the King. Then he need no longer fear his father, for he could take, as it were, their quarrel over his father's head, to Heaven—to the Father who loved him, who had come down in the flesh to die for him."

Baldwin speaks of his own religious crisis in "Letter from a Region in My Mind" as a "spiritual seduction."

victim before that, primarily because his father won't forgive his guiltless impulses. The effect of that victimization in turn is that he is trapped in his childhood. He can't be a Negro or any man. And that fate secures from Baldwin pity and tenderness, beyond which there is no development.

Baldwin's tenderness for John, it should be said, extends to curious shifts. It is Baldwin who completes John's fantasy of revenge and forgiveness, and quite beyond John's knowing anything about it, by making his father really only his stepfather. His real father, safely dead, was, so a flash-back reveals, loving, understanding, graceful, and intellectual, and the victim of irrational injustices. And this is a little fault, a small softness in the story, but a large symptom. If tenderness will substitute for pursuit of character and action, then there will be nothing to do but explain circumstances and bemoan.

It was to just such shifts that Baldwin came in his succeeding novel. *Go Tell It on the Mountain* does drive to some dramatic depth, despite tenderness. *Giovanni's Room* is benumbed by tenderness. It is static. It is static despite its spectacular materials—*Giovanni's Room* is an all-white novel set in seedy parts of Paris; it is about homosexuality; it provides glimpses of a sub-world of tittering fairies and decrepit perverts. The novel is static despite the high adventures in it— broken hearts and a murder. David, a young, and initially a heterosexual, American in Paris, has an affair with Giovanni, which he terminates abruptly when his fiancée comes to claim him. Giovanni, in despair, descends from lover to fairy, to a murder which is the last assertion of his pride. And David withdraws from his fiancée to confront his own guilt. The novel comes to its abrupt end at that point, as it must, because in fact David is not guilty but only pitiful, and there isn't much he can confront. All his impulses are, within the terms of the novel, quite correct, but all his circumstances are against him, and the novel's main task really is to explain away those circumstances and forgive him.

David is accused by virtually everyone he meets, by the elderly pander who converts him to Giovanni and homosexuality, by Giovanni himself, by his fiancée, and certainly by Baldwin, of an unwillingness to give himself in love. His accusers are quite right, it happens, but in a way that is beyond Baldwin's apparent intention, and it happens that his accusers are also wrong, and that too is beyond Baldwin's apparent intention. As love is defined by the novel, David loves.

His deep fault, so the imputation runs, is that he protects his innocence, that he won't risk his virginity. And that, the novel insists, is a national failing, in which David takes part —David's still deeper fault is that he is an American. Americans, Giovanni says, don't believe in "all the serious, dreadful things, like pain and death and love," and Americans think that privacy is a crime. David picks up the tenor of Giovanni's teaching. He observes of his countrymen, on occasion assembled at the American Express office, that the women have neither sex nor age, and the men all smell of soap. Giovanni accuses David, precisely, of wanting to be clean. "You think you came here covered with soap and you think you will go out covered with soap. . . ." Americans, it is said, perpetually smile empty smiles, are obsessed by happiness, have no sense of doom, have no openness toward life, experience, or other people. It is not only the Europeans of the novel, and after them David, who say such things, but even David's fiancée, who should be cast in the role of the angular American temptress, a jazzier Mamie Pocock.

This is all, of course, the vocabulary of the International Theme. David's plight is that he is an American innocent en-

cumbered with a puritanical morality of innocence, and his
salvation then will be in lessons in experience and evil. But
the great joke played on David, considering the way he is
bedeviled, is that he is presented really with no experience
or evil to learn from. The International Theme is in the novel
only a flossy confusion, and not that complicated adjustment
of manners and morals that it has been in the American
literature of tradition. It is here no more than an expansion
of that cliché, that looks as though it might be associated
with the International Theme but which has a much greater
antiquity and a different genesis, that cliché that speaks of
the northern races (Americans) as cold, and the southern
races (Latins) as hot. Giovanni is the more Latin because
he is an Italian, and in fact he objects even to the French
mesure. David's fiancée has learned about love and passion
by traveling in Spain.

And the joke in that is that this Latin passion, of the ancient
cliché and of this novel, is by the novel's definition, precisely,
innocent. The place of David's learning is not the old and
heavy world which is opposite Eden, but just that Eden which,
were David a representative American of the tradition, he
might be expected to carry about in his own soul, an Eden
populated by noble, guileless, faultless savages. This Giovanni
who will introduce him to Sin is indeed more innocent still.
He is, as Baldwin creates him, a gazelle. He is a child. He is
a soul. He carries about with him a penumbra of song and
olive trees and the simple joys and securities of his Italian
village. In this alien Paris he is driven by terror, astonished
by crudeness, and he belives entirely in the passionate communion of loving souls.

David does too, though everybody in the novel says he
doesn't. He responds to Giovanni readily enough, only after
some brief reluctance to make love to a man. And he responds

readily not only to Giovanni, but to everyone available to him in this short narrative. Everyone available to him secures from him a yearning to comfort and protect—motherliness, in fact, which is the mode of his loving. There had been an adolescent homosexual experience with a boy named Joey, who, David remembers, in the morning, sleeping, looked like a baby, "his mouth half open, his cheek flushed, his curly hair darkening the pillow and half hiding his damp round forehead and his long eyelashes glinting slightly in the summer sun." David had felt, along with his guilt and fear, great tenderness for him, and had made his breakfast. Now, the ruined old pander receives David's sorrowing sympathy. And as for Giovanni: David sees "under his beauty and his bravado, terror, and a terrible desire to please; dreadfully, dreadfully moving, and it made me want, in anguish, to reach out and comfort him." He calls him "baby." As for his fiancée: he sends her packing, but in the same moment he says, "Her hair was damp and fell over her forehead, and her face was damp. I longed to reach out and take her in my arms and comfort her."

It isn't David's lack of lovingness that interests Baldwin ultimately. Were David really locked within his virginity, this would be a tougher, certainly, and a more extensive novel. David hasn't, however, done anything bad, and so Baldwin's only possible response to him is pity. David's fault, if it is one, is only that his quick motherliness has been exposed to odd circumstances and so he has got himself into an impossible triangle, of which he is the apex. He isn't guilty.

David's innocence, moreover, exists quite outside the terms of the novel, and it does render him unfit for this world. No one can love as David wants to love, and experience with lovers is bound to thwart him. His love, just like the "identity" of Baldwin's other heroes, is a passionate spark yearning to be a flame, and like Baldwin's "identity" it is likely to be smothered by anything, and certainly by the sobrieties of daily companionship in this world. David ends this first-person narrative with a dream of castration which he gives, not a Freudian, but a theological gloss. He has been imagining himself as Giovanni, now under sentence of death, walking down the corridor to the guillotine. He looks into a mirror and says:

> I long to crack that mirror and be free. I look at my sex, my troubling sex, and wonder how it can be redeemed, how I can save it from the knife. The journey to the grave is already begun, the journey to corruption is, always, already, half over. Yet, the key to my salvation, which cannot save my body, is hidden in my flesh.

It is salvation that David wants, salvation from his corrupt carnality, salvation that is in this world to be approached only through carnal loving. David loves the idea of Love, and the initial discipline in loving *somebody* is for him a cumbersome complication, at best a duty, and it is bound to crush him.

That is not only David's unhappy problem, but it is the signal of Baldwin's too, his seeming inability now to drive his story any further. Or what he is driven to—such is the evidence of his third novel, *Another Country*—is a more insistent shrillness, a greater howling for the communion of innocence, and the sacrifice inevitably of plot, character, and the strong sense of persons achieving identity by moving through their circumstanced lives. *Another Country* is an anarchy of shifting, local intentions, sudden rhetorical inflations, shifting points of view, too many protagonists, too many episodes, and too many rending passions.

The sense of strain—Baldwin's strain, not necessarily that

of his characters—is everywhere evident. The word "terribly," for instance, used as an intensifier, and words like "unutterably," "unspeakable," "ineffable," "unbelievably," "great," are crammed desperately into the crevices everywhere of a crumbling action. A character is made to be "terribly aware" of the forehead of another character, and a pair of lovers are "terribly driven, terribly shy." A young man coming out of the bathroom seems "unutterably huge." The same young man moves in his "great shoes" and on an occasion watches a lady lift from her kitchen cabinet "the great salad bowl." Elsewhere, passers-by on the street cast "ineffable, sidelong, desperate" looks. Forced to an ineffable action, Baldwin is forced—a disastrous thing in a novelist—to an ineffable vocabulary.

And the dialogue of the novel is desultory when it is not stilted. The characters of the novel move through a series of love affairs, searching with more and less terrible awareness for perfect, unutterable union. They can't and they don't have very much to say to each other, other than "Do you love me?" Indeed, Baldwin seizes every opportunity to abandon dialogue, for brooding or rhapsodic reflection. So a love affair is concluded, in the Museum of Modern Art:

> He said nothing, for he did not know what to say, and they continued their frightening promenade through the icy and angular jungle. The colors on the walls blared at them—like frozen music; he had the feeling that these rooms would never cease folding in on each other, that this labyrinth was eternal. And a sorrow entered him for Cass stronger than any love he had ever felt for her. . . . He wished that he could rescue her, that it was within his power to rescue her and make her life less hard. But it was only love which could accomplish the miracle of mak-

ing a life bearable—only love, and love itself mostly failed; and he had never loved her.

It is in fact revealing of the stasis upon which Baldwin has fallen that the one briefly sustained moment when the spoken dialogue of the novel does attain authority is on the occasion of an uninterrupted eulogy by a Negro preacher. Dialogue moves through contingencies and arrives at distinctions. There are no such necessities in sermons.

Strangely enough, given his urge to passionate union, his antipathy to qualifications, and the laxity of his prose, the model Baldwin seems to have before him most continuously in *Another Country* is Henry James, and particularly *The Wings of the Dove*. The novel takes its epigraph from James. A poor Southern white girl in love with a Negro is seen as a kind of anti-Milly Theale, the "unwitting heiress of generations of bitterness." Her opposite, a woman descended from privileged New Englanders, is referred to once as "the icebound heiress of all the ages." In a bit of interior decorating, Baldwin places on a table in a room a copy of *The Wings of the Dove*. It is a book one of his characters is reading.* More largely, it is once again by a number of variations on the International Theme that Baldwin creates his serial attempts at innocent communion. The title of the novel suggests as much—Baldwin apparently intends no reference either to Hemingway or to *The Jew of Malta*. The whole business of the plot is to provide for confrontations—love affairs—between opposing cultural quantities. America meets Europe, not quite so contemptibly, it should be said, as was the case in *Giovanni's Room*. White meets black. Downtown meets Uptown. In addition, men meet women, heterosexuals

---

* On the same table are copies of Blaise Cendrars, Jean Genet, Proust, and *Native Son*. The book list has no particular function in the novel except, presumably, to reveal some of Baldwin's sources.

meet homosexuals, and virtually everyone meets and attempts a love affair with everyone else. And the seeming issue in all of these confrontations, a properly Jamesian one, is the quantity and difficulty of realization that must precede cultural or any kind of union. Only in union is there completeness, and everyone is another country.

That would seem to be the issue. For Henry James it followed that the novelist's task was the creation of more complicated, more understanding moral realizations. For Baldwin in *Another Country* there is no such strenuous consequence. In fact it is assumed, explicity in the relationships between white and black, that no amount of understanding will finally be understanding enough to overcome differences, and it is assumed in the first place that differences between people are the arbitrary, tragic necessities of worldly existence. The novel's protagonists can at best accomplish temporary evasions of them, sometimes by the agency of marijuana, typically by sexual narcosis, the approximate act of love. "Love," one of the protagonists reflects, "was a country he knew nothing about," and it is to that unknown country actually that he and everyone else wants to emigrate. Love will be, of course, the perfect democracy, the new Eden, wherein all complicating distinctions since Eden will have disappeared.

It is to Eden that all the characters of the novel aspire. That finally is the other country, and their journey is toward the past, from innocence to innocence. Meanwhile, social complication corrupts them, and their whole drama therefore is in their "vulnerability," a word Baldwin uses again and again. The more vulnerable the more pathetic, the more they are to be protected from complication, differences, and the social reality, and the more they are to be loved. That is their drama, that is the basis of the relationships between these characters, and that is the novel's architectural principle. First there is Rufus Scott, a Negro jazz musician, a Dionysian innocent who is driven by the social complications of his love affair with a Southern white girl to Dionysian violence and then, before the novel is much advanced, to suicide. His role in the novel is, by imposing his memory as guilt, to test everyone's love. More vulnerable and more innocent, he was most to be protected. Rufus heard in the jazz he played the screaming question *"Do you love me? Do you love me? Do you love me?"* Everyone did, and does, love Rufus, but not enough. His best friend, Vivaldo, a white man, as he attempts to live his own life of loving innocence, comes to know by how much he had failed to love Rufus. He had never taken him in his arms. Vivaldo loves, or tries to love, Ida, Rufus's sister, who has made herself an instrument of Rufus's revenge and by that much reinforces the differences between black and white. Bitterness is the complication she must evade. Then there is Cass, a white woman, a wife and a mother, who had given to Rufus some maternal affections, who is to be taught that true loving involves greater risks. Then there is Eric, a white homosexual now living with a French boy named Yves. Eric had loved Rufus sufficiently to take him in his arms, but his motives, so he now reflects, had been impure, and he had not succeeded in making Rufus believe he loved him. And then there is Richard, Cass's husband, the villain of the piece. "I didn't love Rufus," Richard says, "not the way you did, the way all of you did."

I couldn't help feeling, anyway, that one of the reasons all of you made such a kind of—*fuss*—over him was partly just because he was colored. Which is a hell of a reason to love anybody.

By way, then, of adequately responding to Rufus, by way

of making amends, everyone, except Richard, attempts to love everyone else. *Another Country* is a long novel, as it would have to be to provide for so many combinations. The spirit of Rufus beckons toward Eden. And the spirit of Rufus—Richard, the liberal, is partially blind—does have everything to do with his being colored. Rufus is Baldwin's darker Negro, pre-moral, certainly pre-Christian, possessing greater wildness, greater sexual energies—and possessing, so Baldwin astonishingly says, a natural sense of rhythm.

> *A nigger,* said his father, *lives his whole life, lives and dies according to a beat. Shit, he humps to that beat and the baby he throws up in there, well, he jumps to it and comes out nine months later like a goddamn tambourine.*

And the spirit of Rufus, his joy and his love, despite the complications which have killed him, is of a childlike innocence. All the lovers of this novel, too, call each other "baby." The signal of love is in every case the sudden appearance of a poignant youthfulness:

> She bent her head toward him, leaning more heavily on his arm, as though they were two children.

> With her golden hair down, and all the trouble in her face, she looked unbelievably young.

> She felt his violence and his uncertainty, and this made him seem much younger than she. And this excited her in a way that she had never been excited before. . . .

> This childish and trustful tremor returned to Vivaldo a sense of his own power. He held Eric very tightly and covered Eric's body with his own, as though he were shielding him from the falling heavens.

The women, when they are loved, are gamins. The men, when they are loved, are boys. Lovers, in this novel too, are mothers.

Love is a ceremony of innocence. It follows that it is corrupted by anything, and especially by ordinary carnality. In fact the only successful love affairs in the novel are those between white homosexuals, and the essential component of those affairs is, of course, their purity. It is to such love that the spirit of Rufus beckons, and if Rufus himself, a Negro, is disbarred from such salvation, that is because the social reality has forced on him disabling complications. Others will create Eden for him. Vivaldo, in bed with Eric, succeeds momentarily: "Vivaldo seemed to have fallen through a great hole in time, back to his innocence, he felt clear, washed, and empty, waiting to be filled." But then a moment later, in bed with Ida, he loses Eden: "Her long fingers stroked his back, and he began, slowly, with a horrible, strangling sound, to weep, for she was stroking his innocence out of him." The more perfect achievement rests with Eric and his boy, Yves.

Eric and Yves, mute, perfect lovers, are discovered first in the novel in a villa by the Mediterranean, naked in a brilliant garden. Among all the youngsters of the novel, none is so young, so tormented, or so vulnerable as Yves. He is a "violated urchin," with an "open, childlike grin," a "puppy playfulness," an "adolescent ardor," and, the overt symbolism of the novel makes it clear, he is Eve. Eric is forced to leave the garden, seduced from it in fact, with the urging of Yves, by the promise of a career in the world. He awaits Yves in New York throughout the subsequent course of the novel, and the novel ends, in an ambiguous promise, with his arrival. It began with the slaying of the innocent Rufus. It ends with the descent of the radiant mother of us all, with the Adamic Eric's welcoming of Eve to America. Eden is just about to be lost again, or regained.

So Baldwin would seem to say. And this, now, is where his yearning for an essential identity has brought him. It is perhaps of lesser significance that the Eden to which he looks forward is one created by and available only to homosexuals, though that fact does propose disabling limitations. It is the more significant that Baldwin's progress has been precisely away from the struggle with which he began. To that severe struggle within a particular place and a particular history, Eden is no solution at all, and what is worse, Baldwin's indulgence of Edenic fantasies of purity promise to make him—what he has no right to be—irrelevant.

The two essays comprising *The Fire Next Time* are contemporaneous with *Another Country*. The juxtaposition is of an interest. Baldwin is to be found in the one volume turning one way and preaching Apocalypse, in the other turning the other way and preaching Love. Given Baldwin's initial clarity, this turning and all this oracular grandeur can be nothing other than an evasion.

WRIGHT MORRIS

The American Territory

The typical scene of the novel in America in these years has been a city clutter of discrete things and persons. Its typical hero is an anonymous man beset neither by evil nor good, neither by the faithless nor believers, but by a neutral, a tremendous, and a terribly intricate social complexity. He is a man who, at his best, attempts to locate just that heroic understanding or do that heroic deed that will make the clutter sensible, reveal his own connection with it, and thereby end his own anonymity. The literature of these years has been informed, that is again to say, by a need for accommodation. The need comes long after the information of the wasteland —it takes at least a remnant of faith to discover and certainly to care about faithlessness—after disillusion, and after the lyrical assertion of impossible alienation. And there has been in this literature no urgency such as marked some previous epochs of American literary practice to define American goals —either in terms of Nature, or Socialism, or Culture, or Democracy, or Sex—nor has there been a significant iconoclasm, nor very much poets' unacknowledged legislating, but rather the singular search for the adequate individual illumination.

Except at the remove of such fiction as that, for instance, of Jack Kerouac and John Clellon Holmes, it has not been a bardic literature of large cultural formulation. Things are not what they are advertised to be: the celebrants of the Beat mystique, who present themselves as anarchists, have devoted themselves actually to proclamation of the Americanism they shared, they said, with all Americans;* with only one seeming exception, those whose large participation in American culture has not been questioned have addressed themselves seldom and only secondarily to defining the country.

Wright Morris is the seeming exception. From the beginning, for more than twenty years now of a production more steady than that of any of his contemporaries, through fourteen books of fiction, Morris' scene has most often been the rural Midwest, and the materials in all cases have been those of the home place, the attic of the collected American experience, the lives, contemporary and just a while ago, of its inhabitants. No American of these years has been more deliberately or more conscientiously American than Wright Morris, and no novelist of this time has been more certainly in touch with American surfaces, with such things and such voices as seem to concentrate precisely a sense of the national uniqueness—the rumble of a freight at an isolated crossing, the aspect of the bland store fronts of a Nebraska town, looking, in a metaphor Morris has used frequently, like a row of stubborn old men lined up to be shot, the look of a peeled Mail Pouch sign, the explosions of a superannuated Model

* Of course there is no Beat Generation, but there is something. Kerouac and John Clellon Holmes have exemplified it in utterances ranging from the freckle-faced Americanism of *On the Road* and *The Dharma Bums* to the pedantry of Americanism of Holmes's *The Horn.*

T, the intransigent silences of old farmers, and then in other territories and times of the nation, the clink and whine of a Las Vegas slot machine, the sinuous drawl and intensity of a Hollywood starlet, the haunting heartiness of a department-store Santa Claus—the American artifacts which, taken together, might be cultural formation. No one else has had such eyes and ears for these things nor been so assaulted by the suggestion in them.

Moreover, it was apparently a cultural nationalism that was the intention with which he began to write,* and from the beginning the intention has proposed most of what he has had to say—clearly at least in his first five novels, published in the 1940s: in *My Uncle Dudley* in 1942, then in *The Man Who Was There* (1945), *The Inhabitants* (1946), *The Home Place* (1948), and *The World in the Attic* (1949). These books are emphatically about the discovery of America.

In the first novel the discovery happens through a recapitulation of the American past, and in the other books through an evocation of it. *My Uncle Dudley* was in its beginning, in fact, not entirely direct about the matter, and therefore the novel suffers structural difficulties. It begins in mere picaresque, with the linear adventures of an elder vagabond, Uncle Dudley, who combines something of Don Quixote with a great deal of W. C. Fields, and a younger vagabond, the narrator, whose morality of innocence and misdemeanors makes him Huckleberry Finn. It is not until their adventures are half over that the novel really engages any issues whatsoever—and then Morris clapped on the novel an arbitrary climax simply,

---

* This "intention" doesn't account, of course, for the fact that Morris became a writer. He turned to writing, he has said himself, at the end of a year abroad after college, in 1934, simply because he had tried writing and found he could do it. See Sam Bleufarb, "Point of View: An Interview with Wright Morris, July 1958," *Accent,* XIX (Winter 1959), 34 ff.

it would seem, to stop the diffusion. But what the novel does discover in itself halfway through is an epic of American pioneering, an epic repeated now in the American wasteland with consequent mock-epic revelations. As vagabonds, Uncle Dudley and the boy are participants in the central, democratic, Whitmanesque, Chaplinesque tradition of the Open Road, and as they loaf along they are to prove the democratic spirit. As vagabonds they are also, what the tramps of "The Bridge" were for Hart Crane, the last pioneers. Moreover, they are moved, though suddenly, by that cultural nationalism that had become a movement in the 1920s, by the search for "the usable past." All the signs are present—appeals to Whitman, to Chaplin, to the land, to the quirky natives, to Huck Finn, and there is in these appeals a felt presence of Van Wyck Brooks, Lewis Mumford, Sherwood Anderson, and Hart Crane.*

Morris' pioneers follow a history that has ironically turned on itself. They go from west to east, from Los Angeles toward Chicago. Their covered wagon has become an ancient touring car, and their fellow pioneers, in this time, a tawdry group of paying passengers. They all of them run a gamut of pioneer privations—including a brush with hostile Indians. The car falls apart gradually. The party is reduced through the incursions of the wasteland malaises, lack of spirituality and lack of courage, lack of freedom and lack of endurance. The good and the brave live to cross the Mississippi—only to be

* Morris has said that the writers of the 1920s influenced him only indirectly. "Oddly enough, at the time I began to write, I had not read the great writers of the Twenties. . . . I made contact with the writers of the Twenties, but saturated myself in what I liked about them much later. Almost ten years later." Bleufarb, "An Interview with Wright Morris." Unfortunately Morris did not say in this interview what date it was ten years after that he saturated himself in the writers of the Twenties. In any event, he needn't have saturated himself very thoroughly to have been inspired by this literary nationalism.

arrested as vagabonds by the corrupt policemen of a small
Missouri town. The pioneers founder in the town. They are
caught, one would say, since it is a small Missouri town, by
the legions of Aunt Sally.

The action of *My Uncle Dudley* isn't after all very deliberate or thorough—significant secondary characters simply
disappear when the novel changes direction—and the action
is not sufficient to the novel's belated intention. The large
fault of the novel, however, is in the fact that its intention,
once discovered, immediately seeps away into too much folksy
declamation: Uncle Dudley's beliefs in "the land," "the people," "the little guy," and "bravery," are repeated in too many
wise epigrams. Don Quixote becomes W. C. Fields, and then
when the lessons begin to be urgent, W. C. Fields becomes
Will Rogers. In *The Man Who Was There* and the books
that immediately followed it, there is more control and less
garrulity, effected through a complete reversal of approach.
In *Uncle Dudley* the known past is mounted on the present
and the present itself becomes the backdrop of the drama.
Uncle Dudley stands in the foreground announcing that the
past is the way to the future. After *Uncle Dudley* the drama
is of the present either stumbling upon or deliberately groping
its way to significant mementos of a past which is not so
much taken for granted. The past is now evoked from its
souvenirs, and the technical effort of the novels is to make the
souvenirs present and luminous enough so that they will be
evocative.

But the books are intended, still, to define the country. *The
Man Who Was There* composes three novellas which trace
the spirit and the spiritual heritage left by a young painter
who, now, during the war, is missing in action, who was
himself a searcher after the meaning of the American souvenirs. His heritage, for those who connect with him, is a

reawakened vitality. *The Inhabitants* and *The Home Place* are not quite novels at all, but books of combined photographs and text which together are to illuminate the typical American things. The things are located, in the first book, here and there in a tour through the country. In the second book they are found in and about the town in Nebraska that Morris has named Lone Tree—a town that has some connection, presumably, with his own native Central City, Nebraska. *The World in the Attic* then uses the characters and some of the narrative of *The Home Place* for another return to the home place, a place in this instance named Junction. In both *The Home Place* and *The World in the Attic* a native of the place, a writer named Clyde Muncy who has lived for many years in New York, returns with his acquired city ways and his wife and children to rediscover the traditional, rural, Midwestern America of his home.

All the books Morris has written are, in fact, chapters in what is obviously one work. Characters and events are repeated, reworked, reprocessed in various contexts, from different points of view. Uncle Dudley becomes in *The Man Who Was There* the young painter's maverick uncle who takes his nephew on just such a tour of the country as that used by the first novel, and then his name and something of his audacity is borrowed for a character in *The World in the Attic*. Then much of him reappears in the protagonist of a later novel, *The Works of Love* (1952). In *Ceremony in Lone Tree* (1960) that character's son appears, now approximately of the age and the temperament of the original Uncle Dudley, the character having meanwhile picked up new associations with the Tramp, Santa Claus, and St. Francis. And Lone Tree, Nebraska, located somewhere in the central part of the state, between Ogallala and Callaway, at times a small town and at other times a ghost town, has been Morris'

Yoknapatawpha, only not quite so systematically exploited as Yoknapatawpha. It is the scene of or a point of reference in a half dozen of the novels. The characters, events, and scenes of the books interlock and interweave.

The five books of the 1940s compose, however, a single distinct development within the general work, and they lead to a unique crisis—one which has repercussions, it happens, for all that movement that can be said to have begun with Van Wyck Brooks's challenge to America's coming-of-age, that movement toward a new literary nationalism that had its great day in the 1920s and that was the last great national literary movement we have had.

Brooks had looked for a vivifying of "the dry old Yankee stalk," its stirring and sending forth shoots and blossoms. The image of the lone tree that is in so many places in Morris' work and that gives its name to the town, is the locus of a similar seeking. These five books are a watering of the tree. Even Morris' photographs in *The Inhabitants* and *The Home Place*—of old barns and angular old men, of bedsteads and rockers and the interiors of old barbershops, of barber poles and grain elevators and country churches and tumbled gravestones—partake of that Americanism. They partake particularly of that segment of it that was associated in the 1920s with Alfred Stieglitz and his circle. Whether by subscription or not, Morris was a belated member of the American photographers' Midwestern contingent, and if he was not by subscription a member of that circle, he could hardly have been unaware of its influences later, in the 1930s, in the work of such Americanists of the camera as Margaret Bourke-White, Carl Mydans, and, pre-eminently, Walker Evans and James Agee. Perhaps it is not fortuitous that the painter hero of *The Man Who Was There* is named Agee Ward. In the manifest spirit of this nationalism, anyway, Morris pursued the native America.

He followed it to the point, however, where the gift of the past seemed suspect, and the pursuit of it self-defeating. Whatever the intention of the pursuit, his recapitulation and then his evocation of the native America drifted almost necessarily into American regionalist drama. The necessary dramatic condition of his regionalism was a hint of heroic vitality in a frontier past, the current equivalent of which heroism must be a somber endurance. The drama itself is in the threat to the American past by the new—by the city, by business, in fact by any system of dependence, by any social liberalism, and of course by change itself. And Morris' drama moved from a first instance, *My Uncle Dudley,* which did contain some appeals (albeit safe because anachronistic) to the figures of a native radicalism—appeals to the atheistic Sinclair Lewis and even Eugene Debs—moved from it to a sensibility of deep conservatism and a politics of Midwestern populism.

The Man Who Was There and *The Inhabitants* are books in which the *search* for the past is still the main thing. Agee Ward had put himself to finding his roots and, because he searched, those whom he touches are revivified—revivified in the spirit of the search itself. A young man is worked upon by the legend of Agee Ward and comes to believe that he is Agee reincarnated. Agee's soul searches on. An elderly spinster is mysteriously so touched by Agee that she opens herself up to courtship, to her own seeking of the ancient mysteries. In *The Inhabitants* a series of prose poems, which are not always entirely lucid and not always clearly attached to the photographs they accompany, do the job of mysterious searching. They are teasing, bright vignettes which are not yet quite revealing. They bear the sense of striving for something more. But then by the time of *The Home Place* and its sequel, *The World in the Attic,* the search has come to the point where something must be found—and those books are stories essentially of the city fellow merely astonished and embarrassed by country things. The second half of *The World in the Attic* does move off into something more terrifying, but the large part of Clyde Muncy's adventures is in his coming to regard his country discoveries as "beautiful," full of "character," and "holy."

The search for the meaning of the American things has by this time become merely a spirit of preservation. The books, despite an elaboration within them of country-style joshing, are brooding in tone. The "holy" things are holy because they are of the past and because they are imperiled. Against them modern things and thoughts are inessential or shrill or devious. Clyde Muncy's wife, Peg, is cast in the two books in the role of the modernist antagonist, and she arrives in Lone Tree and then in Junction like an invader. She has no chance, obviously, against Aunt Clara's pickled beets, against the narrow integrity of the real inhabitants, against the pump in the yard, the sense of family, against what in both books is referred to as the holy trinity of "abstinence, frugality, and independence." But the lesson in her arrival is clear. The fiction itself will preserve the past and give the present its comeuppance. Clyde's boyhood friend, Bud Hibbard, is working now in a plant and doing the work of five men because the invading "city people" across the tracks have gone out on strike. He is paid eighty-five cents an hour, after fifteen years, and won't ask for more. "You can't pay a man more than he's worth," he says in *The World in the Attic.* "If you start doing that, where you going to stop?" And Clyde can only agree. Clyde's daughter possesses advanced information about sex, and in the context of these surroundings Clyde remembers righteously, in *The Home Place,* that "the old man would have tarred my bottom" if he had said some of the things she is allowed to say. Clyde's son, in *The World in the Attic,* manages to have the swing pushed for him by Bud Hibbard's son, and this exploitation is "city-kid stuff too."

The difficulty in this confrontation is that it contains no conflict and little drama. The good is doomed—that, in part at least, is what gives it its charm. Bud Hibbard's boy is fast fading into romance. And within such pastoral conservatism there is no progress to be made because there are no ethical judgments to be settled.

But in fact the two books are not so certain of their dogma as they seem. They contain also a subversive skepticism. Peg loses every encounter, but not all her citified objections are answerable nor answered. The narrow integrity of the farm folk, if it is integrity, is still narrow. It allows no new life. "It's *all right,*" Peg says, in *The Home Place,* "for you to share their lives. That's fine. But they don't give a dam about yours." And Clyde can only walk away. The inhabitants, if they keep faith with the past and with their own independence, for that reason become grotesques, fixed in the past. Lone Tree, Clyde knows, is a place that young men leave, and the result, Clyde observes, is that Lone Tree has become inbred and flabby, and therefore is more significantly removed from the home place than are those ex-citizens who have gone to live in the cities. Moreover, Lone Tree is a place that even in its presumably vivid past produced freaks, alcoholics, suicides, men who, bottle in hand, were attracted to walking the railroad ties, men who wanted to leave,* and

* One of them is Tom Scanlon, an old man who spent his days and nights looking down the tracks from his hotel window and who, when he died, defiantly emptied a chamber pot on his head. That gesture

his own father, he recalls in *The World in the Attic,* had dreamed of bringing back a pretty hula dancer "in order to shock . . . the living daylights out of them." The nostalgia for the home place has by the time of *The World in the Attic* become more than a little infected with what Clyde calls "home-town nausea," the sickness of "small-town-Sunday-afternoon." Everything is there in abundance in the hot afternoon to make life possible, but very little to make it tolerable. And it is not just the sickness of the prodigal, but something indigenous in Lone Tree that is stifling. His father, too, he speculates, had suffered from home-town nausea.

The past is not all it is cracked up to be. These novels progressively discover the fact. And then they lead to a crisis that is more informing than that, a crisis in nostalgia itself. At the end of the search for roots there may be, paradoxically, a denial of vitality and of the felt reality one sought. The great trouble with Clyde as a character, as Morris must have seen, is that he is so very passive, and given the drama of this *nostos,* this return, he can't well be anything else. It is his job not really to evoke the past—that is Morris' business, and it is Morris who takes the photographs and sets the scene —but Clyde is to invoke the past that has already been evoked, to call it to witness. Built into that task is a confession of present helplessness. It is a confession which is, moreover, in bad faith, because he obviously wants to rest in his helplessness. While Clyde was still Agee Ward and still engaged in the search, the past proposed a life that could be lived. Agee

is in Morris' iconography precisely quixotic, the chamber pot becoming Mambrino's helmet. Tom Scanlon therefore is to be seen as having pursued the romance that this place prevents. He reappears as a major character in *The Field of Vision* and as the central character in *Ceremony in Lone Tree,* in slightly different guise and equipped with a different pursuit of romance. See below.

Ward was, wisely, missing in action. Had he been present he would have had to make good, in his own person, on the promise of the discovered past. *The Man Who Was There* worked because it was a system of promises of promises. But Clyde, now, really is *there*. He has the past, has his roots so far as they *can* be figured in the present. He inherits the photographs, and his problem, though he doesn't know it, is what he is going to do with them other than treasure them. He is in the position of that other transplanted Midwesterner, Jay Gatsby, had Gatsby married the girl and lived happily ever after. You can't after all repeat the past, and the effort is meaningful only so long as it remains an impossible effort, so long as the past is not available to be lived. The end of this search for the past is now an end of potentiality, and that is the end of all living in the present. The repetition compulsion becomes the death wish.

The crisis of the search for the past and of these five novels is nostalgia itself, the sentimental longing that leads backward into death. The crisis in traditionalism is that mere souvenirs come to displace ordinary reality and disallow the present. Morris has apparently seen in this nostalgia that all but captured his work the crisis, in fact, of his career, and its perils become in his novels subsequent to *The World in the Attic* a large part of his subject. The crisis in nostalgia is the total subject and the basic insight of his critical history of the American literary tradition, *The Territory Ahead* (1958). It is that book's message that Huck Finn's "Territory Ahead" has been for our major writers for something more than a century the world that lies somewhere behind us, a world that has now become a "nostalgic myth":

In the nineteenth century the writer took to the woods or the high seas, literally as well as figuratively. In the present century the same flight is achieved through nostalgia, rage, or some such ruling passion from which the idea of the present, the opposing idea, has been excluded. In the American writer of genius the ability to function has been retained—with the exception of James—by depreciating the intelligence.

The villains of Morris' history are Norman Rockwell and Thomas Wolfe, who in their different ways entirely limit their trade to the unprocessed raw materials of the nostalgic myth. The hero, strangely after all, is Henry James, who was not only, for Morris in agreement with T. S. Eliot, the most intelligent man of his generation, but "the bridge between the past that made sense, the real past, and the present that does not." And he was, Morris says, "the first American of unquestioned genius to escape from the consolations of the past, without recourse to the endless vistas of optimism." He immersed himself "to the eyes in the destructive element. . . ." James is the new Precipitant.*

There is a conflict here really greater than that included in the word "nostalgia"—at issue are two versions of reality— but it is as nostalgia, naturally, that the issue presented itself to Morris. Quite apart from what validity his analysis of the American literary tradition does have, his reading of it is clearly his reading of himself. The development of his own career, Morris has said elsewhere, has been typically American because it has been an escape from the "regressive nostalgic commitment."

---

* Morris' evidence, it should be said, is chiefly *The American Scene.* James is large enough perhaps to sustain almost any generalization, but there are principal works that won't sustain this one: *Washington Square, The Princess Cassimassima, The Aspern Papers, The Ambassadors,* among other works, do turn back to "the consolations of the past."

It is the standard and deep commitment to nostalgia that
almost every American writer has; an effort to come to
terms with it or to capitulate to it. This almost defines
American writing. . . . I had had the same problem, and
I am working it out in my own fashion.[1]

And in *The Territory Ahead,* in fact, in the one instance
when he talks about himself, he says as much:

> Raw material, an excess of both material and compara-
> tively raw experience, has been the dominant factor in my
> own role as a novelist. The thesis I put forward grows out of
> my experience, and applies to it. Too much crude ore. The
> hopper of my green and untrained imagination was both
> nourished and handicapped by it. . . . I had been *there,* but
> that, indeed, explained nothing.

Indeed had Morris in his own career simply gone on going
back there, there would have been no further possibility for
him beyond regionalist romances. Either that, or he would
soon have arrived at that still point his fellow Nebraskan,
Willa Cather, reached, where first all change and then finally
mortality itself became the enemy.

The World in the Attic was, in any event, a critical book,
and not merely because this second return to the home place
confirmed Clyde Muncy's helpless passivity. There is in the
novel an underground fear and denial of the home place, a
denial which is at the end still ambiguous but which in the
second half of the novel, the part called "The Attic," is ob-
jectified in a climax. The story moves, in the first half casually
and then in this second half deliberately, about the reclusive
lives of two old ladies of Junction who themselves enact the
town's deep, hidden disjunction. The more ancient of the
two, Aunt Angie, is incredibly ancient, sturdy, and self-reliant

—and she is in that respect one of Morris' stock figures.* She has endured everything and outlived everyone. Her antagonist is her Southern daughter-in-law, who is her antagonist because the many years ago that she had come to the home place she had brought the South with her. Caddy has graciousness, cultivation, ladylike tastes and charms. She is also a useless woman, a delicate thing, "a primrose among the flowering corn," and she bears therefore that delight and that vitality that have no place in the trinity that this place keeps "holy." She is neither abstinent nor frugal nor independent. The two ladies have lived together alone in one house for twenty-some years, with a locked door between them. Angie's sworn revenge is that she will live as long as Caddy, and then one week longer, and at the end of the novel she does unlock the door to attend Caddy's funeral.

Angie is the very church of the holy trinity, the home place itself. And she is also a harbinger of death—blind and a seer, she announces visions of the passing Dead Wagon. Her triumph of endurance, then, is more terrible than not.

> Facing them, her apron blowing in the draft down the stair well, she felt again what she had known all the time. The folly of it. They were witless. And now they were dead.
>
> In the morning the Dead Wagon would come and for the first and last time put an end to the witlessness of all these years. They were dead. It was time to bury them. She cracked the floor once, twice, with her cane, then slowly moved into the hallway, into the darkness, and before Mr. Purdy stirred himself she was out of sight.

* She, or an equally ancient old man or woman, appears in *The Man Who Was There, The Inhabitants, The Home Place, Man and Boy, The Deep Sleep, The Field of Vision, Ceremony in Lone Tree, Cause for Wonder.*

Angie is not actually Caddy's murderer, but she is deathlike and foreclosing. Her endurance is uncanny, both unhuman and inhuman. She has in effect if not in deed drained Caddy of her flowering vitality by refusing her a reciprocal touch, by disallowing the charm and the humanity that were in what was of course her witlessness.

Angie's craggy endurance is worked upon in the novel to the point where she is not any more just a souvenir of the past, but a carrion-feeder, a vulture. And in this transformation Angie becomes an ultimate reach of Morris' nostalgia. The past is still informative—there is still something heroic in Angie, and Caddy was after all witless—but at the end of the search for the past is the death of any passional vitality, the death, in Morris' formula, of the present and of ongoing life. Angie is the ghost of the past, and she is frightening. With her appearance the whole of Morris' regionalist drama turns about. The home place is not now so much threatened by modernity as the present is imperiled by the past. Characters in the subsequent novels will be impaled on a moment of the past. They will squirm, when they are aware, to be free of it, to find a connection with the immediate present. When they are not aware, they will suffer a dreadful illusion that they are living a continuous present.

And there is an abrupt shift in the next novel after *The World in the Attic, Man and Boy* in 1951. It is the first of Morris' novels to be principally located in, if it is not confined to, the present. It is the first of his novels—in fact, though, it is the only one—to be principally concerned with social satire. It is the first that is witty rather than joshing. And its locus is not the Midwest. In the novels that follow the shift does not indeed remain shifted all the way all the time. Lone Tree is to be revisited and the things of the home place are to be examined again, but the intention has significantly changed. There are to be no more dramas the principal actions of which are pious evocations of the American mementos, hymns to the tradition, lessons in conservation. The putatively usable past is now permanently suspect.

The intention toward the past has changed. But in fact "nostalgia" never had totally comprehended Morris' intention, as it does not comprehend the "failure" that he sees, in *The Territory Ahead,* in the American literary tradition.* The past was searched because it was to have revealed something: a quality of living greater than this ordinary, wasteland, present-day living, a reality more luminous, more real than this reality, something heroic, vital, and something, of course, enduring. And what was sought is, after this turn, still sought. Ironically, the past *had* largely showed forth what it was to show, but the realization of the romance of the past was also a captivity. Inside it there wasn't any human life. You can't repeat the past. You can't because to repeat the past is to deny the present, to leave the present, and that is to deny human life. It is Gatsby's dilemma after all, only it is now proved that the way to the timeless, if it is to be approached through the past, is killing. In *Man and Boy* and especially in the novel that follows it, *The Works of Love* (1952), the effort is, then, in the opposite direction, to rescue out of the past a sense—there can be now only a sense of it—of the timeless, the Real, the heroic, for use in the present.

The present of *Man and Boy* is not quite the wasteland, but the look of death is upon it and it needs the touch of the Real. The protagonist and the authority of the place, neither the Man nor the Boy but the woman simply called Mother, has subdued the place virtually by the exercise of her sterility.

---

* The tendency in American writing, Morris says, is "to start well then peter out." Failure is the "accepted American practice. Failure, not success, is the measure of an artist's achievement."

Her connection with the Boy, her son and a war hero now missing in action, is entirely formal except when it is exploitative. Her relationship to her husband is imperial. Mother is engaged in causes. Mother has pushed a quail-refuge bill through the House, and Mother is always pushing things through the House. Her talk is a compound of bromides and Latin tags. The field of her expertise is modern inventions. She is an adept of the telephone and of Air-Wick. "Modern man is," Mother knows, "obsolete," as she knows that "there is no pyorrhea among the Indians," and that "all men are brothers." Pulling at the dangling cord above her head, Mother says: *"Fiat lux,"* and there is light. And Mother is the woman, in this instance rendered in a fine dry point, whom James Thurber had long ago discovered, who, since Philip Wylie's *Generation of Vipers* gave the term currency, has accounted for "momism." Her husband, meanwhile, has suffered a translation of gender. He drudges and cooks and cleans and shops, and admires Mother.

The novel's apparent design is to provide through the Boy, who is like Agee Ward, another man who is not present but who is there, a vivifying and transforming influence. But the design is not completed except by declaration. The Boy is not this time an agent of the past, and there is nothing else very large or precise substituted for him to transmit—only a taste for self-reliance, a cool appraisal of Mother, and an involvement with nature more complete than Mother's concern for quail. He is not quite comfortable in the novel and he is not really necessary to it. His one effect is that, through love and memory of him, the Man mounts a little rebellion.

The protagonist, despite Morris' clear intention, is and remains Mother, and the novel's principal action is in Morris' struggle with her. In fact nothing really happens to Mother. Her character, her desiccated rhetoric, and her politicking re-

main constant, but the context in which she is to be judged
is reworked. At the end her husband crumples back into admiration, but one is now to feel that the admiration is legiti-
mate. And the change is in the revelation midway in the
novel that Mother, modern as she is, continues out of a past.
She is the daughter of a frontiering family—her dowry had
been a symbolic old hickory log. Beyond that, the war she
wages in behalf of quail and against men continues, no matter
at what remove and with what poor tokens, a mission of the
frontier woman. She had had in her girlhood, it is revealed,
the benefit of something like a frontier experience, and it
had taught her that men destroy and that she was engaged in
a war. On a Texas ranch once long ago a little boy had
rushed at her with a glass dagger, and then she had watched
a man bagging wild ducks with a double-barreled shotgun.
If in her warfare now she is unfeminine, the action is conducted for a principle of preservation, a woman's principle,
and it is therefore heroic. Mother is febrile, imperious, and
not a little silly, but the old hickory is in her and constant.
She has in this present rescued out of the past something
that is Real.

Or Morris has done the rescuing for her. *Man and Boy*
submits finally to some arbitrariness of intention. *The Works
of Love,* however, goes in a straight line from the wilderness
into the wasteland, and it is altogether more stringent, as it
is more problematic, in its try at transferring to the real life
of the present moment the past's wholeness and heroism. Its
protagonist, a man named Will Brady, is this time really the
son of pioneers, born in a sod house on the Nebraska farm-
ing frontier, and therefore without the necessity of reaching
back for himself. And he does not, in the manner of those
sturdy ancients of Morris' early Midwestern novels, practice
his heroism simply by enduring, by resting still within the

past. His job is to do what history actually did, to move East and into the twentieth century. The past fast recedes, and the particular frontier of his birth fails. His parents had died when he was young and he is forced early to his own, other pioneering. Because he is the orphan of a broken bit of history, the field of his striving is naturally—what it was for Morris—in renewed connection with the world. The metaphor of his striving, then, is love, and his story is to be of his love affairs.*

He sets forth to find connection. He attempts connection first with an elderly prostitute, whose charm, though Will Brady is hardly aware of it, is that she predicts an ultimate truth of all earthly loving. She reminded men "of what the situation really was." Men do not live and make love forever. But she forbears this innocent's proposal of marriage and thereby withholds that information, thereby forcing him to make his own discoveries. He contracts a marriage with a proper, respectable wife, who is frigid. He marries, then, a young and improper girl, who is tawdry and promiscuous. He has on his way picked up a son, not his proper son, to whom he tries in all the recommended ways to be a father, and of course he fails. At almost the furthest extreme of his love-making, he buys kisses on a street corner from a dirty-faced little girl, and then loses her, too, naturally, when she turns to boys her own age. At one further extension, an old man now with an extreme record behind him of the mortality of love, he takes a job in Chicago, "in the Wasteland," as a department-store Santa Claus. Then in a crazed, blind mo-

* That is not to say that *The Works of Love* is a novel about love. At least one critic who reads it as a novel of love is obliged therefore to find a love motif throughout Morris' work, and he finds himself soon exploring the attitudes Morris' protagonists bring to insects. See Wayne C. Booth, "The Two Worlds in the Fiction of Wright Morris," *The Sewanee Review*, LXV (Summer 1957), 387–94.

ment, filled with a vision of Chicago as an inferno sizzling with life, he walks out toward the city, to meet it. But the Chicago canal is in his way, and he drowns.

He dies, of course, for love, and in his failure is his success. He has at least loved. But the novel has still larger proportions. Love is merely the metaphor of Will Brady's striving, as it is merely the vehicle for his moving into common life. He begins with his greatness upon him, only a greatness which is located out of this world, which he is to unite with this world. The place of his birth was, his father had once said, "God's country," but his mother, herself a stranger to the frontier, had said it was "a godforsaken hole," and Morris' stated intention for Will Brady is that he is to "combine these two points of view." He is to combine heaven and hell, clearly, by moving out from heaven through hell, and then back again. At the moment just preceding his passion he stares out over the city from the platform of a railroad tower and "he felt that he was back—where he had started from." He seems to be back because he has done the great and heroic thing, because he has in these other circumstances continued the higher life of the pioneer. The higher life of the pioneer touches upon that higher Reality which is all one Reality. Will Brady, by participating in the works of love, has participated in Love, which is another counter of the Real.

But then his success is after all not so certain—and that is the point finally to which Morris seems to want to come. Will Brady's getting back to where he started from will, in the next moment after he feels he has arrived, cost him his life. That is the impossible and certain price of this Reality. He has, all the while he has been adventuring with love, moved more deeply into the world—he becomes in the course of the novel a substantial man of affairs, in both senses, until the world is taken from him, and he goes from his wilderness to hamlets to towns to larger and larger cities. It is here and now, in the wasteland, that he is to find connection. This is where love is to be enacted—the story is of Aucassin, who knew that the great lovers are in hell. There is a moment when Will Brady, in a park in Los Angeles, watches an old fool feeding the pigeons. Feeding the birds is an act repeated throughout Morris' novels, and it is always a spiritual act, a Franciscan act, a way of connecting with the ideal, and it is an act of love. But in this instance the value of the act is particularly qualified. A voice suddenly speaks to Brady from above:

> "Old man," this voice said, "so you think you are a lover?"
>
> Did Will Brady smile? No, he kept a sober face.
>
> "Speaking of heaven," the voice went on, though of course they had not been speaking of heaven, "I suppose you know there are no lovers in heaven. I suppose you know that?"
>
> "No lovers in heaven?" Will Brady replied, but the voice did not answer. Will Brady thought he heard it sigh, but it might have been the wind. "Then why go to heaven?" Will Brady said.
>
> "I don't know," said the voice, "I've often wondered." Then it added: "But I suppose the small lovers like it. They like it up here."
>
> "And the great lovers?" Will Brady said.
>
> "There's no need," said the voice, "for great lovers in heaven. Pity is the great lover, and the great lovers are all on earth."

That "Pity" is the great lover is an idea intrusive in this novel—Morris somewhat elaborates it in later work—but this second thought about heaven compacts the whole of the present problem. That Love which Will Brady is to demonstrate is, like the Reality into which he was born, out of this world, and that, in a word, is what is wrong with it. In order to love at the pitch of the highest he is forced to utilize that which is out of this wasteland world, where love is compromised by a civilized propriety that is frigidity, or by a freedom that ends in vulgarity, or by money, and always by mortality.

He answers the department store's advertisement for a Santa Claus because the job requires "a man big enough, fat enough, and of course out of this world." Santa Claus in fact is, or should be, the very reconciliation of heaven and hell. He is the man able to "live in this world, so to speak, and yet somehow be out of it." He is a living myth, both fat and a saint, both mortal and immortal. But Santa Claus really, in the order of ordinary reality, is just a dressed-up decaying old man. There isn't any Santa Claus, not in this world, and Will Brady's error is that he persists in his belief to death. As Santa Claus, in order to redden his cheeks and smoothe his wrinkles, he gives himself sun-lamp treatments which first blind him, then fill his nostrils with the odor of carbon that he mistakes for the burning life of Chicago, and then result in his death. The treatments, he says when he begins them, make him feel "suspended—out of this world"—and that is *only* where this cheating of mortality leads.

In his last, large act of Love, Will Brady merges with the Real, but that is something that, in the design of the novel, he had before been merged with. He had set forth, rather, to find connection. What has happened in the novel is that a man intended to reconcile two worlds, a man suited to the task, has attempted to the limit in one of the traditional ways to make that reconciliation, and he has, of course, failed. The

story, that is to say, is about reconciliation and not about a
pursuit of the Real. It is still Gatsby's platonic dilemma, or
for that matter the Christian dilemma, but reversed. The
Real, like the past, in order to be usable, must be usable in
the present. Will Brady is still heroic because he had tried
to live at two levels of experience simultaneously, because like
all Morris' other heroes by designation and heroes by implication, the artist, the photographer, the seekers, and the endurers, he had lived according to an idea of that higher order-
ing of things. But his fate is worse because the testing is more
resolute.

The Works of Love does come to a complete and resolved
end, and in that it is unusual among Morris' works. The problem is how *in the world* to engage the Reality that is the
definition of another world, and the end, simply, is that you
can't. And at this point, then, the Real is to be obtained neither
in the progressive present nor in the past. The road to it, in
both directions, is out of this world. But then, given this
metaphysics, that complete answer doesn't eliminate the question. Rather it is the answer that is impossible, and once
possessed of it, it is to be supposed, Morris was smack at
the end, not only of the quest, but of the subject he had
entertained now through seven novels. The end of *The Works
of Love* presents not only an impossible philosophical dilemma,
but a narrative impossibility as well. This is, given this
metaphysics, as *far* as Morris possibly can go—and it is as
far, in any event, as he has gone. Stories of more strenuous
reconciling of the Real with the real can lead him now,
whether he goes backward or forward, only to quicker suicides. And because this is the only possible ultimate resolution of the story he tells, Morris won't be attracted again to
the straightforward and urgent linear action of *The Works
of Love,* and he won't try to come again to unifying,

thoroughly tested solutions. The work will be rather in dramas
that exploit a character or a number of characters who know
the tension between the details of unheroic ordinary life on
the one hand and on the other the feeling apprehension of
the greater Reality.

After *The Works of Love* that tension itself, indeed, is the
thing, created in one metaphor and another—that tension
rather than the mounting details of the heroic quest. The
next novel, *The Deep Sleep* (1953), is, Morris himself has
said, the "quintessential" one. Although it is outside the
stream of his Midwest concerns, it is, he says, "very instruc-
tive and casts some light on all my books, anticipating them
. . . in the techniques employed."[2] In fact it is not precisely
the "quintessential" book. It casts little light backwards except
that the mechanics of its narrative technique was promised
in *Man and Boy*—simply a number of related persons reflecting and circling upon a central, ordinary, but ceremonial
event. But *The Deep Sleep* was clearly for Morris a pivotal
novel. Its technique, if it is not entirely new, is natural for
him now that his attitude had undergone a marked adjustment. In the novel now everything is felt to be circular and
continuous, and every end is a beginning. There are significant, climactic realizations, but no complete actions. Everyone is held within the informing tension—and moreover, just
because it is everyone, because there are no antagonists, there
is a tone and an approach now that is distinctly different.
The tone is mellow and the approach is comic. There is still
the radical discontinuity between exigent ordinary life and
what is felt to be Real, and the dilemma is of course in no
way solved, but it comes to rest through being perceived in
multiple instances, and it is accepted.

The Deep Sleep and the novels that follow it are wise
rather than agonistic, written in the perspectives of wisdom,

with amplitude of vision, from the vantage point of experience
had and consolidated. Comedy is that mode that says this is
a life of impossible dilemmas but after all one can and one
does live it. This mellowed comic mode must have been for
Morris the means, precisely, of an accommodation. Since
there is no possible reconciliation of the two worlds of his
drama, since his hero is bound to suffer disconnection from
one world or the other, only a technique by which, or a vision
in which the hero can be held in constant suspense between
the two will allow life at all, and Morris' contracted intention now would seem to be just that, to allow life. That ambition is his participation in the spirit of the times, the spirit
that succeeds demonstrations of radical rootlessness, frag-
mentation, rebellion, disconnection, alienation. The terms in
Morris' work are unique, but Morris' development, too, is
toward a marriage of the individual in all his individuality
with the everyday life of his everyday community. The history of his development is exemplary, proceeding from an
impulse to heroic rebellion to a point where further rebellion
is merely suicide. At the extremity of isolation there occurs
a necessary casting about for the means of return.

The new heroes themselves are still, most often, heroic
agonists, either compulsively repeating the past in search of
some moment of higher living, or reaching to tear away the
veils that hide some greater validity, or deliberately attempting some impossible formula of reconciliation, but now
Morris holds them within their lives. Their strivings now are
their stories and not Morris'. For him the work is in an accommodation to the frustrating facts of life. And the protagonists now, significantly, are neither young seekers nor
old endurers, but mostly middle-aged men and women who
both seek and endure. The tension is the thing, the living
that goes on between the poles of life and between the poles

of reality. The society of the novels is hereafter more various, and, as distinct from the earlier genre paintings of the rural Midwest, there is more society, a fuller and more intimate sense of individuals struggling between individuality and engagement. The scene of the principal action, moreover, is the present, a present that is never again called "the waste-land." Even to call it that represents an imposition of the past, and a story of the wasteland requires a questing knight who will by his example reveal it for what it is. Morris' story is no longer so partisan, and it is much more domestic. The necessity is to allow ordinary life.

The ostensible subject of *The Deep Sleep* is, once again, heroic Love and the way it is frustrated in this world, but the subject the novel comes to is an accommodationist one, marriage. The "Deep Sleep" is Adam's, the one in which he exchanged his rib for a wife. The Lover in this case is a man who, just beyond middle age, has just died. He was an important man, a respected Judge, a good neighbor to his neighbors in Bryn Mawr, Pennsylvania, a faithful husband and father. And he was, an initial turn of the story reveals, a man who all his life was driven by secret yearnings for something more, some delight greater than this life per-mitted him. Around him now are the mourners, his ninety-nine-year-old mother, the old handyman, his daughter and his son-in-law, and most of all his wife. They circle about and reflect upon the ceremonial event of the funeral arrange-ments, and provide the narrative.

What is to be expected is romantic exposé. All the ma-terials for it are present. The Judge's son-in-law is a painter and therefore equipped to be Morris' registering sensibility. He is in touch with the life of the soul. Judge Porter himself had lived the life, to all appearances, of a higher George F. Babbitt, and he has died young, to all appearances, of a struggle to get out of this death. His wife is all bustle about the practical and the social details of the funeral and has hardly a moment for backward-looking sentiment, and she is to all appearances the primary agent of the wasteland which killed him. His daughter is left to pity him, the old handyman left to chronicle his small rebellions, his ancient mother to unite his death with his birth.

But the progress of the novel actually is a serial qualification of that romantic story. What is apparent is not entirely false, but it is not either entirely true. The Judge, clearly another but a more effectual version of the Man of *Man and Boy*— even to having a war-hero son missing in action—had conducted all his married life a war for independence. His wife is another, slightly less desiccated version of Mother—even to an addiction to Air-Wick and to a membership in the Dawn Busters. The Judge, like the Man, had been domesticated to household duties, but unlike the Man he had on the sly stashed away a bottle of Old Grand-Dad, the more symbolically because he didn't drink. And there is a lonely islet down the river to which he had secretly and silently resorted, and he had stolen away to the attic for a smoke, and almost his last words had been, *"In the name of God, will you let me die?"* But then it turns out that despite the fact that he had lived and died in cramped rebellion, the Judge had really lived with his wife, according to a settlement the terms of which his sensitive son-in-law will in the course of the novel only barely perceive. As he will just perceive that the Judge's wife had been and still is true and necessary to Judge Porter. It is the son-in-law's job, because he is a painter, to get what he calls "the picture," and that is of course the novel's job, and the picture is more than its story line. It is a composed balance of interdependent forces. The son-in-law, who is, it happens, an orphan, must take lessons in the way

opposite forces do compose. He must learn both what a picture is and what a family is.

His own wife, the Judge's daughter, anticipates him by
qualifying her own pity for her father, by redressing the balance in favor of her mother. Her mother, she discovers, has
all these years played out her proper role and played it without a hitch. She has maintained and preserved the house. She
has invented and kept the rules of the house, ambiguous and
inexpressible and even arbitrary as they are. When at night
she washes dishes, her daughter suddenly realizes, her mother
enjoys herself because dish-washing is a part of the functional
ritual by which the house is maintained. Her father had been
driven from this house, but nevertheless his wife had been his
necessary counter. Their marriage had not been a happy one,
but it had been an imperative one. "She could not, that is,"
she thinks, "see how it might have been otherwise."

> The unjust thing was that it was just. The horrible thing
> was that it was not horrible. They had each been true to
> some sort of conscience, they had each made some sort of
> peace with their souls, and the really senseless thing about
> it was that it made sense.

And that, finally, is the novel's whole ambition, to reveal
that this impossible marriage, like the impossible metaphysical
dilemma it contains, does make sense. The two unreconcila-
ble worlds that were from the beginning the forces of Morris'
fiction are in this instance, not brought into a unity, but resolved in the way of marriage. Marriage is the comic metaphor of their resolution. Between these two worlds there
should be a fight to the death, but instead, in fact, in their
struggle they balance each other out, and in their struggle
they define the continuous life of the human world, the life
that really does go on. The Judge had stretched forth hero-

ically, out of this house, out of this world, and that is right and necessary. His wife had tempered him as she had tempered all feeling, for the sake of discipline, responsibility, propriety, the woman's principle that is equally real and that is as well necessary and right. Her necessary opposition, the son-in-law begins to see, is something which the Judge himself, even as he had sneaked away to the attic for a smoke, had understood, and it is a principle to which he had assented. In the attic, along with the telltale cigar butts, there are, the son-in-law discovers, letters from his wife and children which the Judge had carefully preserved.

Along with those mementos he discovers as well an expensive gold watch, which clusters the novel's meanings and which is to provide what climax the novel has. The Judge had bought the watch abroad—not strictly speaking on his honeymoon, the Judge had once said, but at the time when his marriage "came to a head." The Judge had then lost it. His wife had found it and returned it to him. He had put it away in a safe place, and now his wife has been looking for it. Her role is, of course, to keep that household, worldly time in which alone the Judge could have striven to escape to the timeless. She had preserved that ordinary life in which alone he could have struggled for the extraordinary. The watch, ticking away in the attic, hidden but preserved tacitly by both of them, is the marriage, and at the end of the novel the Judge's son-in-law returns it, he fancies in the spirit of Judge Porter, to Mrs. Porter.

Nothing is solved by the gesture. The Judge lives on in his son-in-law and their mutual gesture marks, in fact, a retreat from an ideal. But it is a large action nevertheless, a heroic idealist's assent to this provisional world in which one does live. And it is a gesture made, it may be said, in Morris' behalf. For him, now, the tension is the thing, the equal pull of opposite poles, and so the hero who is heading out of this world is pulled back to it. *Vice versa,* too, but for the moment it is the heroic agonist to whom the opposing force is to be applied.

That opposition is as well the large action of Morris' next novel, *The Huge Season* (1954), conducted in different circumstances and in a different metaphor—the metaphor being Nostalgia, Morris' favorite disease. But in this instance the nostalgia is for a different home place. The "Huge Season" is the season of the Lost Generation and it, this one time in Morris' works, provides the circumstances and the aim of the backward-looking of his protagonist.* Hemingway and Scott Fitzgerald, not quite in their persons but in close approximations, people the world of the protagonist's backward involvement. At the center of his past is a rich playboy whose chief and unrelenting fascination, on the one hand, is that he was very rich and therefore very different from us, and whose chief legacy, on the other, is that he died after being gored in a bullfight in Pamplona. He contains in himself, as it were, a complete dialogue of the 1920s. And around him there are echoes: Charles Lindbergh and Babe Ruth, the Lone Eagles, flappers and philosophers deracinated in Paris, college boys and girls who are both reading and living *This Side of Paradise* and *The Sun Also Rises,* all of whom lived, so the memorial goes, in a context of aspiration for "the great style" and "the habit of perfection." Whatever their individual suc-

---

* It is strange, perhaps, not that Morris did not this once use the Middle West as the locus of his drama of Nostalgia, but that he has to date used the 1920s only this once. He is apparently involved in the 1920s. *The Territory Ahead* is another testimony. But then the simple commercial matter must have presented itself to Morris, that the huge season of this nostalgia has in recent years been processed many times. In this novel, in fact, an editor says to the hero, Foley, "Good deal fresh interest in the twenties," to Foley's dismay.

cesses, they were the "rainmakers" of a supposed wasteland. The protagonist, Peter Foley, is a professor of classics and therefore a professor of the persistent past. He is writing a novel, which is as much his career as his indulgence, based on his youth in the Twenties.

His book will be perhaps just another, though presumably a truer, memorial to the glamorous season. But Morris' isn't just such another tribute. The Professor's book is to be called *The Strange Captivity,* the title to betray the fact that the Professor does perceive that this huge season is captivating in at least two senses, but it is Morris who exploits the pun, and the climactic gesture Morris arranges for Peter Foley is his burning of his manuscript, the end of his long captivity and his entry into this time. The novel is by that much another of Morris' advices that the usable past, in order to be useful, must be used. It is less a tribute than a warning. One of the things Peter Foley seems to learn from *his* hero is that you can't fight bulls in a safe bull ring in which there is no bull. That, in one of his hero's token words, is merely "bullshit." And there is no bull nor Moment of Truth in what is not a present peril. That other world of that other Reality, that is to say, may be achieved only by an aesthetic discipline practiced in this moment. Foley is aided in his lesson by the present example of one of his friends of the huge season, another derelict but one who seems to have shed his nostalgia for the sake of a current heroism in a current arena. His friend has become a voice, significantly, of the Voice of America, and now he is being investigated by Senator McCarthy. At the end of the novel, as Foley burns his manuscript, he looks forward to entering, too, that ring in which Senator McCarthy was the bull.

That will be really to use the past and not submit to it. But then Foley's burning of his past is not so complete a gesture, after all, as it seems—the novel engages wider issues than the one that this climax climaxes. Foley's realization, which looks like his rebirth in middle age, is not so much a denoument issuing out of a dramatic problem as a new beginning within the same problem, and this Nostalgia which Foley has battled and conquered is merely a metaphor for the larger battle, in which the best success is to win a draw.

The novel is a day in Foley's life—May 4, 1952—and the action of this day is his visit to the present as well as the past, and to principles for which present and past are local names. On the one hand, in the past, there was the hero, the rich-playboy-turned-bullfighter, who had lived and died for "the great style," but on the other there is Foley's friend, the voice of the Voice of America. His friend had once seemed and had apparently thought himself to be the hero's chief satellite, but he is, the perspective of years reveals, his very opposite. For one thing, he is a Jew, and in the intervening years, Foley observes, he has become "more Jewish." He has really not so much shed his nostalgia for the huge joyous season as suffered the erosion of time.

All the soft gentile topsoil, the non-furrowed regular guy, the comical Jewish clown, had eroded away. Leaving bedrock. A flood-scored Jewish bedrock showing beneath.

And that is his friend's principal action and the principle for which he stands. Like Mrs. Porter, like Mother in *Man and Boy,* for that matter like Peg in the books of the home place, he is a figure of the present time which is the time of this world. Even more extremely than those others, he finds his place in this world. His vision is of the imperfection of this world and his response is pity, the kind of love that will draw him deeply, too deeply, into it. The mode of his heroism is martyrdom.

There are still the two worlds, and all that Foley will at the end achieve is a place between them, in a stillness created by the equal pull of opposite forces. That is how life can be allowed. The playboy-bullfighter on the one hand and the Jewish martyr on the other are equally heroes, but neither of them allows life. The bullfighter, after he had been gored, had shot himself—for "perfection, the terror of it," Foley observes. The Jew, ironically, had shot himself once also, though not to death, for the sake of pity and imperfection. As he is a martyr, he is suicidal. One died of a flight out of this world, the other is dying of a struggle to get all the way into it, and both ways are the ways of heroic, romantic death. Foley's more prudent success is that he can see both heroes and thereby be informed by these opposite lines of force. He sees himself at the very end of the novel as living, miraculously, in the field of a magnet whose opposite poles are the bull-fighter saint and the Jewish martyr, and when that image presents itself to him he has come, implicitly, to his lesser but authentic triumph. His triumph is that he will go on living in the field of the magnet, that he does live.

It is a triumph which unfortunately he expresses only par-tially by his burning of his manuscript, the rest being left to reported illumination. The climactic action is a perception of only one of the poles of the magnet. But then that is the one that exercised for Peter Foley and Morris both, obviously, the more dangerous fascination. Motion toward the point of equipoise is for Morris more likely to be motion toward this world, as is to be expected considering where he has been. And it is motion toward this world that is to be discovered in the novels that come after *The Huge Season: The Field of Vision* in 1956 and its sequel, *Ceremony in Lone Tree* in 1960, *Love Among the Cannibals* in 1957, and its extension, *What a Way to Go* in 1962, and then *Cause for Wonder* in

1963. The present remains problematic in them, but the novels are nevertheless located in the present, and the past is far more untrustworthy.

The line of his development has been, Morris has himself said, from the past toward the present, his arrival signaled by *Love Among the Cannibals*. So he said in an interview just after the novel was published:

> The present and the past play a kind of fugal development in [my] novels. Then the past begins to be questioned, and over a period of eight novels, the past first dominated, then was compelled to recede. *The Cannibals* is the first book in which the past does not exist. We begin with the present, we live in the present, and it is an effort to come to terms with the present, in terms of only the present.[3]

The theme *Love Among the Cannibals* actually develops is not, for all that, without confusions, but the novel does conscientiously equip itself with furniture of the present. Its characters—a pair of Hollywood songwriters and their girls—are newcomers to Morris' territory and they are as current as they can be, and so is the Hollywood that is the novel's initial setting. Moreover, there is in this novel a spirit of greater willingness, or perhaps simply friendliness, than there is in any of Morris' other work. The novel is not only comic, but it intends to be funny. It is not only of the present, but it is determined to have a good time. Therefore one of the songwriters is equipped with a gaudy sea-green beret, uses Man Tan, and is inarticulate in a modern way. " 'Man,' he will bark, 'it's great!' "

This fun is suspended from the novel by davits, in fact, perhaps only to provide for shipwreck, and the novel isn't "an effort to come to terms with the present, in terms of only the present." That effort of coming to terms is anyway not implict in its mechanism but is at best a goal, and one at which the novel does not arrive. And certainly the past is present in it. The book does exalt what Morris elsewhere, after D. H. Lawrence, calls "the immediate present," under the obvious inspiration of a Lawrentian vitalism.* But this immediate moment is itself just what the spirit of the past has always been for Morris, and it is just as unattainable, and the book's real presentness is only in its final hedging against this moment. The book's modern characters and setting and idiom have been set by Morris, it would seem, in balance against the past that has always for him weighed more, but really the novel only shifts the constant metaphors. What is really achieved, once again, is a magnetic field between the opposite poles.

The protagonist, the lyricist of the song team, is proposed as a "master of the cliché." Clichés, he says again and again, are his business, and he seldom invents new ones when he can transform old ones. He is a middle-aged master of second-hand sentiments mostly amorous, and his story is that he falls in love really and is forced therefore to a problem in original expression. What is intended for him, clearly, is an act of transformation, an imaginative adventure in which the cliché will be made to reveal the authenticity that it contains. The girl as she appears to him once like a Madonna forces him to realize that "Every cliché in the world once had its

* In *The Territory Ahead*, Morris quotes Lawrence: ". . . there is another kind of poetry; the poetry of that which is at hand: the immediate present. In the immediate present there is no perfection, no consummation, nothing finished. The strands are all flying, quivering, intermingling into the web, the waters shaking the moon." P. 230.
   Morris has said: "Temperamentally, I now lean very strongly to such an imaginative figure as D. H. Lawrence who in his later years defined to me the serious predicament of a man coming to terms with the present and using the past, not abusing it, in an effort to make this imaginative act possible." Bleufarb, "Interview with Wright Morris."

moment of truth," and when he takes her to a beach at Acapulco, the novel's other scene, he wonders whether he hasn't
come to the end of the perfect cliché. Then he thinks that
whether he has or not, this moment seems to be what he
wants.

The "cliché" is the novel's most conspicuous problem, and
the word has since become a focus of Morris' criticism and
narrative. It will adumbrate the materials of *What a Way to
Go*. The book immediately after *Love Among the Cannibals*
is *The Territory Ahead,* a primer on the cliché. The cliché
is the raw-material past as it has been tirelessly reprocessed.
The trouble with Norman Rockwell, for instance, is that he
substitutes clichés for the authentic raw material. The begin-
ing of the problem is that we are surrounded by clichés, that
we accept them for the real thing, but then that is just the
beginning of the problem. The cliché is phony, but palpable.
The lyricist of *Love Among the Cannibals* locates the old,
impossible dilemma in these new terms: "The phony *is,*" he
discovers.

> I mean it's here and now, and all that once was or is yet
> to be *isn't.* You've got to take what's phony, if it's all you've
> got, and make it real.

What we've got, then, here and now, is the sentimentalized
past, and the problem is to recapture by an imaginative transformation of the cliché the reality that was in the past before
it became a cliché.

And if that, finally, is this lyricist's job, he is not at all to
be seen as coming "to terms with the present." From his
location in the present, he is reaching for the past.

But in fact that is a job provided only by a discontinuous
intention in the novel. In fact the cliché becomes only a metaphor for whatever in this world prevents his attaining what

is Real. He does no actual transforming of anything. Rather, he disburdens. The principal metaphor of the Real has become in this novel primitive desire, a Lawrentian idea of love as unqualified communion—another metaphor for which is cannibalism. The protagonist as he is a hero strips, and is stripped down, to it. He goes to Acapulco and loses his luggage, then his car, then his civilized habits of sanitation, then his pride, and he tries to lose his mind to the point where there will be left only flesh feeding on flesh. When he achieves that cannibalism, clearly according to the intention of the novel, then he will be in the immediate present. Therefore it would seem that the dead mementos of the past, the clichés, which is to say the accumulations of civilization itself, are to be sloughed off for the sake of the basic, the essential Real.

The novel looks for Reality in opposite directions. But then that Reality that on the one hand is said to be contained by the clichés, the raw past, and the Reality on the other hand that is of the immediate present, are the same Reality, that which is out of this world. That is where this lyricist is heading, and at the end, inevitably if he is going to be allowed to live, he is chastened. His partner gets married and so sinks back into the clichés. He doesn't follow his partner, but his own girl, who is all primitive sex, conveniently walks out on him because he hasn't been able to slough off enough. She walks out more conveniently than he knows. He is left with the resolve to cast off one more stitch of pride and mind, and to seek her out again. He is left therefore where he was in the beginning, only more knowing. He is between this world and the other, caught between the impossibilities of both, in movement in the field of the magnet. Only the metaphors have been shifted, with the pole of this world called the "cliché" and the other indicated to be sex.

But then the trouble with *Love Among the Cannibals,* beyond the facts that it just isn't as funny as it wants to be and that the intentions behind it hobble the conflict it comes to, is that the primitivism it opposes to the cliché is itself a cliché, a literary sentiment exhausted and more than exhausted by D. H. Lawrence. The girl of this songwriter's dreams, who is no better than she should be, is an appropriate symbol after all: this raw material has been processed and overprocessed before. Moreover, Morris uses primitivism only as a cliché, a convention that one is to understand, accept, and not bother about—as indeed he had to unless he were to repeat Lawrence altogether, to wind more rhapsodic diadems of violets in more pubic hair. And because it is just a cliché, this time the Real does not reverberate its reality, and behind this songwriter's glazed phenomenal world there is only another inert phenomenon.

What a Way to Go reworks what are essentially the same materials, with consequences only not quite so frustrating because this time the cliché is presented in, and obscured by, the guise of myth. The songwriter becomes a Prufrockian professor in search of what is now called "The Wisdom of the Body." The great primitive life force, the immediate present, the wisdom of the body, is figured forth now by a fabulous bobby-soxer, with whom the professor's researches end. The songwriter had called his girl "Greek." The professor, Arnold Soby, goes to Greece, and the girl who will be his is made explicitly to contain—what he is looking for—Botticelli's Primavera, Nausicaä, the siren, the mermaid, the *ewig weibliche,* the Wild Goose. She is "something," once again, "out of this world," and she represents the eternal continuity of the Corybantic glory that was Greece.

Professor Soby, on his sabbatical, goes first to Venice, and then to Greece, places which, like Hollywood and Acapulco,

have become clichés. The secret of immediate appropriateness
to be found in the stones of Venice and also in Greece,
"buried," as a character says, "under half a century's fall of
photographic ash," is that which is miraculously to be found
in his fellow passenger, another cliché, a slangy Oberlin fresh-
man, Miss Cynthia Pomeroy of Winnetka, Illinois. Soby
knows as much in the first place, he finds what he is looking
for, and that, except for an abrupt and significant hedging
at the end, is his whole story. But meanwhile these particular
clichés provide Morris with an illimitable fund of mythical
and literary references, so many that to name them over
allows him to give his theme authority without being put to
the task of testing it.

For a while, until the end, it is almost enough to keep the
novel going to create an intricate system of cross references.
If Cynthia is Nausicaä, then Soby is the elderly Odysseus,
but Cynthia is also Cleopatra to Soby's Caesar, and she is
Lolita to Soby's Humbert Humbert, and Humbert Humbert
is therefore Caesar and Odysseus. *What a Way to Go* is, with
much enjoyment of its indulgences, a very literary book. *The
Odyssey* by the method of *Ulysses* brings to mind *Lolita,*
"The Love Song of J. Alfred Prufrock," *Death in Venice,*
the legend of Pygmalion, the passions of Petrarch, the life
of Goethe, and the career of Henry James, among all its other
documents, and all the references refer to each other. Morris
doesn't name Katherine Anne Porter's *Ship of Fools,* but
that novel, for good measure, would seem to be present, too.
He approximately re-creates characters from it—principally
that of La Condesa—and scenes; there is the same close urging of Dionysian energies wanting to be released, the same
scheme of the voyage, the same scoring of Germans. And
then everything is carried forward and elaborated in an arch,
elliptical style which is largely a parody of James:

"My dear—" Soby said, "I think you forget—"

She probed his sleeve with the blade of her knife. Forget? Leaning toward him, her breath pear-scented, "What I do not forget!" she cried, "is who is Italian! For an Italian nobody is too old!" The prospect hovered between them, palpable, fluttering its wings. Soby was the first to turn away from it, lidding his eyes.

But the literary play plays mostly, in fact, about the figure of Gustave Aschenbach. Not only Soby but virtually everyone else in the novel, including a toothless, balding old tomcat, is given the image of Aschenbach, and Cynthia is Tadzio to everyone except the cat. *What a Way to Go* is by apparent intention a comic version of *Death in Venice*. Soby, like Aschenbach, like the Socrates of the *Phaedrus,* is to go the sense way, the artist's way, the lover's way to the spirit, along the path of perilous sweetness, and it is an open question whether beauty, which alone is divine and visible, will lead to wisdom and true manly worth or to the abyss. The dilemma imposed by the question forced Aschenbach to wanton perversion, and then it killed him. Soby, after many reluctances to make himself ridiculous, succumbs and marries the girl. *What a Way to Go* is *Death in Venice* without the death.

Without the death Morris is compelled one more, unfortunate, step forward. The plague by which Aschenbach was carried off, an appropriate symbol of the rage upon which he had fallen, in a manner solved everything. If Soby is to live on with the dilemma and if the novel is to be brought to an end, then adjustments will have to be made. Morris abruptly changes the terms of the dilemma. With Soby finally in bed with the girl, the drama becomes suddenly just a mortal matter: "A pair of cool fish, scared of drowning, but

no longer so scared of each other, they crouched. . . ." In a
final moment Soby paraphrases to himself that passage of
the *Phaedrus* that occurred to Aschenbach just before his
death, but the paraphrase leads him far from the original
quotation. "My dear Soby do you not think," he says, "—for
I leave the point to you—that this is a path of perilous sweetness? . . . Getting back to the Greeks has its hazards, doesn't
it?" And he answers himself:

> If it's something immortal you're after look behind the
> eyes, not at them. But that can be a strain. We're men after
> all, not fish. However, if it's something mortal you're after
> —and I take it that it is—what you see before your eyes can
> be good enough. In your case, if not in hers, eminently
> satisfactory, but don't offend the Gods by ignoring your
> luck.

The novel concludes, then, with some wedding announce-
ments, the hazards involved in getting back to the Greeks or
in following the path of perilous sweetness or in discovering
The Wisdom of the Body reduced to a tepid, for all dramatic
purposes superfluous, warning. Cynthia regarded in a certain
way did resemble Nausicaä, a little, around the edges, but
she is really just Cynthia, and what she can propose now
will be a middling problem, just a problem of marriage.

And she will have to be merely Cynthia, because if she is
Nausicaä, Morris will have to find in her something like the
primitivism of *Love Among the Cannibals,* another aspect of
the Real, and there is a technical danger in the quest for the
Real. The end of it, like the end of Morris' earlier souvenir-
hunting, is if not a swoon then a rhapsody which is bound
to be second hand. There are a limited number of ways to
say that the ultimate undifferentiated good is wonderful,
that the Real is real. Morris' hero indeed is polarized between

clichés, and quite in Morris' sense of the word. What alone
is fresh, given this metaphysics, is the ongoing life between
them, as what is fresh and exciting in Morris' work is his
grasp of this dynamism rather than his bardic proclamation.

Altogether his richest work is in the linked novels, *The
Field of Vision* (1956) and *Ceremony in Lone Tree* (1960),
which are expositions simply in multiple instances of this
impossible polarity as the principle of ordinary life. The
principal characters of these novels, middle-aged Middle
Westerners, are all somewhat in and somewhat out of this
world, struggling, with death on either side of them, for a
full sense of life. The novels compass five contemporaneous
generations. They look into the long past and the long future,
but their center is in this middle age in this middle place
between and informed by the extremes. It is the tense middle
vision that is productive of life.

These novels are ripe work as well as rich work, a settling
and a consolidation of much that has gone before. We are
back to Lone Tree, the home place of the inhabitants, though
now it is reduced to a single obstinately enduring inhabitant.
He is taken whole from *The World in the Attic,* and in
Ceremony in Lone Tree the son of Will Brady comes along
in search of his father, a man conceived to have been *there.*
The bullfighter of *The Huge Season,* in a different name and
in a wreck of middle age, is figured again, and there are
transcripts of the Man of *Man and Boy,* of Mrs. Porter of
The Deep Sleep, of Mother, whose principles were born of a
perception of cruelty. A boy who made a momentary appearance in *The Man Who Was There* is in *Ceremony in Lone
Tree* one of Agee Ward's possible successors. Moreover, there
is a gathering of all the names and roads to the Real: the
past, pioneering, vagabondage, bullfighting and the moment

of truth, masculinity, love—with the addition, now, of murder, but that is made no more conspicuous an action than the others. They are novels for that matter almost without action other than a system of intersecting reflections, their richness made by the number of lives in motion they gather in a single field of vision. It is virtuoso work in a landscape and with characters Morris knows to every nuance, and the great trick turned in it is that so many persons in their individual voices and bound to various metaphors, do consolidate and cohere about a constant theme.

Morris has himself spelled out the theme, in some jacket copy he wrote for *The Field of Vision:* These Middle Westerners, assembled for the moment in Mexico to watch a bullfight, see in the bull ring a mirror which reflects the fragments of their own lives. They seem compelled to come to imaginative terms with them. "This book grows from the belief that this imaginative act is man himself." And indeed the two novels are ceremonies of the imaginative act. But they are just that, with the act seen to be compulsive and perpetual and always incomplete. The stated theme is really an extension of the meanings of the presented drama, and not the meaning of the drama itself. These people don't actually *accomplish* the imaginative act. They don't create their lives except as the pattern of their lives is in the repeated act of re-creation. And the meaning of the drama itself is that the patterns of their individual lives, lived in largely exclusive circumstances, is the same pattern. It is the way and the motion of their imagining that is the meaning.

In fact what Morris in the same copy seems to propose as merely the dramatic device of his theme, comes closer to the meaning achieved. "In my effort to dramatize this idea," he says,

I have dealt with the imagination of the plains, where corn is sometimes grown, dust sometimes blows, but the bumper crop is still fiction and romance. I have tried to suggest what a changing world does to the unchanging drives of this imagination—drives which seek to transform an ever changing set of facts to their own terms. The range and nature of the plains imagination—its audacity, however ill advised, and its practicality, however illusive—contain elements that are peculiarly American.

It is after all a most cautious statement, but the achieved subject of these two novels is an image of the American imagination, concentrated in the place where after all it is most likely to be found, in Morris' home place.

It is quite the same home place, with both the same radiant artifacts and the same defeating narrowness, apprehended now, however, neither for the romantic promise in the one nor for the strangulation in the other, but seen in a comic vision of its vitalizing contradictions. "Audacity" and "practicality" are merely other terms once again for the two worlds that had always polarized the home place wherever it was found. The multitude of characters in these novels are so many pendulums between these polarities, their movement being the act of the imagination, and their imaginations being their lives. There is Boyd, who is as much as anyone the protagonist of *The Field of Vision* and who is a principal of *Ceremony in Lone Tree,* who has lived a life proposed by audacity, delinquency, the pursuit of the higher vitality. He had once tried to walk on water, he had kissed his best friend's fiancée, he had ripped the pocket from Ty Cobb's uniform, and in the action of the first novel he squirts soda pop into the muzzle of one of the fighting bulls—his life has been a series of poor but meaningful gestures of his dedication and his failure, and his need now is to make some practical meaning of his life. His best friend, McKee, has meanwhile lived a life dedicated entirely to conservation, compromise, and practicality, and his need is to find within the fragments of his life some principle of audacity, some reality to let him know that he is alive. The novels go from their center in middle age backward into the life of Tom Scanlon, the old man rescued from *The World in the Attic,* a nonagenarian who is really twice his age because he thinks he is his own father. They go backward through his birthday and funeral—the twin ceremonies of the *Ceremony in Lone Tree*—to the pioneering past. And they go forward through his grand-children and his great-grandchild to the present, where heroic pioneering is the disallowed necessity. The great-grandchild is projected further forward in *Ceremony in Lone Tree* in another young man, who predicts one of his possibilities, who runs amuck in Lincoln, Nebraska, and shoots and kills ten people because, as he says, he wants to *be* somebody. Both backward and forward there are masculine principles of vio-lence, which are to be opposed by the necessity of everyday life, opposed by Morris' constant guardians of ordinary life, the women. Tom Scanlon, moreover, is a man frozen in the past, who is to be rescued into the present, while his great-grandchild is frozen, as it were, in the future and is to be rescued by the information of the past. And all these lives and all the lives attached to them are in one direction or the other in motion between the two worlds that are equally impossible.

And that is the vision, finally, of the American Territory that Morris has come to, full and wealthy with felt life—and yet circular in a way that is perhaps beyond Morris' inten-tions. It is a comic vision, after all, of failure. If, because the mode of apprehension is comic, these characters are allowed life, and if what is perceived is a principle by which they can

live, still the lives they lead are pathetic because they are
bound to be fruitless. They are all agonists whose total adventure is that they are batted back and forth between impossibilities. These novels are rich and ripe and full and wise,
kept well within this life by their gathering of the real voices
and things of this life. But even so there is in them a manipu-
lating of all these things into symbols which say again and
again that this life is *only* between the loci of the real realities,
and it will surely have to be Morris' effort to prevent the
collapse of his immediate present into a confusion of merely
symbolic evocations. Morris' naive and marvelous sensibility
for *things,* in all their inertness, is luckily persistent, but
meanwhile this felt life has become for him theoretically
implausible.

The redeeming importance to him of the American things
in their imprisoning density, concreteness, and inertness becomes manifest, indeed, as Morris applies the same theory to
other things. In *What a Way to Go* the artifacts of ancient
Greece are ornaments at best, and in Morris' subsequent novel
about Americans abroad, *Cause for Wonder* (1963), the
European setting would seem to be responsible for making
everything suddenly slack and merely ruminative. The setting, a crumbling Austrian castle, is a caprice, a whimsical
invention for the sake of whimsical speculation, and as such
it contains no danger. It really is a way out of this world,
lacking as it does any historical authenticity. The novel does
end, again, in a signal of continuance—the chatelaine is seen
arranging and sorting apples, in the way she is used to doing.
The protagonist is left contemplating what he has been contemplating, namely the oddities of this castle and the quirks
of its castellan. But since it is just quirkiness that fascinates
him, just something that Morris has made up, there is no

reason for him not to end his life triumphantly by following the example put before him.

In fact, *Cause for Wonder* begins by repeating what for Morris have become the old impossibilities. Warren Howe, his hero, is a man very much like Clyde Muncy and like Peter Foley and like Gordon Boyd. He lives between deathly symbols of time present and a sense of a strangely captivating time past. Moreover, except for the castle itself, the materials offered to him consist of fragments chipped from the other novels. By way of figuring the present, for instance, there are signs around him of preparation for nuclear war. Boyd, in *Ceremony in Lone Tree,* had been entranced by a placard in a Nevada motel, reading WAKE BEFORE BOMB. Howe speculates on the title of a play about fallout shelters, *No Place to Hide,* and a friend of his sells survival kits. Another friend, a progressive educator, like Mother in *Man and Boy,* is so in love with gadgets that he converts everything into clichés. According to the deathly system by which he lives, the past is useless. On the other hand, Howe is presented with a pioneering uncle, the stock ancient of Morris' fiction, who brings to the present the sustaining virtues of abstinence, frugality, and independence. And he is presented with a fragment of *Love Among the Cannibals* in the character of a Hollywood junk dealer, a man whose study is the dead effects —the clichés—of movie stars. And Howe, a writer, is presented with a fragment of *The Huge Season* in the character of his agent, a man fatalistically named Gatz. The narrative is set into motion, once again, by a funeral. The funeral is for a nutty old Frenchman named Etienne Dulac who lives in the Austrian castle in which Howe once, some thirty years earlier, had been forced to spend a few months, but Dulac is made in good part of the ideas that went into Will Brady and Tom Scanlon. Howe thinks of him as being Santa Claus, Don Quixote, and as being "out of this world." And the castle itself, in which in a manner Howe has always lived, to which he now returns, is a broad symbol of the past much like Morris' other symbols. It is like Lone Tree even to having an old barber chair to complement its lone survivor. Like Peter Foley's 1920s, the place exercises a "strange captivity."

But then these souvenirs and these odds and ends of ideas don't compose into the kind of surface by which Morris is captivated. Paradoxically, the strange castle and the strange Frenchman free him precisely into a symbolical mode of thought so comprehensive that there is nothing left to symbolize and therefore nothing left to fear. The novel is divided into two parts, "Time Present" and "Time Past," which are obviously meant to be informative of each other. In the first part Howe receives a notice of the death of Etienne Dulac and goes about finding someone who will accompany him to the funeral. In the second part, at the castle, Howe discovers that the notice was a little premature; Dulac is so close to death as to be infantile, but he doesn't actually die until the last pages of the novel, having arranged for Howe to be present. At the end the moral might be simply that the past imposes itself on the present and therefore—the novel pilfers extensively from "Burnt Norton"—that all time is eternally present. In an interview at the time the novel was published, Morris indeed proposed that the duty of the serious novelist was to show the larger effects of a modern consciousness of Time. "Today," he said, "we no longer have the narrative sense of time our fathers had . . . we feel time in the moment; time has no flow—it is atomized." [4]

Unfortunately, the novel comes to that realization and then, because there is little to restrain it, it proceeds to still larger effects. Howe indulges in much too much talk about

time in a style made up of much too much portentously
rhetorical questioning:

> What time was it? Could any time be said to have stopped?
> In Monsieur Dulac's case the answer was yes. Dead he
> was. His time had stopped. But could it be said that he was
> now out of time's reach?

> What he had brought along with him—the time on his
> watch, the time better described as time-passing—that time
> whatever it was, seemed inadequate. As he passed the old
> man time-present seemed identical with time-past. Cause
> for wonder—or so it seemed to Howe.

> At sixty miles an hour time and space seem to wind on
> the spool beneath me. Or within me, which is more accu-
> rate. Dimensions of time: I see it rushing toward me,
> worming slightly, then I see it unraveling behind me. A
> stretch of time? A piece of space? Or one and the same,
> weaving together.

While Howe realizes, repeatedly, the atomization of time,
the drama in which he should be engaged turns static. There
is so little flow that most of the characters of "Time Present"
are simply dropped when the novel moves into the castle,
and what conflict was proposed is abandoned.

The sad truth both Morris and Howe unwittingly discover,
however, is that the past contained in the castle is haunting
just because it is incredible. The castle as such is not an arti-
fact but only a sketchy setting for Dulac, and Dulac, it turns
out, is a madman whose life has consisted of a series of
audacious but meaningless japes. There is an idiot in the
castle, Dulac's protégé, who roams about playing practical
jokes. Dulac himself thirty years before had liked to bury his
visitors in snowdrifts. Among his effects there is to be dis-

covered an elaborate menu going from nuts to soup. The funeral to which Howe has come is an elaborate joke—Dulac has been playing dead. And the novel comes quite explicitly to value the sheer nuttiness of it all. By being nutty Dulac, as Morris has a character say, has turned fiction into fact. By that much he has flown out of this world. By that much he has conquered time, become immortal, and created a place to hide. And by that much Morris has solved everything.

The resolution to the maintained tension of Morris' later novels is at this point a solipsism. The achievement of *Cause for Wonder,* therefore, despite its whimsicality, is a deathly restfulness, purchased by a denial of all contingencies and the qualities of all things, a denial which is disastrous for Morris considering where he has been. The strenuousness and the seriousness of Morris' fiction have been in his perception that symbols are attached to things, things which are imperative and dangerous. That perception, especially in *Field of Vision* and *Ceremony in Lone Tree,* has kept his characters alive, and if Morris has come to the point where he must make their lives not only possible but fruitful, surely he cannot do that by blinking at everything he has known. The sense in their existence will have to come from Morris' continued awareness of the American Territory.

～VI～

BERNARD MALAMUD

The Sadness of Goodness

The radiant artifacts of Bernard Malamud's fiction have been the shrouds and the graves of Jews: rusty caftans and rusty black derbies, decrepit tenements, gloomy grocery stores smelling of poverty, of age, and of inviolate failure.

The tutelary elders among his distinctive inhabitants have worn the whiplash marks—sparse teeth and hollow eyes and yellowed, ragged beards—of ancient suffering, improbable survival, and sure transition. Their language has been taut and uncomfortable, a language which wants release into incantation or ritualistic gesture or moaning, outside the qualifications of speech. His guides to the spirit have been, characteristically, scrawny old Jews, skeletal *nudniks,* the agents of oblique commands and Yiddish paradoxes, whose very presence is a visitation.

Malamud's home place has in fact not been the traditional Jewish community as it really exists in Brooklyn or the Lower East Side or anywhere else. Malamud has seldom exploited the local color of the ghetto, and he has actually situated his fiction almost anywhere else. But the Jewish community as a place which has traditionally denied the priority of existence, has been the constant condition of his sensibility. Malamud's fiction has depended upon the *shtetl* problem and the *shtetl* sense, as Irving Howe and Eliezer Greenberg have described it, of permanent precariousness, of proximity with the mythical past and with the redeeming future but of distrustful detachment from history.[1]

No one in America in these years has lived further from the ordinary contingencies of middle American culture, certainly, than Malamud. His lyricism, his ideas of beauty and of the nature of the spirit, his apprehension of time and of circumstance, his pity, and his humor have all been fastened, even when Malamud has seemed merely American, to the unreality peculiarly proposed by Jewish life. Despite the fact that he has made many and often successful excursions, and despite his literary sophistication, Malamud's real knowledge has been intense, parochial, isolated, and exotic. Moreover, his special note has been a mysticism which compels all the discrete actualities of his knowledge to extremes. The fiction has hurried reality into myth, or into parable or exemplum or allegory, and its typical process has been a sudden transition of particularities. So the shriveled Jewish light-bulb peddler of one of Malamud's early stories, "An Apology,"[2] a wraith composed of bony shoulders and large eyes, haunts a policeman who has done him a minor injury until he wrests an apology from him, and the policeman, when he looks again, sees nothing. "The long, moon-whitened street had never been so empty." So the marriage broker of "The Magic Barrel" has a trick of appearing in the shrubbery, and his office, it is said, is in the air. "Idiots First" rushes to the moment when Mendel, a starved Jew at the last moment of his life, will force from the angel of death a moment of pity. The angel manifests himself as a trickster ghost named Ginz-

berg. In his last agony clinging to him, Mendel sees his own
terror reflected in the angel's eyes. And then

> he saw that Ginzberg, staring at himself in Mendel's eyes,
> saw mirrored in them the extent of his own awful wrath.
> He beheld a shimmering, starry, blinding light that pro-
> duced darkness.

The perception in this fiction is through mirrors, and it
renders reality problematical. And even when Malamud's
characters have not been Jews by designation, and when there
are no sudden obliterations or vanishings, there has been no
settled earthliness either. The materials are in the first place
different, and in the second place it has been the constant
tension in Malamud's stories that the materials, as Alfred
Kazin has pointed out, are always just about to disappear.[3]

Malamud has lived far from the middle of American culture and, because he has been an emphatic moralist, indeed a
fabulist, he has not participated either, except in some few
deliberate gestures, in what has been the chief manner of
fiction in these years, that constant acrobatics of living within
this world with its too many things and its too many complications. Malamud seems by every token of manner to be
a special case.

But there is nothing so smooth and determined and decided
in the manner that the manner could really be a strategy.
Indeed, what might otherwise be Malamud's mere gothicism
or his mere moralizing—and he has not been either a conspicuously shrewd or a stunningly original moralist—is prevented by a continuous, deep uneasiness in the fiction, and
it is not after all the special world of his imagination nor the
brilliant manner that composes the large truth about Malamud. In truth, the brilliance of the manner is not continuous.
Malamud is not an especially deft writer. His talent is for the

extraordinary, for annunciations and epiphanies, the suspenseful second of revelation, and not particularly for the other, lesser demands of imaginative composition. Only a man with a heightened talent for the extraordinary, for instance, or no talent at all, could have a character (in *The Assistant*) say, "Your Jew ass is bad, you understand?" and believe he had rendered a colloquialism, and the instance is not at all unique. It is only at those times when his fiction allows him to talk in the derived dialect that he has made his literary speech that Malamud's performance does have absolute authority. Not infrequently he forces those times. But just this uneasiness of craft, deep and integral, is actually his strength, and it would seem to imply his real truth. The fiction is pressed to move along much too rapidly, and there is a telling awkwardness in it. The manner is an extremity to which the fiction is forced, and the real story that Malamud's fiction tells, when it is at its best and really no matter what it means to tell, is the process of its being forced to extremities.

For Malamud, too, that is to say, the informing motive is the necessity of accommodation to this world, and the difference in the materials and in the manner is a difference primarily in his original distance from the world. The motion of the characters in his fiction is indeed one of compulsive urgency to be out of this world and in a more certainly felt reality—one often contained, it happens, in a special folklore. And their adventure is precisely their frustration; the end of straining and the beginning of heroism, if achieved, is the beginning of acceptance, one foot still stretched out of the world, of the inevitability of retreat into this world. It is just the fact that everything is about to disappear, that the historical reality of this world is problematical, that provides Malamud with his drama.

The motive of the fiction, if not at all its home place, is

indeed quite that of Wright Morris, who would seem in every way to be Malamud's exact opposite. For Malamud, as for Morris with his accomplished apprehension of American surfaces, this world is the fatality which must be engaged because all the forms of the more cogent Reality—perfect love, perfect freedom, the life of the spirit or the life of the self— are out of this world. For both of them, it follows, the hero is a man awakened and in quest of a discipline, one which will inform this life with that Reality. For both of them the actual terms of that Reality are vague, easily interchangeable, and finally less important than they should be. For both of them, the hero is doomed to his struggle by the nature of his knowledge, and, because he is in this world, doomed to failure.

Malamud and Morris in fact come into odd conjunctions. It is odd, given the absolute difference in their sensibilities, but then it is perhaps inevitable, that they both rely on the same merely conventional representations of Beauty and the Spirit—it is not the shape of the Spirit but rather its tantaliz- ing impossibility that is the beginning of adventure. So they both deal extensively in flowers and birds. Just beyond Mala- mud's icy streets there is continuously the flutter of wings, and when there are no birds, birds are there in some other way. In *The Natural* (1952), Malamud's first novel, the god- dess who sends the hero on his quest is named Harriet Bird, and in *A New Life* (1961) a particularly dull student of English composition is named Albert O. Birdless. And it is the more unlikely, given the milieu from which Malamud derives his fiction, but then it is perhaps inevitable, that, just like Morris, he should sometimes discover his hero in St. Francis. Frank Alpine's patron saint, in *The Assistant* (1957), is St. Francis, the Assisian, and the Franciscan life is the ex- ample toward which he yearns. In the story "The Last Mohican," revelation turns on recognition, by the protagonist, of St. Francis in a painting by Giotto. The hero for both Malamud and Morris is of course a man who recognizes the provenance of the birds—although the Franciscan marriage to poverty provides Malamud with another convenience of symbolism. And it is perhaps the more inevitable that they should agree on this figuration just because they are neither of them theologues. St. Francis is surely the most secular of saints and, after Santa Claus, the simplest and the most available. It is not first of all the particularities of the discipline of reconciling this life with the other that moves either of them, but its necessity and its aesthetic.

Malamud has become an emphatic moralist, and he might therefore be different in this time, but he is a moralist who has little interest in moral conflict. His constant and his total moral message is, quite simply, the necessity in this world of accepting moral obligation. The message was implicit in his earliest stories, and it became explicit in his later fiction. He has sometimes described his fiction as telling the story of personality fulfilling itself,[4] and he has sometimes made his characters assert the paradox that moral conduct, derived from love, is freedom, but really the energy and the authority in his moralizing about personality is entirely in the fact that morality is a necessity, one which a man will be reluctant to acknowledge, and it is not a creative choice. Morality is a reluctant mode of accommodation. Morality is simply the *name* of the discipline, for those who are not saints, and Malamud is not much concerned with the details of the discipline. Morality, like the world itself, is a fatality—there are better possibilities available to the imagination, but they are not here and now.

The story to be told, consequently, is of the hero who becomes heroic either by rising to acceptance of moral obligation or descending to it, but in either case he proceeds from the comfort of some more certain contemplation. It is at that point that Malamud's story typically ends. And that is the basic plot from which all of Malamud's fiction derives. The moral act, no matter what moral act it is, is itself charged with significance because any moral act is difficult and unlikely. That is to say that it is a difficult and unlikely business to accept ordinary humanity. The urgency of the awakened spirit is to soar. His hero's heroism is his hero's loss. And the luminous moment for Malamud, that moment toward which his talent rushes, is always that in which the loss is revealed.

The whole of the message, except perhaps for the specific, positive announcement of moral obligation, was implicit, indeed, in Malamud's very first publication, in 1943, a brief short story called "Benefit Performance." [5] The story was intended, certainly, as little more than a comic character vignette. For just that reason it is revealing. An elderly unemployed actor on the Yiddish stage, Maurice Rosenfeld, comes home to his shabby apartment one afternoon after fruitless job-hunting. Second Avenue, he says, is like a tomb. His twenty-eight-year-old daughter is in the apartment, in bed with menstrual cramps, and awaiting her suitor, a plumber. His wife has left him a dinner of a warmed-over hamburger, some potatoes, and carrots. His action in the story is then his bumptious, guilty assertion of himself. Midst, and against, his unlikely circumstances, he acts the part of an actor, striking large poses. "You got a father," he shouts at his daughter, "whose Shylock in Yiddish even the American critics came to see and raved about it. *This* is living. *This* is life. Not with a plum-ber." And his action is funny because the speech by which he asserts the transcendent loftiness of the actor's spoken word is crude, guttural, broken-edged, and bursting with his crude circumstances. "All right," he says, "So *I* don't make a steady living. So go on, spill some more salt on my bleeding wounds."

The comedy is, apparently, the most of Malamud's deliberate intention in this mere vignette. The subject is Rosenfeld's language. But in fact it happens that Rosenfeld, when he reaches the maximum of his rant, is moved to a rhetoric that is less certain in its intimations. The language is still rant, disproportionate to its occasion, top-heavy with clichés, swooning in its rhythms, and sabotaged by dialect. But still it comes to a grandiloquence that is not more than once removed from eloquence. Crossing his arms over his breast and then raising them ceilingward. Rosenfeld begins to speak in fluent Yiddish:

> Hear me earnestly, great and good God. Hear the story of the afflictions of a second Job. Hear how the years have poured misery upon me, so that in my age, when most men are gathering their harvest of sweet flowers, I cull nothing but weeds.
>
> I have a daughter, Oh God, upon whom I have lavished my deepest affection, whom I have given every opportunity for growth and education, who has become so mad in her desire for carnal satisfaction that she is ready to bestow herself upon a man unworthy to touch the hem of her garment, to a common, ordinary, wordless plum-ber, who has neither ideals nor——.

Rosenfeld is not what he pretends to be, but the sudden intimation of the story is that his pretense is not what it has seemed, either. Rosenfeld *is* noble and beautiful. Chained to his tomb, his circumstances and his daughter's plum-ber, he aspires. The subject is still Rosenfeld's language—what he aspires to is rhetoric uncircumstanced, entirely formal— Beauty itself. And if in the next moment after its flight his rhetoric plummets to the earth—when he crashes into that dreadful word "plum-ber"—that is not entirely funny. It is also an imperative of his living here midst his circumstances. Certainly Rosenfeld is no longer involved in a classical comedy of deflated pride. The loss of his eloquence is a real loss.

Rosenfeld is not a hero, of course. In the next, final movement of the story we find him posturing before his hamburger, and his acceptance is signaled by his saying with awful quietude: "Tonight I will eat chopmeat." One bite might introduce him to heroism, but the story does not go so far. Still, the hero's story opens before him, and so does all of Malamud's subsequent production. In fact Malamud published only a few stories in the next almost ten years, but then his first novel, *The Natural,* published in 1952, conspicuously different as it is in all its circumstances, its milieu, its literary sophistications, and its rhetoric, is still a smoothly relevant extension from Rosenfeld's benefit performance. Its world—professional baseball—is as far from Second Avenue as might be. Its protagonist, Roy Hobbs, a bewitched slugger, is as distant from Yiddish bombast as he might be. One of Malamud's ambitions, certainly, in *The Natural* as in some of the stories in the years before it, was to prevent himself from parochialism. But different as the novel is in every way, nevertheless Roy Hobbs's career is created by the same universal imperatives Rosenfeld knew. It is as well, and again, Hobbs's misfortune that he is chained to a complexity of trivial, degrading circumstances. He moves, although with special equipment, toward the higher, and his story, too, consists of the inevitable frustration. Roy is out to break all the records—to do, that is to say, what no man has ever done, to soar—and he founders in the common corruption.

The Natural was suggested, Malamud has said, by one of Arthur Daley's columns in the *New York Times,* which raised the question, why does a talented man sell out? It is one of the awkwardnesses of the novel that it does not in its basic plot do much more than just encounter the question. Roy is offered a bribe and, so far as his experience in the novel teaches him his own motives, he accepts the bribe by reason of a circumspect regard for money. Baseball players have short careers. Roy in his virtue has not received the money he might have expected. That much is Roy's own accident. But there is a universal imperative in Roy's degradation, certified by the fact that he is made to suggest his mythical archetypes.

In fact he is all but obscured by them. *The Natural* is a deliberate and an artful novel. Roy, the would-be king of the diamond, is more than he is. He is also Achilles before Troy, and he is the Grail Knight at the Castle, and for a moment at the beginning he is young David and also the son who must replace the father. The mythical methodizing is discontinuous—and it is another awkwardness of the novel that Malamud won't take full responsibility for it—but nevertheless it is determined. Like Achilles, Roy fails his team by a long slump, and he is given to sulking in his dugout. Roy's bat has been scorched by lightning, the heavenly fire of Hephaestus. There is a Thersites, a deformed fan, in the bleachers to deride Roy's glory. Roy makes his visit to the nether world—a night-club named the Pot of Fire, populated by masked devils and screaming, half-naked girls—and his Hades is the gambler who rules the place, a man called the Supreme Bookie. His Helen is a girl named Memo Paris, who won't forget her first seducer. A lady bearing the name of the goddess Iris recommits Roy to battle. His Hector is the pitcher he chases from the mound.[6] And then as he is Sir Percivale, the Knight of the Grail, Roy is originally a backwoods bumpkin who reaches the climax of his career when he fails the Fisher King. The manager of Roy's team, the New York *Knights,* is Pop Fisher, a man who is mysteriously ill and who possesses a shameful past—the guilty passion of Anfortas becomes "Fisher's Flop"—and he rules, as he says, in "a blasted dry season."

> No rains at all. The grass is worn scabby in the outfield and the infield is cracking. My heart feels as dry as dirt for the little I have to show for all my years in the game.

Meanwhile, Roy's bat, which is the sword of Achilles, is at the same time Percivale's lance, and it is moreover Percivale's sword which was designed to break on just one occasion. Roy's Thersites is also his Sir Kay. Like Percivale, Roy must earn his first glory by defeating the current champ in single combat—he strikes him out. Like Sir Percivale, he adventures in eerie forests, he is surrounded by omens, and he is besieged by besieged women. He even finds the emblem of his love, like Percivale, in a white flower—Percivale's queen, Blanchefleur, is proposed twice for Roy by the ladies Harriet Bird and Iris Lemon, both of whom peculiarly ornament themselves with white roses.

And, in addition to these certified myths, Roy's career is manipulated to suggest a folklore of baseball, a folklore that might be raised, just by its involvement in this multiple narrative, to the authority of myth. Like the hero Babe Ruth once, Roy promises a home run to a kid in the hospital, and hits it for him. The baseball park in which Roy strives is a hierograph of the Ebbets Field of folklore. After Roy has thrown the pennant game and his corruption has been revealed, a newsboy cries at him, in the manner that a newsboy is said to have cried at Shoeless Joe Jackson after the Chicago Black Sox scandal, "Say it ain't true, Roy."

It is a difficulty with this procedure that when it should

inflate Roy Hobbs, perhaps comically, into a mythic figure, at the same time it comically reduces him and all his mythical archetypes with him. The novel works, it must be with Malamud's consent, to crystallize an image of Sir Percivale swatting homers against the walls of Troy. Of course Malamud is aware of the fun, and he takes deliberate advantage of it—*The Natural* is a comic novel. Unfortunately, the fun, is not in the fact that Roy Hobbs, a baseball player and an unlikely hero, is really the exemplar of something much larger than himself. The fun is in the fact that Roy Hobbs, an unlikely hero, tangles the larger myths into an unlikely confusion. The Grail Castle becomes a baseball park, rather than *vice versa*. But there is a still larger difficulty with this procedure—the mythical method does not, either, explore the possibilities of Roy Hobbs. Why does a talented man sell out? The myths don't really say. In the freewheeling action of the novel it happens, surely by deliberation, that Roy commits every one of the Seven Deadly Sins, from pride to lust, from gluttony to sloth, and any one of them might account for his tumble into an absolute of corruption. Any one of them might be his corruption. But by their very number they cancel each other out, and then none of the myths adduced to confer significance on Roy provide, or are followed out so systematically or with such responsibility that they might provide, a moral answer to the moral question. Not even the myth of the venal Shoeless Joe. There is only the one allusion to him. Rather, what weight there is in the myths is wholly in the fact that they contain acknowledged heroes who in one way or another failed to sustain their heroism, and the whole intended function of the myths in the novel is, apparently, to invest Roy's fate with so much corroboration that the moral issue will disappear into a feeling of inevitability.

Roy Hobbs is a man who, in this world, is provided with the talent to do what no man has ever done, and his ability is a matter not merely of his natural talent. If he is a "natural," he is quickly, by the first lady of his life, transformed into a disciplined quester. Harriet Bird shoots him—with a silver bullet—at the moment of his lust, and thereby ordains him to fifteen years in the bush leagues. Roy learns what it is to travel endlessly and fruitlessly in this world—trains provide him with a special symbol of forlornness. He learns to suffer in this world. It is significant that the novel actually skips those fifteen years of travel and suffering, and takes Roy up again at the point where he will almost emerge into the glory for which he has quested. The particularities of the discipline are not Malamud's concern, and they are described only generally, obliquely, and in parentheses. But when he emerges, and although Roy does not know it, glory is still his inspiration. And he must seek it within his circumstances. He does have glorious moments—rendered symbolically, of course, because there is no other way to describe all that Roy really is after. Ordered once to "knock the cover off" the ball, Roy steps up to the plate and does literally that, but then it is most important that "the ball plummeted like a dead bird into center field." A moment later, rain abruptly falls on the wasteland ball park. Again, in the outfield once, raising his glove to snag a fly, so he thinks, Roy catches a canary. Those are the moments, or the tokens, or at the very least the promises of his real heroism. Playing within this ball park—which, it must have occurred to Malamud, is not unlike a bull ring—Roy touches the ultimate. And he cannot sustain his heroism—because, finally, no one not a saint ever could sustain such heroism, not Achilles nor the Grail Knight nor Shoeless Joe Jackson.

Roy sells out by the rule of the same imperative that dashed

Rosenfeld into the word "plum-ber." It is the feeling for that
fatality that governs the progress of the novel, and not anything Roy does and not anything in particular, either, that
Achilles or Sir Percivale did. Roy does, in truth, very little—
the very pace and multiplicity in the action prevent his in-
dulging any failure or sinfulness long enough for it to take.
All that holds his adventures together and gives them direction is the sense that the heroic quest always is bound to
failure. His lady Iris picks Roy out of his slump and tells him,
on one occasion, that she is interested in him "Because I hate
to see a hero fail. There are so few of them." And once the
identification is explicit, this hero has reached the apogee of
his accomplishment and the rest for him must be a descent
into failure.

Indeed, the novel sacrifices everything to the large feeling
of fatality—character, plot, even style. Or rather, given the
feeling of fatality, nothing else is demanded and anything else
is permitted. Roy himself is only a symptom and so *he* has not
much sensibility for anything, and Malamud achieves for
him little intensity of character. On the other hand, the novel
is open to all sorts of marvelous inventions—Harriet Bird;
the Supreme Bookie, who engages Roy, in the Pot of Fire, in
a contest of magic; the evil owner of the baseball club, Judge
Goodwill Banner, a Merlin who lives in a dark, slanted tower,
who obscures his evil designs in a pious oratory of bromidic
mottoes—minor characters who do have a vivid, if momentary, life to them. The plot is free to reach out for weird,
virtuoso, and not strictly necessary moments, and, just because everything is ruled by a fatality that isn't going to be
argued in the intricacy of character and event, the style too
can be fanciful. It is sometimes terse and colloquial. It is
now and again a rhapsodic blend of sports-columnese and
Chrétien de Troyes:

The third ball slithered at the batter like a meteor, the flame swallowing itself. He lifted his club to crush it into a universe of sparks but the heavy wood dragged, and though he willed to destroy the sound he heard a gong bong and realized with sadness that the ball he had expected to hit had long been part of the past. . . .

A Negro porter talks about his travels in a litany derived from Vachel Lindsay:

"Why Chi?" Eddie asked. "Why not New Orleans? That's a lush and Frenchy city."
"Never been there."
"Or that hot and hilly town, San Francisco?"
Roy shook his head.
"Why not New York, colossus of colossuses?"

And other characters and events are indulged in other caprices of language.

Everything might be indulged, and everything is indulged, except a circumstantial, scrutinizing realism. And it is the total weakness of *The Natural* that what realism might provide, a detailed knowledge of the detailed human difficulties of the quest, is not there. Even the myths upon which Malamud draws have a closer reality in them. But then this weakness is so entirely appropriate to the story Malamud has to tell that it becomes Malamud's curious strength—Roy Hobb's questing is Malamud's own, and they both would avoid the lower things in order to concentrate upon the higher. They both, that is to say, suffer a distrustful detachment from history. That is why they can be so arbitrary with it. And tragedy for both of them is in the brute fact that circumstances—not any particular circumstances, but just circumstances—are. For Malamud, if not for Hobbs, there is an additional strategic danger in such apprehension. If all circumstances, except perhaps the extremes of love and death, are tragic just because they exist and because they prevent the higher, then all circumstances are equally tragic. Therefore they all earn the same undiscriminating apprehension, which is sentimentality. Sentimentality is avoided, then, in the same trick of vision by which circumstance itself is avoided, in making everything, even the specific contents of the great myths, illogical and of little account—everything except the one Reality. So long as this silly accident of a real world can be generalized and distorted, it does not yet exist. *The Natural* is playful with the lesser reality, but Malamud's playfulness, here and elsewhere, has a somber force to it. It is not, as has been suggested, a Kafkaesque distortion that is indulged.[7] It is not an actively persecuting, baffling world that is presented. But quite the contrary. This world is terribly neutral, easy to understand, but hard to take, and so the distortion is made, subject to the final fatality, in order to prevent its happening. The story *The Natural* tells is the process of a sensibility forced to extremities in order to withhold acknowledgment from the world.

Because this novel lacks a density of realistic motivation, the ending must also be arbitrary, and it is, except that fatality finally closes in. Along with Rosenfeld, Roy Hobbs is not quite the explicitly moral hero of some of Malamud's other fictions, perhaps because he isn't very certainly anything except, by designation, a quester. But at the end, when Roy loses his last chance for the Real, he is pointed toward an acceptance. He is made in his fall to adopt what is for Malamud, elsewhere, the sign of moral acceptance. Iris, a girl who has been around, tells Roy at one point that experience makes people good because it makes them suffer, and suffering, she says, leads to happiness. Iris is nothing if not elliptical—she says in addition only that suffering "teaches us to want the right things." Roy himself is not the hero to explore a gnome, and he won't be convinced. He doesn't like to suffer. But in his very last moment, when he walks away from his ball park and his shame, he thinks to himself that now he will have to suffer again.

Suffering is the sign, and Iris's wisdom, although there is nothing more in the novel really to make it intelligible to Roy, is therefore finally not wasted on him. The content of this wisdom, and therefore the full content of the ending of this novel, is elsewhere in Malamud's work. And elsewhere, suffering is the mode of goodness and happiness and right desire because, given Malamud's metaphysics, suffering is the one possible mode of engagement both with and in this world. All circumstances are in the first place tragic because circumstance is itself the name for the loss of what is higher. Therefore to be engaged with this world—to love this world, or to love in this world—is to suffer. For the hero who can imagine something higher suffering is the one possibility of love. Therefore it is morality itself. Suffering is good-willed and deliberate acknowledgment and acceptance of the common life of men. It is expression of the way in which men are bound together, in their loss. Indeed all of Malamud's heroes who are of a thoughtful turn, when they reach their highest awareness, in whatever particularities of situation, either cry or, what is the same thing, take upon themselves a deliberate regimen of self-punishment, and the significance of their suffering is always in the fact that it is larger than any particularity of situation. All and any experiences make men suffer, and suffering is their achievement.

So in a very early story, "The Place Is Different Now," [8] Wally Mullane, the neighborhood bum, returns to his neighborhood after an absence to discover that it is entirely closed to him. His mother doesn't recognize him, his sister screams at him, and his brother beats him up. Only the local barber, an elderly man who is reminded by Wally of the son he had himself once failed in love, is affectionate and protective. In the final action of the story, Wally, while the barber shaves him, remembers the neighborhood as once it had been for him, a place where he could dress up and go out on the town on Saturday nights. He whispers, "Everything's kinda changed. The place is different now." The barber too is occupied in remembering a better time of love. And looking down, he sees that tears are rolling down Wally's cheeks. Tenderly, he mixes the lather with Wally's tears. And this static, intense ending—the kind of ending toward which Malamud's fiction characteristically moves—might simply be elegy, elegy further intensified because reduplicated. But elegy is in the loss of something, and just this reduplication actually cancels the reality of the something by making it inconsistent: Wally and the barber recall quite different things. What is important, rather, is that they have a common recognition of all experience. What they achieve, then, is a communion in tears, a commonalty in their sense of the way things are. The place is always different now, no matter that it was different before for different people. In the imagined distance there was something better which experience has canceled. Loss is continuous and universal. And to acknowledge that truth, in suffering, is to discover both the world and communion in it.

"The Place Is Different Now" rushes through its actions to the moment of luminous suffering, when suffering will shine forth as the way of love and goodness, and by that much it establishes exactly the procedure of most of Malamud's later fictions. The pure cases are in such stories as "The Mourners" and "The Loan," stories so intense and so quick

in their concentration of all materials into the final moment
that all specificity of situation disappears. In "The Mourners"
a dirty and lonely old Jew refuses to be evicted from his tenement flat. The events of his struggle force him to a trance of
ritualistic mourning. The landlord realizes suddenly that
the man he would have victimized is mourning him and,
alone with him in his bedroom, he tears a sheet off the bed,
wraps it about himself, sinks to the floor, and becomes a
mourner too. There are ironies in his mourning which he
cannot know—the old Jew has been weeping not for the guilt,
the spiritual death, of the landlord, but for the wrongs he has
himself throughout a lifetime committed. But it is just to the
point that the landlord should be mstaken, that he should be
led by someone else's private suffering to an apprehension
of his own, private experience, and through that apprehension
to a voluntary act of suffering. Ironies and contingencies disappear, and what is achieved is suffering. And in "The Loan"
the story itself, in the same way, disappears in the brilliance
of its last moment when two old Jews, remet after many years
and a confusion of circumstances have forced them apart,
embrace for the last time, and sigh over their lost youth.
"They pressed mouths together and parted forever." And
what alone matters is the desperate momentariness of this
last kiss. The kiss is not love but the recognition which serves
for love, of the nature of experience. Love is suffering.

It is to that recognition that most of Malamud's fiction proceeds. It is the lesson learned in all of his novels, somewhat
more explicitly in *The Assistant* and *A New Life* than in
The Natural. It is the lesson learned in what is by all measure
the richest of his stories, "The Magic Barrel." And when it
is not the lesson learned, the lesson to be learned is only its
opposite and therefore the same thing: not to admit suffering
is not to love. The heroes either admit suffering or, by reason

of some preoccupation, they don't, but in all cases suffering is the one possible expression of true goodness, and suffering is always the ultimate problem. In so unlikely and so happy a farce as "Angel Levine," a story in which an elderly Jew is saved from ruin and misery by the intervention of a Jewish-Negro angel, a shift of protagonists occurs, and what is accomplished is the angel Levine's salvation. He learns to suffer in this world and therefore he secures heaven. Levine is a probationary angel who must earn his way. Only after he has been sufficiently rejected by the Jew he has come to aid can he perform miracles and then fly up to heaven like a bird. Then in so seemingly documentary a story as "The Lady of the Lake," which appears to, and does, shake a reproachful finger at a Jewish boy who courts girls without admitting that he is Jewish, the issue is not finally poor Henry Freeman-née-Levin's cowardice, but his embarrassed avoidance of the history of Jewish suffering. The Italian princess he would love is really, it turns out, a refugee from Buchenwald who, as she says, treasures what she suffered for. Henry cannot be her lover or, by implication, anybody's lover, because he lives in hypocritical freedom from the pain to which he was born.

The lady of "The Lady of the Lake" doesn't look Jewish—which is why Henry miscalculates—but of course it is of absolute importance to Malamud's purposes that she be Jewish rather than, say, merely poor. If Malamud is not a local colorist of the ghetto, except incidentally, still, Jewish tradition provides him with an inevitable metaphor. Its inevitability is tested in the fact that his characters when they are not Jews tend anyway to talk in Yiddish constructions. "He enjoyed to be poor," says Frank Alpine of St. Francis, and "He was born good, which is a talent if you have it." On occasion Malamud has himself spoken of the similarity of sensibility he finds existing between Italians and Jews—he is reported also to have said that all men are Jews—but it is the case that his Jews never sound like Italians. Jewish life, with its exemplary alienation from the ordinary life of the world, is obviously basic to his sensibility. Jewish idealism, in the very vagueness and variousness of its notion of "the higher things," provides Malamud with a handily vague idealism. Ghetto character—involuted, prickly, distrustful in one moment, in the next lyrical and impractical—provides him with a plot. Jews, Malamud has said, "are absolutely the very *stuff* of drama." [9] And the Jewish history of suffering provides Malamud, finally, with his lesson in reconciliation. The lady of "The Lady of the Lake" *must* be Jewish because it is Jews who know how to suffer. The Jewish expertise is in suffering.

Whether or not Malamud's Jews are real Jews in their sociological and psychological detail, they and all of Malamud's other heroes contain Jewish history. They contain the separate Jewish history as it is condensed in the traditional, bitter Jewish joke on the chosen-ness of the Chosen People: For what are the Jews chosen? They are chosen to suffer. And that is to say, given Malamud's vision, that the separate Jewish experience is a lesson in the only love, the only goodness, there is in this world. Frank Alpine, who will be a convert to Judaism before his novel is over, asks the grocer Morris Bober why Jews suffer so damn much. It seems to him that they like to suffer. He asks, "What do you suffer for, Morris?" and Morris Bober says, calmly, "I suffer for you." Suffering is the communion of people under heaven. The separate Jewish experience is a paradigm of that communion.

The Assistant, Malamud's second novel, is his principal working out of the matter. It is entirely the story of the apprenticeship of Frank Alpine, a purposeless and confused drifter, to the discipline of Jewish suffering. Frank begins in a sort of itchy neutrality, in a generalized need for discipline, for a way of life in this world; he apprentices himself to a Jew; and he ends, as an apprentice should, by replacing his master. He learns to suffer. The suffering he comes to make his own is the more Jewish, moreover, because it is pure. It is constant and hopeless. This suffering begets merely suffering. Suffering is the way of life, and it is not even a spiritual investment. Indeed, the singular achievement of the novel is its yoking of Frank simply to a dead weight of disenchantment about the nature of suffering. His master, Morris Bober, who has given his life to his grocery store, thinks just before he dies: "I gave away my life for nothing. It was the thunderous truth." And the whole significance of the impoverished grocery store in which Frank is to discover both the Jewish experience and experience itself is that it slowly, inexorably denies all other possibilities. The grocery store is the alien circumstance in which a man must live. It is mortality itself, and a living death—the Grocery Store has been a constant reference of Malamud's fiction, described repeatedly as a prison, a tomb, an open grave, with a dead smell and a constant chill in it. It is the very denial of heaven and of all higher things, and it forces a discipline of human community by excluding everything better.

Frank's assistantship begins with his briefly assisting not Morris, but Ward Minogue, a boozy, occasionally vicious neighborhood bum, who is derived directly from Wally Mullane. He assists him in robbing Morris one evening of fifteen dollars, an event that puts him to the necessity of earning forgiveness and therefore, though he is never fully aware of his motives, to moral questing. Already "a moody gink," as a neighboring storekeeper describes him, and already given—like the Jew he is to become—to much sighing and muttering under his breath, and besides with a head full of St. Francis, he insinuates himself into Morris' store, gradu-

ally to become Morris' assistant. Frank's intentions in the beginning are muddled, but they are none the less splendid. He
will aid his victim. He wants to confess. He wants definition
within moral being. All his life, he tells Morris, one wrong
thing has led to another, and all his life he has been on the
move, unable to accomplish anything worth while. The very
motionlessness of the grocery store, it turns out, appeals to
him. And he comes to it as to a shrine.

The grocery store will in fact be the right thing for Frank,
an end to the moral shiftlessness he has known. But then the
discipline it imposes on him, far from leading to the accomplishment of his vague "anything worth while," is a system
of endurance of endless frustrations. The grocery store is
the world he has already avoided, but now constricted to the
point where there is no escaping it. It is the world intensified
by being made more bleak. In this world there is, for instance,
no justice, but instead a brutal economy of luck. In this
narrow, petty economy, Morris' neighbor, Julius Karp, a man
without brains or rigor, grows rich in direct relation as Morris
grows poorer, and Morris reflects that Karp's "every good
fortune spattered others with misfortune, as if there was just
so much luck in the world and what Karp left over wasn't
fit to eat." During the robbery—which had of course been intended for the gluttonous Karp—Ward Minogue hits Morris
with a gun, and as the blow descends, Morris thinks that it
is fitting, that this is his luck, others had better. The true God
in the grocery store is bad luck. The grocery store provides
Morris with no sure sense of ownership. In this world all
hope of betterment is a fraudulent tease. So Frank in his
enthusiasm, and in the long action of the novel, scrubs the
floors of the store and the windows, and paints, and brightens
the shelves, and brings a hearty energy to the customers, and
supports the store by taking an extra job, and at the end he

sits in it alone, visited only by a bulb peddler who tells him that things are *schwer*. And in this world, history is a record of losses, of loss even of all chances for improvement. Romantic love, Frank will discover, is a sad confusion. The very spring of life is blighted—Morris suffers his fatal heart attack in April, shoveling snow.

The grocery store is the sheer, staggering quantity of existence, revealed perhaps nowhere more bluntly than in Malamud's discovery that sleep was Morris Bober's only refreshment, that "it excited him to go to sleep." This grocery store will crush Frank into moral discipline, and the more frightfully because this gloom does allow illusions. There are flurries of business. For a moment there seems to be an opportunity to sell the store. And for Frank there is Morris' daughter, Helen, who does return his love. But it is first of all a grocery store kind of love that she offers, hedged by fears, hopelessly hopeful, based on much experience of failure. Helen is apparently the principle against which the validity of Boberism, that grim morality of misfortune, might be and should be tested. She is the love interest. And Helen is old at the age of twenty-three, knowledgeable about the transience of lives, oppressed by a sense of mourning which she fights to a practiced draw. The love she offers, like the tenacity of her ambition to finish evening college, like her earnest reading, is an idealism already reduced to endurance. And then her lovingness is so sensitive to hurt that there is little possibility for her or her lover of practical achievement. She is peculiarly apprehensive about her breasts—as are indeed a peculiar number of Malamud's heroines. Caresses pain her. Her little experience with physical love, in this world which is sordid, teaches her to despise herself.

Helen ends by imposing on Frank exactly what the grocery

store has already taught him to accept. The ritual of his acceptance is of course a circumcision—Helen, who is well read, has once called Frank "uncircumcised dog," and what he needs in order to be Helen's proper companion is a pain between his legs, a pain which, in the last words of the novel, "enraged and inspired him." Morris has once, in the beginning, told him that he can learn from the grocery store only one thing, "a heartache," and what in both events he learns is a regimen of pain. To exercise one's affections is to suffer, and to suffer doggedly. Frank comes to his knowledge, in both events, with much dreamy good will. He contemplates with satisfaction the aesthetic of great discipline. The images in which he conceives love are only initially, and briefly, lustful—he carves a wooden rose for Helen, and he courts her by telling her how St. Francis had made himself a wife out of snowy moonlight. He wants to be a man of fine character. He wants to be honest and loyal. But what he does not know is that the self-denial which is the price of moral being really hurts and without relief. Frank is a great backslider. Even as he apprentices himself to Morris, he pilfers from the cash register. At a moment of high moral fervor, he rapes Helen. And it turns out that, evader that he is, he has much easy pleasure in guilt, in the calisthenics of conscience. The novel acts to leave him, then, in a state of rigorous and unrewarded goodness, a Jew in a grocery store, still and forever earning Helen, hopelessly patient.

The novel acts to plant Frank deep in the alien world, thereby to disabuse him about the nature of suffering. The sign on the door of this novel is, in fact, Naturalism. Malamud's initial description of Morris Bober echoes, not surprisingly after all, Stephen Crane: Morris Bober is a man who, in the long dark tunnel he inhabits, "rarely saw the

sky." Given just slightly different circumstances, Thomas
Hardy might have owned and operated this grocery store.*
But then it is a curious and finally more telling a fact than
anything in Frank's adventures that, dreary as this landscape
is, it is really not so dreary as the quantity of Malamud's
response to it implies. The novel is to be a paradigm of
Jewish suffering, and Malamud's apprehension of the suffering in ordinary circumstances is, it would seem, much more
extreme than any possibility, in this context, of his invention. If, after the grotesqueries of *The Natural,* the method
of *The Assistant* is a more or less disciplined naturalism, the
novel still is uncomfortable within its discipline. For Malamud, if not quite for Frank, this grocery store is a great deal
more than a disabling humiliation—it is the dark night of
the soul. The quantity of Malamud's own response is indeed not in Frank Alpine at all, but in Morris Bober, a
character so steeped in suffering and therefore so fixedly and
so hyperbolically good that there is no referring him back
to the detail even of his constant misfortune. He is much
more than he is—he is in fact The Jew—and there is so much
of him, all so static and so merely exemplary, that indeed the
novel is in its effect as frequently as not a lyric of praise to
him rather than a sequence of adventures.

Morris is unnecessarily dutiful. He has risen at six A.M.
every morning for fifteen years in order to sell a single roll to
a vaguely anti-Semitic Polish woman, and even then he un-
dercharges her. When the sudden blows descend, Morris will
not complain. Morris, old and broken, will shovel snow in

---

* Malamud has made particular study of Hardy, who is the subject of
his master's essay. See "Thomas Hardy's Reputation as a Poet in American Periodicals," unpublished (Columbia University, 1942). Despite its
title, the essay is, for the most part, a critical examination of *The
Dynasts.* It is to be noted that in Malamud's *A New Life,* a taste for
Hardy becomes in an instance a sign of sensibility.

April because "It's Sunday, it don't look so nice for the goyim that they go to church." But Morris is larger even than his own extravagances. He is mythic, a mythicized secular history of the Jews. He is the vessel of the Jewish Law—the novel makes it incumbent upon him to tell Frank the meaning of the Law, which is "to do what is right, to be honest, to be good."

> This means to other people. Our life is hard enough. Why should we hurt somebody else? For everybody should be the best, not only for you or me. We ain't animals. This is why we need the Law. This is what a Jew believes.

And when Morris dies, the substance of his epitaph as spoken by the attending rabbi is, of course, his exemplification of the Law.

> Yes, Morris Bober was to me a true Jew because he lived in the Jewish experience, which he remembered, and with the Jewish heart. Maybe not to our formal tradition—for this I don't excuse him—but he was true to the spirit of our life—to want for others that which he wants also for himself. He followed the Law which God gave to Moses on Sinai and told him to bring to the people. He suffered, he endu-red, but with hope. . . . He asked for himself little—nothing, but he wanted for his beloved child a better existence than he had. For such reasons he was a Jew.

But in fact at every point in the novel Morris Bober is The Jew more imperatively than he is Morris Bober. He is constantly identified in his Jewishness. And then he is somewhat the more mythic in his dimensions by the fact that he is in part Leopold Bloom—Morris too dotes on the memory of a son dead in infancy, and Frank, his heir, is his Stephen Dedalus.

At every other point the novel threatens therefore to become a Jewish testimonial. Morris' hardships aside, there is something undeniably cozy in Malamud's treatment of the character. But Morris by his awkward disproportionateness, by the very fact that he is more exemplary than he is human, hints at a kind of apprehension that is anything but cozy. The fact is that Morris, the emblem of good, patient, hopelessly hopeful endurance, does not endure. And not only are the circumstances in which Morris lives ruled by bad luck, but throughout the novel his circumstances inexorably retreat from him—Morris' history is one of loss. His circumstances, that is to say, have progressively less reality, and ultimately they disappear altogether. What is conveyed, finally, is an extreme notion of the uncertainty of all circumstance. Morris' existence is at least half mythical, but if his existence is disproportionate to his discrete circumstances, those circumstances themselves only half exist. Morris is problematically related to what is only problematically there. He begins as a man who "had no sure sense of property," and his sense of things is confirmed by a mode of perception only slightly subterranean throughout the novel. Character, existence, and property—not only Morris', but everyone's—are rendered continuously throughout the novel in images of leaking away, dribbling away, being blown away by the wind. Frank observes of Morris that "His pity leaks out of his pants. . . ." Frank is oppressed by the sense of his own leaking away, "of the slow dribbling away, starting long ago, of his character," and he observes of himself as well that "He was blown around in any breath that blew, owned nothing, not even experience to show for the years he had lived." The store is a "bloodsucking store." Business is "up today, down tomorrow—as the wind blew." Karp reflects that "if Morris Bober found a rotten egg in the street, it was already cracked and leaking," that "if Morris earned a dime he lost it before he could put it into his torn pocket." Helen thinks of her father that, "At the end you were sixty and had less than at thirty," that "he couldn't hold onto those things he had worked so hard to get."

If Morris Bober tends to be a mythic generalization, so does the circumstance in which he is discovered. Things are seen not in themselves, but in their motion toward disappearance. True suffering, then, and endurance and life itself, come to be an extreme poise at the edge of dissolution. Morris' tenacity in holding on to his failing grocery store for years is meant certainly to imply something of this sort. The matter is somewhat more apparent in one of the early stories from which *The Assistant* is derived, a story called "The Cost of Living," in which a poor grocer forced finally to give up the store in which he has suffered, by that much gives up his significant life. Engagement with circumstance is suffering, which is to be preserved against always imminent loss. Frank, hearing that Morris and the bulb peddler, Breitbart, have in a moment wept together, thinks: "That's what they live for . . . to suffer. And the one that has got the biggest pain in the gut and can hold onto it the longest without running to the toilet is the best Jew." Which is precisely to the point. Being a Jew, given Malamud's uses of Jewish experience, is ultimately a holding operation.

Morris does not hold. The characters in *The Assistant* who do hold are still more Jewish, more desperate, and more extreme. They are minor characters—Breitbart, and then a grotesquely impish arsonist who offers his services to Morris— but it is revealing that they are present in this naturalistic novel at all. The narrative stretches beyond itself to the information about living in this world that would seem basic to Malamud's apprehension, to the information that Frank's story cannot contain and that they in their perilous living in this world will almost disclose. And brief as these characters are, they are the most striking figures in the novel. They do live at the very edge of dissolution. The arsonist's whole trade, for instance, is in his knowledge of the way things disappear without a trace. He is at home with the prospect of dissolution, and he has almost but not quite been caught in it himself. A skinny man in an old hat and in an overcoat down to his ankles, with a long nose and wisp of red beard, he speaks in a coarse, gritty, discomforting language: "Insurinks you got—fire insurinks?" The secret of his trade is "celluloy," a word that he hisses. He is in fact a goblin. Breitbart, a figure taken whole from "An Apology," composed of a gulping Adam's apple and bony shoulders, visits Morris and then Frank in spells that are in effect visitations. He silently brings news—he bears on his shoulders enormous cartons of light bulbs and a case of the seven-year itch. "The world suffers," Morris says. "*He* felt every schmerz." And Breitbart's whole case is in the fact that he continues to exist within the last severity of fatigue and suffering, at the edge of the void which his very existence postulates.

The human task is to make and preserve a home in this world: to suffer in it, to contain every *schmerz,* thereby to love, thereby, for lack of any better present possibility, to make the moral conjunction that ,will accommodate human beings to it. But it is a murky, swampy world that Malamud in the first place knows—thick, oppressive, ominous, but also amorphous, liquescent, every seeming solidity treacherously uncertain. And the fiction has been most taut when it has been able to propose in an uninterrupted vision the cost of living, of holding on, the comically desperate obligations of being, carried out in a world that exists just this side of nothing. The world does not come easily to Malamud, everything is on the verge of not being, and the process of his own holding on, rather than any moralizing he does, is indeed the excitement of his fiction, and its tension.

He holds on nowhere more extremely against the extreme flowing away of things than in his story "The Magic Barrel," and it is the most exciting fiction he has written. The moral adventuring in "The Magic Barrel" is in fact not so different from that in *The Assistant*. An apprentice once again, in this case a rabbinical student about to graduate, whose previous moral drifting has taken place in his purely academic apprehension of The Law, is led by the story into this alien world which is again a place of suffering and death. The "place" is in this case localized in a carnal young lady. The story ends short, at the moment of the apprentice Leo Finkle's symbolic entrance into the world she is, but still the young lady performs for him the same function that the grocery store performed for Frank Alpine. Although young, she impresses Leo with "a sense of having been used to the bone, wasted," and at first sight of her photograph he thinks that she has "somehow deeply suffered." She is, although not precisely in the grocery store sense, lowly. Something about her suggests —Leo shudders when he realizes it—filth. He is told that she is "dead," and when Leo meets her in order to marry her, the marriage broker of the story will chant a prayer for the dead. Quite like the grocery store, she is an open tomb, into which Leo leaps. Leo Finkle's particular mode of apprenticeship in the story is his search for a wife. He hires a marriage broker, Pinye Salzman, whose role, if not entirely his significance, is just that of Morris Bober. This guide will eventually trick Leo into knowing that love and life and suffering and lowliness and death inhabit the same place. When Leo accepts that much, violins and lit candles will revolve in the sky, he will in effect be ordained, and he will in effect become a Jew.

And this moral adventuring is carried out with a swiftness, and therefore with a sweeping urgency, that is missing in *The Assistant*. But the great energy of the story is in something else, in the effort necessitated by the contingent, continually indistinct reality within which Leo's adventures take place. The very thinness of furnishing in the story, whether or not by Malamud's explicit intention, makes Leo's need. So it is integral to his story that Leo has no home, no place in which circumstances might accrete and take shape for him—as a Yeshivah student he inhabits a cell which has specific identity only in that it contains many books. And much of Leo's story occurs within this lack of place.* Leo is at best uncertainly attached to anything. He is without companions, and without companionship except for that of a landlady who has mistaken ideas about him. The first girl with whom Leo tries himself insists on addressing abstract pieties to him—he goes courting in a black fedora and a heavy black Saturday coat, and so he earns what he receives—and rather than offer him anything, she leads Leo to the realization that he is not attached even to the God Who has been his study. If Leo is to be introduced into the world, the real world is not apparent and easy to find, and then it is presented to him at the end in what is after all only a brief and symbolic evocation. The effect of, if not the moral intention in, his taking his carnal young lady, is that he clutches with lyrical relief at *something,* as an alternative to nothing. The girl has momentary but sensual and palpable presence, as nothing

---

* Such lack of place becomes conspicuous in Malamud's occasional stories about homelessness. See "Behold the Key" and "The Last Mohican."

else in Leo's life and landscape has. The apprehended landscape within which he is throughout the story made to be,
between The Law in which he has abstractly roamed and the
girl of his dreams, is neither dreary nor not, but purely
intermediate, and therefore one is left at the end of the story
with the power of the desperation of his clutch.

Malamud's own full response to this present landscape is,
once again, in the old Jew in the role of guide. Like Morris
Bober, Salzman actually contains more of the story than
does the apprentice hero. The sensibility of the story rami-
fies from him. Unlike Morris, he is an adept in a world
where nothing is certain, and indeed the kind of mastery this
master presents presupposes a spectral uncertainty of reality.
He is one of Malamud's wraiths, a demonstration of insub-
stantiality, slight and animated, missing a few teeth, and
smelling of fish. He is "a skeleton with haunted eyes." By the
end of the story he is "haggard, and transparent to the point
of vanishing." He is besides either a magician or a demon.
He makes mysterious entrances and exits. He lives everywhere and nowhere. Searching for him, Leo is told that his
office is "in the air," but he appears, like a genie, when he is
wanted. Courting his first girl, Leo senses uneasily that Salzman is somewhere around, perhaps high in a tree flashing
signals to the lady, or dancing invisibly before them. Salzman
exists outside all ordinary determinations. As a marriage
broker, he is an anachronism. As a marriage broker, with
his magic barrel of photographs of clients, he mysteriously
controls the source of life, but there is nothing fecund nor
generous nor reliable nor easy about him. He is a tease. He
provokes Leo into love, virtually by the process of his unreliability—by giving Leo what he does not want and with-
holding from him what he does want. He lies. He evades.
He denies his lying. And by his fleshlessness, his agility, his

unexpectedness, Salzman is a figure who holds on in a world where uncertainty, evanescence, and unreliability are the rule. He lives the truth of this world. Therefore, and by the extreme sacrifice of all illusions of anything more solid, he can exist.

Salzman is a sufferer, of course, and, by virtue of his job, a minor deity of love, whose love and whose suffering have made him thin and swift. He is, moreover, like all of Malamud's exemplars, a sufferer who for the sake of engagement in this world has abandoned a prior dedication to higher things. He has ransomed his flesh to this world—the scarlet lover to whom he finally and reluctantly introduces Leo is his own daughter, and he makes her available knowing that she is no bride for a rabbi, that he is introducing this student of The Law into death. And Salzman's suffering is clearly Malamud's. This world is a fatality, purchased at the cost of something better. Life and humanity in it are to be created by self-denying commitment to a reality that is not Real. This world does not fascinate Malamud. He works hard and under the rule of a self-imposed obligation to discover it. His suffering makes his fiction swift, too, and not infrequently thin, and therefore it would seem he is put to still more deliberate and extreme attempts to discover a felt ordinary reality, to saturate his exemplary hero in it.

The Assistant insofar as it is naturalistic drama would seem to be such an attempt. *A New Life,* an academic picaresque composed directly, so Malamud has said, according to the influence of Stendhal,[10] is certainly a discipline, strenuous but comic, in real things. The "new life" his hero, S. Levin, seeks, is, it turns out, an alternative not merely to his past life. Levin sighs much in the novel about the encumbering presentness of his past, but that past, as he deals with it directly and briefly just once, is a vague history of drunkenness and a fairly tale of family horrors, in effect a non-life. The new life is life itself. And it is to be life with possibilities much more extensive than those provided by Malamud's claustral grocery store.* Levin is set down in a place where, for one thing, nature is present—nature, Morris Bober had reflected, "gave nothing to a Jew." Moreover, this place will contain a community, a variety of private histories and domestic troubles, jobs, politics, a presence of American history, and, because the place is an academic community, it will provide as well for a clear encounter with large social forces and ideals. *A New Life* is oddly enough one of the few novels not journalism, of the mid-century, that contains specific speculations on Korea, the cold war, McCarthyism, Hiss and Chambers, loyalty oaths, the plight of liberalism, the definition and the duties of radicalism. Levin's speculations on these matters are not indeed analyses, but the materials are there as materials for his adventures, and it is the point of his adventures that he is to engage them, along with all the other present realities.

Near the beginning of the novel, Levin knows and he chooses to avoid the events and the meanings of current history. "America was," he says, "in the best sense of a bad term, un-American," and he is "content to be hidden amid forests and mountains in an unknown town in the Far West," and then, "Teaching was itself sanctuary—to be enclosed in a warm four-walled classroom." Toward the end of the novel, he commits himself to social leadership. In the same way, the novel moves Levin to a close engagement with nature, from New York City and an abstract, distant love of it. Levin's new life is a matter, indeed, as he repeatedly expresses his

* Levin's ambitions obviously parallel Frank Alpine's. Indeed it was Frank Alpine who first discovered for his ambitions the phrase "a new life."

ambition, of coming out from his privacy, and virtually every pattern of events in the novel is designed to illustrate his coming out. Levin wears a beard, and at a certain point in the novel he shaves it off. He wears a hat and a raincoat and carries an umbrella, when none of the rugged Westerners do, and the progress of his consciousness, like Lear's, urges him to stripping in the wilderness. Levin learns to carry golf clubs, to rake leaves, to fire a furnace, to drive a car. He learns to distinguish friends and enemies. And he falls in love and learns how to have a family.

Levin is a young man from the capital, it happens, who in order to secure his initiation moves to the provinces. That would be the way of a contemporary American Julien Sorel. It is specifically to the Pacific Northwest that Levin goes, a place called Eastchester in the state of Cascadia,* where it might be expected that the American civilization could be discovered pure. Quite by the spirit of Stendhal, he is introduced there to manners and morals, passions, intrigues, hypocrisies, the workings of power, and the things of civilization, all of such a civilization as this is. The spirit is Stendhal's, as Malamud has said, but the facts are different ones. Quite like Julien Sorel's Paris, of the Bourbon Restoration, Eastchester is fallen into betrayal of the ideals of its own recent past, but the ideals are, or were, radical democracy, progress, and enlightenment, not empire and glory. And the circumstances of its past are different. In the spirit of Stendhal, Levin is introduced not to a surviving aristocracy, but to nature—nature, as Levin says on an occasion, is Eastchester's true history. And the social facts which this young-man-from-the-capital is in his new life to engage are those of a

* Levin's locale has some relation, presumably, to Oregon State College in Corvallis, Oregon, where Malamud was a member of the faculty from 1949 until 1961.

civilization no longer creative, but not sophisticated, either, and this is a civilization that has gone stale but that is without the certainties either of institutions or of social nuance upon which a Stendhal could depend.

The spirit is Stendhal's, but neither the problem nor the manner nor the voice could be. Remarkably, Malamud does discover a great deal and he does get it down on the page. For the first time in Malamud's fiction, the real things have a real and, more to the point, a continuous specificity. The physical descriptions are frequent, detailed, and exact. The place in which Levin finds himself makes demands. And there is a felt social organization available to him, re-created by a scrupulous, and a consistently ironic, attention to its manners. *A New Life* is indeed, one half of it at least, vivid social satire. But it is social satire in the manner and the voice—astonishingly, considering Malamud's dedication to a European literary tradition—not of Stendhal but Sinclair Lewis. But then inevitably. These are fallen democrats to whom Levin is to be given, whose society is not an institution complicated and refined by the ages but a relatively simple process of enthusiasm generated by loneliness. Their salience is their protective heartiness, and the literary apprehension which as a society they demand is caricature, just enough so that the hollowness may be heard. "People aren't too formal out this way," Levin is told as he arrives. "One of the things you'll notice about the West is its democracy," and his answer, tart and Yiddish, is "Very nice." And that, the hollowness of the democratic gesture, is just the demonstration to be made. Eastchester is not Gopher Prairie, of course. For one thing it contains Levin. But it would seem not to be far from Gopher Prairie, and in any event Malamud's procedures and perceptions are those of a somewhat harsher Sinclair Lewis.

So it is a completely amiable society that is to be seen, a society under an iron discipline of amiability. It is a society whose members nevertheless are in hot, fussy pursuit of petty ambitions. The imagination, the ideals, the sap have gone out of it. Its tone is a broad charade of its worthy past. The satire serves the purposes, since this is an academic novel, of an academic exposé, another exposé of the English Department, but the locale has larger uses. Because culture is this community's business, the past will be the more uncomfortably and the more tauntingly present. And this is a society whose members are all good guys, just a little on edge, open, sincerely devoted to harmlessness, pietistic about certain things, and, it will turn out by function of their organized effort toward triviality, altogether vicious. The basic materials are those of Gopher Prairie. Given them, the voice and the very inventions of specific character must be echoes of Sinclair Lewis. Levin's immediate superior and principal antagonist, Gerald Gilley, in their first talk talks boosterism:

You're our twenty-first man, most we've ever had full-time in the department. . . . Professor Fairchild will meet you tomorrow afternoon at two. He's a fine gentleman and awfully considerate head of department, I'm sure you'll like him, Sy. He kept us going at full complement for years under tough budgetary conditions. Probably you've heard of his grammar text, *The Elements of Grammar?* God knows how many editions it's been through. The department's been growing again following the drop we took after the peak load of veterans, though we've still got plenty of them around. We put on three men last year and we plan another two or three, next. College registration is around forty-two hundred now, but we figure we'll double that before ten years. . . .

We've been hearing from people from every state in the Union. For next year I already have a pile of applications half a foot high.

And in the next moment he talks cautionary self-exculpating Babbittry: "I like your enthusiasm, Sy, but I think you'll understand the situation better after you've been here a year or two. Frankly . . . Cascadia is a conservative state. . . ." And then, Gopher Prairie *redivivus,* the Department is "service-oriented." Professor Fairchild, the community exemplar, resonates one-hundred per cent American clichés.* The community spirit has its opportunity in the college's football and basketball teams, and therefore they are a serious concern. The underground, as one should expect, consists of a couple of village atheists, one old and one young, both of whom confine themselves to cautious ironies. And even Malamud's heroine, Pauline Gilley, the wife whom Levin will steal from Gerald Gilley, emerges in the image of Carol Kennicott— she is a rangy girl vaguely dissatisfied with the narrowness and the restriction of the community, willing to take a chance, vaguely ambitious for something not very clear.

A New Life, Malamud predicted,[11] would be something new for his readers, and it is. The half of it that is social satire is, much of it, broadly funny. The fun is sometimes very good fun—Professor Fairchild, who will expire with the words "The mys-mystery—of the in-fin—in-fin—in-fin—In-fin-i-tive," in the beginning tells Levin an endless moralizing tale of his drunkard father who on his way to Moscow, Idaho, succumbed to drink and never got there, a tale that sounds like a biography by Tolstoy of W. C. Fields. And then the

---

* The monger of pious clichés is a constant character in Malamud's fiction. Professor Fairchild's forebears are to be seen in the owner of the baseball team, Goodwill Banner, in *The Natural,* and in Julius Karp in *The Assistant.*

fun is sometimes corny—Levin meets on the road an old hayseed of a farmer who hands him a pair of pliers and asks Levin to pull his tooth: "Got an achin' tooth here at the back of my mouth. Could you give it a pull with these pliers?" And Levin declines. But fresh or corny, the fun is fabricated from perceptions not usual to Malamud. The perceptions are social and they are directed toward manners and they have breadth. It is here an American humor that, apparently, Malamud is after, to be discovered in a folk, in some Americans as they are in the first place typical, as they typically constitute a certain society, and then as they have just in back of them a certain folk tradition. This humor is far removed from the desperate uncertainties of the *shtetl.*

Levin's new life, then, is to be a serial engagement with the West, with nature, with a community, with some facts, current and traditional, of American history, with social forces, with American civilization and the American folk, all credibly realized. But then the fact is that though the real things are, at least in instances enough, really there, Levin never does come to the point of participating in them. More than that, Levin's adventures consist really of lengthy and private speculations leading to a series of fumbling and abortive attempts at engagement, followed by long retreats, culminating in a plunge into a situation which is meant to represent for Levin and for us a fullness of real life because it is unpleasant. The novel was to be written according to Stendhal, so Malamud said before he had written it, and it was to be, so Malamud also said, "a romantic love story, with warmth and richness." [12] The two intentions are not dissimilar. They meet in an intention toward engagement. And at the end of *A New Life* Levin does get the girl, all right, but in the end he no longer wants her, and at the end his love is neither romantic nor warm nor rich, but sternly dutiful. The story that Malamud

tells in *A New Life* is at the end the old story: the real
things propose not themselves but a moral imperative, and
the hero plunges uncertainly after the things for lack of anything else. And what then is demonstrated is the extremity of
the hero's attempt.

One half of *A New Life* is social satire and the other half
is Levin, and the verve of the one is made uneasy by the
melancholy of the other. Malamud does not accomplish for
Levin the forward movement that will bring him progressively into the world, and that will, incidentally, bring the
novel together. Levin's desire for a new life is in the first
place merely desperate, an urge forced from the impossible
dreamy loneliness of his past, a matter of discipline, and his
true history is, so the evidence will come to suggest, his inevitable frustration. One of the items of his desperation is his
need not for lovers but simply for a friend or two, and some
good part of his early adventuring in the novel is his searching for some casual friendship. Levin as he knocks on the
doors of his various colleagues is in one instance after another
rebuffed, but then more significant than his defeat is the fact
that he is never in his search brought to any climatic confrontation. The matter simply tires itself out and is dropped,
and what is dramatized, no matter what is intended, is a
great weariness in Levin's searching and an inevitability of
defeat.

What is dramatized in every other instance is a conviction
of the inevitability of frustration, the consequence of which is
inertia, against which by main force Levin stumbles and
fumbles for engagement and discovery. Nature is a large part
of the reality which Levin is to engage, and he does learn to
perform some chores of gardening and such. Indeed he is
moved to lyrical appreciation of natural beauties in such a
way as perhaps only a boy from Manhattan might be. But

the intimate connection, the real engagement, despite Malamud's forcing of a couple of moments, just never takes place.

The test is in those moments. Levin would seem to be
derived in part from his namesake in *Anna Karenina*.[13] Like
that Levin, he is provided in a set scene in an open clearing
in a woods with opportunity for a redemptive insight. The
scene in *Anna Karenina* apparently contains a special sug-
gestiveness for Malamud. Frank Alpine was made to happen
upon it in his reading and to be "moved at the deep change
that came over Levin in the woods just after he had thought
of hanging himself," and Frank had reflected that unlike
Anna, at least Levin wanted to live. Malamud's Levin, on a
spring day miraculously burst in the middle of January, in
the middle of the novel, with some temerity enters a local
woods to do some bird-watching. Bird-watching has consequences in Malamud's fiction, and here Levin meets and
for the first time makes love to Pauline Gilley. This is an
important scene, an anagnorisis. Levin has fumbled unhappily after other girls, but this is love. This forest, it happens, is a place where foresters are trained. And the moment,
so Levin reflects, is marvelous. He has become at once a lover
and Natty Bumppo. "In the open forest," he says to himself,
"nothing less, what triumph!" He has discovered the promise
of life.

Or that should be and would be the case except that the
moment, brief as it is, is so qualified by ironies as to be con-
tradicted. This time in nature is, first of all, a time out of
nature—midwinter spring is its own season. The unusual
weather for January indeed prompts Levin, as he sets out for
the out-of-doors, to speculate with "a touch of habitual sadness" on "the relentless rhythm of nature," the eternal sameness which prevents human freedom. And whatever insight
this day will offer, it will not offer nature as it is. Nature-as-

it-is hovers near-by to cancel the illumination. Moreover, then, the promise of life, as it should be certified by Levin's love-making with Pauline, reneges on itself. Pauline, as her husband will much later tell Levin, is no bed of roses. And Levin finds out now that she is unfortunately flat-chested, a fact which, were Levin permitted to know Malamud's iconography, he would recognize as a symptom of failure at love.* In his passion clutching at her breasts, which is to say clutching after engagement with her, Levin seizes nothing. And then finally such joy and freedom as there is in this love-making is qualified by the secretive messiness of adultery it looks forward to. The sun shines brightly as he and Pauline leave the forest, but Levin opens an umbrella over their heads. And in the quick course of things the forest will shrink to a double bed in Levin's bachelor room.

The episode is forced—what Malamud asserts, he takes back. And then it is in its achievement the more suspicious because it should be redundant. The episode follows shortly upon another in which Levin, having suffered from a cold and from a long bout of dreary loneliness and from a recidivous thirst for alcohol, walks abroad to discover a magnificent Western sunset. He felt, so it is said, "like a man entering a new life and entered." But that is the abrupt end of that episode. In fact Levin's harmony in the woods is followed shortly by still another greeting from nature, occurring when he admits what he thinks he knows, that he is in love with Pauline Gilley.

Above the tops of budding trees he watched the flaring, setting sun, wanting to abolish thought, afraid to probe

* In a preceding episode Levin himself affirms, if he does not recognize, Malamud's pectoral iconography. A sexual encounter with a lady named Avis Fliss is frustrated because the lady, having suffered a fibroma, is sensitive in her breasts.

the complexion of the next minute lest it erupt in his face
a fact that would alter his existence. But nature—was it?—
a bull aiming at a red flag (Levin's vulnerability, the old
self's hunger) charged from behind and the Manhattan
matador, rarely in control of any contest, felt himself lifted
high and plummeted over violet hills toward an unmapped
abyss. Through fields of stars he fell in love.

The experience does not, however, alter his existence. In the
next moment, in the very next paragraph, he will retreat back
into his habits of anxious speculation, the moment of his full
engagement still before him, the reiteration necessary because
the moment refuses finally to occur.

Levin reflects in the beginning, after some preliminary attempts at gardening, that "he had come too late to nature,"
and in fact all his efforts are conducted against a sense of
something—whether or not his particular past—dragging him
back. The Levin presented is a lonely, bearded Jew, locked
in himself, desperate to get out, after great effort coming too
late to everything. The best of an external reality that Malamud
will allow him is one at second hand. So Levin buys a secondhand car, observing that "he had come too late to mechanics," as later he observes more largely, in the middle of
his woodland adventure, that "he had come too late to the
right place." He will reflect still later that he is no Chingach-
gook; wherever he had been, someone had been before. This
new life after which he will finally plunge is forced from
a sense of its opposite, and then if it isn't just the old life
again to which Levin falls, it doesn't either contain anything
entirely new. At the very end of the novel, Levin will drive
off in his secondhand car with his secondhand wife and with
the children she had in the first instance adopted. Pauline is
pregnant with Levin's child, and that might be something

new, but the child is only another possibility of the future, for which Malamud does not make himself responsible.

There is something secondhand and stale even in the objects of Levin's purely social commitment. There is no doubting the sincerity or the urgency of his idealism. "I worry," he says to one of his teaching colleagues, "I'm not teaching how to keep civilization from destroying itself," and if the statement is faintly pretentious, as Levin admits it is, it is also so blunt as to prove conviction.* And Levin's idealism should be of special usefulness to Cascadia College, which is "service-oriented," which (like, it is to be said, America) lost the liberal arts shortly after the First World War, which has lapsed into a viciously self-protective narrowness of political reaction, and which is on its way toward destroying the civilization by which it was nurtured. But Levin's passionate idealism accomplishes no revolution and it is impossible that it might, despite the fact that Levin actually does urge himself to the point of running for the position of head of the English Department, despite the fact that he actually does enter himself into such politics as there is. His idealism is a matter of his subscribing himself passionately to ideals—democracy, humanism, liberalism (and the liberal arts), radicalism, freedom, art, and intellect. The words are ever and easily at his lips. And splendid, and necessary, as his ideals are, they exist pure and at a tremendous distance from the social facts. Levin becomes aware of that distance, as apparently Malamud became aware at a certain point in the novel. Malamud presents Levin with, indeed, some particulars of social action. As Levin is a reform candidate, he urges

---

* There is no doubting Levin's sincerity furthermore because he echoes Malamud's statement of his own purpose as a writer: "The purpose of the writer . . . is to keep civilization from destroying itself." *New York Post Magazine* interview.

upon the English Department: elimination of the Department's grammar text and also the examination in grammar, elimination of "censorship of responsibly selected texts," recommendation that every instructor teach a course in literature, and some other similar matters, all to an effect comparable to Trotsky lecturing at the local P.T.A.

Between Levin's ideals and the social facts there is tremendous distance and a total absence of social analysis. His ideals are not tested in the large social complication they require, and certainly they are not forged from social experience. Levin's ideals are the convenient instruments of his idealism, and what his idealism accomplishes, aside from elimination of the grammar text, is its own integrity. His idealism is not what it seems to be and should be, the way of his engagement with the new life out there. Confronted in his idealism by the facts, Levin is in fact apt to be foolish. So when he is told of a photograph of a man and woman swimming together naked, he refuses, quite with Malamud's assent, to believe that they were lovers, on high juridical grounds of reasonable doubt. There is in such idealism something not merely naive but also forced. It has no sensible commerce with the world, and what about Levin's idealism is effectively dramatized is its uncertain relevance to the real world.

But of course Levin will be a man who believes that ideals, as he says, "give a man his value if he stands for them," just as he will be a man for whom love is finally neither a joy nor an enrichment nor an emotional fulfillment, but a stern moral imperative. The world doesn't beckon to Levin. He and Malamud invent disciplines by which to secure an accommodation to what is only uncertainly there. So Levin's final plunge after Pauline is, as it must be, entirely dutiful, and merely desperate. After adventures in adultery, he no longer wants her. Moreover he has discovered reason to believe that she does not love him, but, instead, a previous lover whom he resembles. Then, in a final interview, her husband rubs Levin's nose, as it were, in Pauline, a woman who, as Gerald points out, was born dissatisfied, who is thrown off balance by almost anything, who is not a good housekeeper, who is unpunctual, who is afraid of growing old, and who suffers chronically from constipation and menstrual troubles. And the children Levin will inherit are not easy to live with either. He will love Pauline nevertheless because he can discover, so he tells her, no reason not to. He will love her without feeling, and on principle, and because, so he says to Gerald, he can. And off he then goes, with a car full of luggage, two children, one crying for its real daddy, the other, suffering eczema, covered with ointment, and his bride in a white dress.

Stendhal would have written a different ending, with irony less excruciating and a resolution more secure. At the end of *A New Life* nothing, no experience, has yet really happened, and the end is just a more extreme attempt by which Levin is to be got into life, under the rule of a stern discipline, and out of himself. But the record of Levin's failure is Malamud's startling strength. Malamud is not a Stendhal or a Balzac and—it is exactly his informing trouble—the world does not tumble in upon him, and so he is forced to extremes to discover it. The strenuosity of such a hero as Levin is of the mood of Malamud's taut balance, elsewhere, on the edge of supernaturalism, and it is created in an apprehension of a world in which nothing certainly exists.

∽VII∾

AFTERWORD

The something new in these writers, I have wanted to say, is to be defined historically, which is to say in terms of the relevance of these writers to the age. It is something that resides not in any messages buried in their works, nor necessarily in any explicit realizations, nor even in any individual cunningness of apprehension of the age. And it does not reside in any formal inventions or in any preferences of technique. Bellow, Ellison, Baldwin, Morris, and Malamud constitute no *school* of thought of fiction, but they do, along it would seem with numbers of other novelists, have in common a knowledge that we are all on the edge of dissolution and that at this point in history things must be salvaged. Human living must be made barely possible. The fiction they write, for all that is tends away from explicitly social subjects, is shaped by the social and political pressures of an age that is the most desperate in all history.

Something assuredly is missing from this fiction: not only the exhilaration of assault on the smug and somnolent community, but the conscience that such assault once implied. Once, to be an alienated artist-intellectual was to have clear and passionate convictions about social values and about the nature of good and evil. To assault the community from a position of alienation was to bring witness to wrongs—which were recognizably wrong—perpetrated by hypocrisy or ignorance or stubborn Philistinism or narrow-mindedness or self-interest. To be alienated was to be right-minded and aggrieved.

Something is missing: the old grievances don't begin to comprehend the evil with which in these years we have lived. That which was evil has given way to what the late Isaac Rosenfeld named "the terror," and with respect to the terror, good conscience itself is only mildly relevant. The culture is now without doubt still less habitable for the artist-intellectual, or anyone else, than it was. The boobs are gone, but replaced by the arrogant middlebrows, the *fonctionnaires,* of the Media. Dayton, Tennessee, is replaced by Little Rock and Birmingham. An imposing Puritanism has been sublimed into IBM machinery. A cruel industrialism has been replaced by a rampant scientism. And meanwhile the nation's creative energies are given to sport, the famous race with the Russians, which there is no danger of our losing because everything depends on the way one keeps score. But such is the nature of the terror, that what in the culture is wrong, stupid, and evil becomes trivial. Evil is not so important as once it was.

The terror beyond evil is the murder that occurred in the Second World War together with the prospect become familiar of entire and utter annihilation. We are all half-dead of it already, and there is to be opposed to it only a more strenuous and a more vivid sensing of human community. There is to be opposed to it only the assertion that despite the hatred in everyone, despite violence, despite weakness and sickness, despite the uncertainty of ordinary reality, despite mortality and the seductions of a myth of eternity, despite everything, the human community is possible—and that, so I have wanted to say, is the theme and the occupation, begot of the terror, of a literature of what I have called "accommodation." It is a literature that exists between the extremes of an easy nihilism and a bland hopefulness—between, for instance, the gamboling grotesqueries of such a statement as Joseph Heller's *Catch-22,* and laureate platitudes to the effect that man will endure— because there, between those extremes, is where the humanity that is to be asserted goes on.

"Accommodation" is restoration and love in their ordinary, domestic, painfully contingent instances, and it makes up in plain necessity what it lacks in conscience.

NOTES

I. INTRODUCTION

1. Van Wyck Brooks, "Letters and Leadership," *Three Essays on America* (New York: E. P. Dutton & Co., Inc., 1934), p. 184. The essay was published originally in 1918.

See, for examples of Brooks's earlier attitudes, *The Wine of the Puritans: A Study of Present-Day America* (New York: Mitchell Kennerley, 1909); *The Maladay of the Ideal: Obermann, Maurice de Guerin and Amiel*, published originally in 1913 in England, the first American edition printed Philadelphia: University of Pennsylvania Press, 1947.

2. "Letters and Leadership," p. 184.

3. "The Literary Life in America," *Three Essays on America*, p. 205. The essay was published originally in 1921.

4. Randolph Bourne, "Twilight of Idols," *The History of a Literary Radical & Other Papers* (New York: S. A. Russell, 1956), p. 257. The essay was published originally in 1917.

II. SAUL BELLOW

1. *The Living Novel*, Granville Hicks, ed. (New York: The Macmillan Co., 1957), p. 3.

2. "The Swamp of Prosperity," a review of Philip Roth's *Goodbye, Columbus, Commentary*, XXVIII (July 1959), 79.

3. "Isaac Rosenfeld," *Partisan Review*, XXIII (Fall 1956), 567.

4. "The Uses of Adversity," *The Reporter*, XXI (Oct. 1, 1959), 44, 45.

5. "The Sealed Treasure," *Times Literary Supplement*, July 1, 1960, 414. Reprinted in *The Writer's Dilemma* (London: Oxford University Press, 1961), pp. 60–67.

6. *The Hudson Review*, IV (Summer 1961), 225–26. Reprinted in *Nelson Algren's Own Book of Lonesome Monsters*, Nelson Algren, ed. (New York: Bernard Geis Associates, 1963), pp. 142–48.

7. See Richard G. Stern, "Henderson's Bellow," *The Kenyon Review*, XXI (Autumn 1959), 659, 660.

8. *Partisan Review*, XVII (November-December 1950), 793.

9. See, for instance, Richard Chase, "The Adventures of Saul Bellow," p. 324; Delmore Schwartz, "Adventure in America," *Partisan Review*, XXI (January-February 1954), 112.

10. *Partisan Review*, IX (May-June 1942), 178–94. The story is reprinted in *More Stories in the Modern Manner from Partisan Review* (New York: Avon Publications, 1954), pp. 235–52, where a biographical note says it was Bellow's first published story. But it was preceded by "Two Morning Monologues," *Partisan Review*, VIII (May-June 1941), 230–36.

11. "A Talk with the Yellow Kid," *The Reporter*, XV (Sept. 6, 1956), 41–44.

12. See, for instance, Bellow's translation of Isaac Bashevis Singer's story "Gimpel the Fool," in *Gimpel the Fool and Other Stories* New York: The Noonday Press, 1957), pp. 3–21; his review of Sholom Aleichem's *The Adventures of Mottel the Cantor's Son*, "Laughter in the Ghetto," *Saturday Review*, XXXVI (May 30, 1953), 15.

13. See Irving Howe and Eliezer Greenberg, "Introduction," *A Treasury of Yiddish Stories* (New York: Meridian Books, Inc., 1958), p. 39.

14. "Laughter in the Ghetto," p. 15.

15. *Partisan Review*, XVI (May 1949), 455–62. Reprinted in *Fiction of the Fifties*, Herbert Gold, ed. (Garden City: Doubleday & Co., 1959), pp. 66–73.

16. *Thus Spoke Zarathustra*, trans. Walter Kaufmann, in *The Portable Nietzsche* (New York: The Viking Press, 1954), pp. 137–40.

III. RALPH ELLISON

1. See Saunders Redding, "Negro Writing in America," *The New Leader*, XLIII (May 16, 1960), 8.

2. James Baldwin, "Everybody's Protest Novel," *Zero*, I (Spring 1949), 54–58; reprinted in *Partisan Review*, XVI (June 1949), 578–85; reprinted in *Notes of a Native Son* (Boston: Beacon Press, 1955), pp. 13–23.

3. Ralph Ellison quoted in Rochelle Girson, "Sidelights on Invisibility," *Saturday Review,* XXXVI (March 14, 1953), 20.

4. James Baldwin, "Autobiographical Notes," *Notes of a Native Son,* p. 5.

5. James Baldwin, "The Discovery of What It Means to Be An American," *New York Times Book Review,* January 25, 1959, p. 4; reprinted in *Nobody Knows My Name.*

6. See, for instance, these reviews of Baldwin's *Go Tell It on the Mountain:* Henry F. Winslow, "'Church Sermon,'" *The Crisis,* LX (December 1953), 637. Robert K. Bingham, "Baldwin," *The Reporter,* VIII (June 23, 1953), 38.

See these reviews of Ellison's *Invisible Man:* William Barrett, "Black and Blue: A Negro Celine," *American Mercury,* LXXIV (June 1952), 100. Richard Chase, "A Novel Is a Novel," *The Kenyon Review,* XIV (Autumn 1952), 682. Henry F. Winslow, "Unending Trial," *The Crisis,* LIX (June-July 1952), 397, 398. Robert Langbaum, untitled review, *Furioso,* VII (Fall 1952), 58. Harvey Curtis Webster, "Inside a Dark Shell," *Saturday Review* XXXV (April 12, 1952), 23. Delmore Schwartz, "Fiction Chronicle: The Wrongs of Innocence and Experience," *Partisan Review,* XIX (May-June 1952), 359. Heinz Rogge, "Die amerikanische Negerfrage im Lichte der Literatur von Richard Wright und Ralph Ellison," *Die Neueren Sprachen,* VII (1958), 56–69, 103–17.

7. Alain Locke, "The New Negro," *The New Negro: An Interpretation,* Alain Locke, ed. (New York: Albert & Charles Boni, 1925), pp. 3–4. Italics mine.

8. See Robert A. Bone, *The Negro Novel in America* (New Haven: Yale University Press, 1958), pp. 65–94, 114–16, 178–91.

9. Arthur P. Davis, "Integration and Race Literature," *The American Negro Writer and His Roots: Selected Papers from the First Conference of Negro Writers, March, 1959* (New York: American Society of African Culture, 1960), pp. 34, 35.

10. "The Art of Fiction XVIII: Robert Penn Warren," *Paris Review,* IV (Spring-Summer 1957), 135.

11. Carl Milton Hughes, *The Negro Novelist: A Discussion of the Writings of American Negro Novelists 1940–1950* (New York: The Citadel Press, 1953), p. 148.

12. Margaret Just Butcher, "The Negro in Modern American Fiction," *The Negro in American Culture* (New York: New American Library, 1957), p. 148.

13. J. Saunders Redding, *On Being a Negro in America* (Indianapolis: Bobbs-Merrill, and Co., 1951), p. 26.

14. Saunders Redding, "The Negro Writer and His Relationship to His Roots," *The American Negro Writer and His Roots,* p. 8.

15. See, for instance, Ralph Ellison, "Richard Wright's Blues," *The Antioch Review*, V (June 1945), 207–09. The hostility of Negroes toward Negroes, especially within the family, is a theme of James Baldwin's *Go Tell It on the Mountain*, and it is a constant theme in Baldwin's short stories. See especially: "The Outing," *New-Story No. 2*, April 1951, pp. 52–81; "Come Out the Wilderness," *Mademoiselle*, XLVI (March 1958), 102–04; "Sonny's Blues," *Partisan Review*, XXIV (Summer 1957), 327–58. See also Baldwin's play, *The Amen Corner*, a portion of which was printed in *Zero*, II (July 1954), 4–8, 11–13.

16. *Notes of a Native Son*, p. 112.

17. Ralph Ellison in an interview by Alfred Chester and Vilma Howard, "The Art of Fiction VIII: Ralph Ellison," *Paris Review*, No. 8 (Spring 1955), 57.

18. F. Cudworth Flint, "Fiction Chronicle," *The Sewanee Review*, LXII (Winter 1954), 176.

19. *Paris Review* interview, p. 68. See also Ellison's statement to Rochelle Girson, "Sidelights on Invisibility," p. 49; "Invisibility has to do with the failure of most of us to regard the individual we contact as a human being. . . . On the other hand, you have the failure of the individual to exert himself to be mature, to run the risk of humanity. . . ."

20. "Negro Prize Fighter," a review of *Walk Hard, Talk Loud*, a novel by Len Zinberg, *The New Masses*, XXXVII (December 17, 1940), 27.

21. "Camp Lost Colony," *The New Masses*, XXXIV (February 6, 1940), 19.

22. "A Congress Jim Crow Didn't Attend," *The New Masses*, XXXV (May 14, 1940), 5.

23. See, for instance: "Argosy Across the USA," a review of *The Argonauts* by five members of the American Youth Congress, *The New Masses*, XXXVII (November 26, 1940), 24; "The Way It Is," *The New Masses*, XLV (October 20, 1942), 9–11; "Judge Lynch in New York," *The New Masses*, XXXII (August 15, 1939), 15–16; "Transition," a review of *Blood on the Forge* by William Attaway, *The Negro Quarterly*, I (Spring 1942), 87–92.

24. Ellison quoted in Eloise Perry Hazard, untitled biographical note, *Saturday Review*, XXXV (April 12, 1952), 22. Ellison quoted in *Paris Review* interview, p. 56.

25. His first contribution to *The New Masses* seems to have been "Practical Mystic," a review of *Sojourner Truth: God's Faithful Pilgrim*, a historical novel by Arthur Huff Fauset, *The New Masses*, XXVIII (August 16, 1938), 25–26. His last seems to have been "The

Way It is," *The New Masses,* XLV (October 20, 1942), 9–11. The first issue of *The Negro Quarterly,* Spring 1942, lists Ellison only as a reviewer. In the next issue, Summer 1942, he is listed as Managing Editor, under the Editor, Angelo Herndon. The fourth issue of the magazine, appearing for Winter-Spring 1943, is apparently the last.

26. *The New Masses,* XXXVI (July 2, 1940), 16–17. Reprinted in *Negro World Digest,* I (November 1940), 61–65.

27. "Transition," *The Negro Quarterly,* I (Spring 1942), 88. Ellison had some months before already reviewed the novel: "The Great Migration," *The New Masses,* XLI (December 2, 1941), 23–24.

28. "The Way It Is," *The New Masses,* XLV (October 20, 1942), 11.

29. "Recent Negro Fiction," *The New Masses,* XL (August 5, 1941), 25.

30. For some of Ellison's reflections, implicit and explicit, on Hemingway, see: "Negro Prize Fighter," p. 27; " 'Big White Fog,' " a review of a play by Theodore Ward, *The New Masses,* XXXVII (November 12, 1940), 22; "Stormy Weather," p. 20. For some more recent reflections, see: "Light on 'Invisible man,' " extracts from Ellison's National Book Award acceptance speech, *The Crisis,* LX (March 1953), 157; "Sidelights on Invisibility," p. 20; "Twentieth-Century Fiction and the Black Mask of Humanity," *Confluence,* II (December 1953), 17; "Society, Morality, and the Novel," *The Living Novel,* Granville Hicks, ed. (New York: The Macmillan Co., 1957), pp. 74 ff., 84–86.

31. "The Darker Brother," *Tomorrow,* III (November 1943), 55.

32. "Editorial Comment," *The Negro Quarterly,* I (Winter-Spring 1943), 296, 298.

33. See: "Stormy Weather," p. 20; "Recent Negro Fiction," p. 22; "New World A-Coming," a review of *New World A-Coming* by Roi Ottley, *Tomorrow,* III (September 1943), 68.

34. *The New Masses,* XLI (November 4, 1941), 19–20. Reprinted in *Negro Story,* I (July-August 1944), 36–41.

35. *Common Ground,* III (Summer 1943), 30–37. Reprinted under the title "Mr. Toussaint" in *Negro Story,* I (October-November 1944), 3–11, as a sequel to "Mr. Toussan."

36. *New World Writing* #9, 1956, pp. 225–36.

37. "Light on 'Invisible Man,' " p. 158. Ellison says much the same thing in *Paris Review* interview, pp. 70–71.

38. "Twentieth-Century Fiction and the Black Mask of Humanity," p. 15. This essay, though not printed until 1953, was composed in 1946.

39. "Society, Morality, and the Novel," p. 69.

40. *Tomorrow*, III (July 1944), 41–44.

41. *Cross Section*, Edwin Seaver, ed. (New York: L. B. Fischer, 1944), pp. 469–85.

42. "Editorial Comment," *The Negro Quarterly*, I (Winter-Spring 1943), 298. In his interview with Rochelle Girson, "Sidelights on Invisibility," p. 49, Ellison says that he had intended after the war to write a novel about a flyer. This story would seem to be its beginning.

43. *Tomorrow*, IV (November 1944), 29–33.

44. For an index of the symbols of vision in *Invisible Man*, see Charles I. Glicksberg, "The Symbolism of Vision," *Southwest Review*, XXXIX (Summer 1954), 259–65.

45. "Change the Joke and Slip the Yoke," the second part of an exchange with Stanley Edgar Hyman on "The Negro Writer in America," *Partisan Review*, XXV (Spring 1958), 220.

46. So Ellison says: "Change the Joke and Slip the Yoke," p. 220.

47. Ellison himself has compared Rinehart to the Confidence Man. *Paris Review* interview, p. 70.

48. Leslie Fiedler, "Come Back to the Raft Ag'in, Huck Honey!" *An End to Innocence* (Boston: Beacon Press, 1955), pp. 142–51. Ellison discusses the essay in "Change the Joke and Slip the Yoke," p. 215.

IV. JAMES BALDWIN

1. Act One of the play appears in *Zero*, II (July 1954), 4–8, 11–13.

2. "Down at the Cross: Letter from a Region in My Mind," *The Fire Next Time*, p. 112. Italics mine.

3. "In Search of a Majority," *Nobody Knows My Name*, p. 137. Italics mine.

4. "The Black Boy Looks at the White Boy," *Nobody Knows My Name*, p. 232. Italics mine.

5. "A Question of Identity," p. 137; "The Discovery of What It Means to Be an American," *Nobody Knows My Name*, pp. 3–4.

6. "The Northern Protestant," *Nobody Knows My Name*, pp. 178–79.

7. *Nobody Knows My Name*, p. 117.

8. "A Negro Assays the Negro Mood," *New York Times Magazine*, March 12, 1961, p. 104. Reprinted as "East River, Downtown: Postscript to a Letter from Harlem," in *Nobody Knows My Name*.

9. "Nobody Knows My Name," p. 114.

10. "The Harlem Ghetto," *Notes of a Native Son*, p. 64.

11. "The Black Boy Looks at the White Boy," p. 217.

12. "The Crusade of Indignation," *The Nation*, CLXXXIII (July 7, 1956), 21.

13. The essay was first printed in *Zero*, I (Spring 1949), 54–58; reprinted in *Partisan Review*, XVI (June 1949), 578–85; reprinted in *Notes of a Native Son*, pp. 13–23; reprinted in *Perspectives USA*, 2 (Winter 1953), 93–100.

14. "Preservation of Innocence: Studies for a New Morality," *Zero*, I (Summer 1949), 21.

15. "Notes for a Hypothetical Novel," *Nobody Knows My Name*, p. 144.

16. "Many Thousands Gone," p. 42.

17. "Stranger in the Village," *Notes of a Native Son*, p. 173.

18. "Encounter on the Seine," *Notes of a Native Son*, p. 123.

19. ". . . this depthless alienation from oneself and one's people is, in sum, the American experience." "Encounter on the Seine," p. 123.

20. See "Notes for a Hypothetical Novel," pp. 149, 151, and "The Northern Protestant," p. 180.

21. "In Search of a Majority," p. 137. Cf. "Encounter on the Seine," p. 123.

22. "Many Thousands Gone," pp. 37–38, 42–43.

23. "The Negro at Home and Abroad," *The Reporter*, V (November 27, 1951), 36.

24. "Stranger in the Village," p. 166.

25. *Commentary*, VI (October 1948), 336–37.

26. *The Atlantic*, CCVI (September 1960), 44–45.

27. "Many Thousands Gone," p. 24.

28. Partisan Review, XXIV (Summer 1957), 327–58. Reprinted in *Fiction of the Fifties*, Herbert Gold, ed. (Garden City: Doubleday & Co., Inc., 1959), pp. 32–64.

29. "Autobiographical Notes," p. 6.

30. "Stranger in the Village," p. 165.

31. "Many Thousands Gone," p. 38.

32. *Mademoiselle*, XLVI (March 1958), 102–04, 146–54.

33. "Encounter on the Seine," p. 122.

34. "Alas, Poor Richard," *Nobody Knows My Name*, p. 215.

35. "Notes of a Native Son," p. 112.

36. *New-Story No. 2*, April 1951, pp. 52–81.

V. WRIGHT MORRIS

1. Sam Bleufarb, "Point of View: An Interview with Wright Morris, July 1958," *Accent*, XIX (Winter 1959), 45.

2. *Ibid.*

3. *Ibid.*

4. *New York Times Book Review,* September 22, 1963, p. 5.

VI. BERNARD MALAMUD

1. Irving Howe and Eliezer Greenberg, "Introduction," *A Treasury of Yiddish Stories* (New York: Meridian Books, Inc., 1958), p. 7.

2. Commentary, XII (November 1951), 460–64.

3. Alfred Kazin, "Bernard Malamud: The Magic and the Dread," *Contemporaries* (Boston: Atlantic-Little, Brown, 1962), p. 205.

4. Bernard Malamud in an interview by Joseph Wershba, "Closeup," *New York Post Magazine,* September 14, 1958.

5. Threshold, III (February 1943), 20–22. The materials of this story are reworked by Malamud in his play, *Suppose a Wedding.*

6. For somewhat more detailed exposition of the Homeric parallels see Norman Podhoretz, "Achilles in Left Field," *Commentary,* XV (March 1953), 321–26.

7. See Leslie Fiedler, *Love and Death in the American Novel* (New York: Criterion Books, 1960), pp. 469–70, and Alfred Kazin, "Bernard Malamud: The Magic and the Dread," p. 205.

8. *American Prefaces,* VIII (Spring 1943), 230–42.

9. *New York Post Magazine* interview.

10. *Ibid.*

11. *Ibid.*

12. *Ibid.*

13. For a briefly extended comparison with *Anna Karenina* see Eugene Goodheart, "Fantasy and Reality," *Midstream,* VII (Autumn 1961), 102–05.

SELECTED BIBLIOGRAPHY

The following bibliography includes citations, in chronological order, of the first editions of all books by the five major subjects of this book. Most of these titles are currently available in paperback editions. Uncollected stories and essays referred to in the text are cited in the notes.

SAUL BELLOW
Dangling Man. New York: The Vanguard Press, Inc., 1944.
The Victim. New York: The Vanguard Press, Inc., 1947.
The Adventures of Augie March. New York: The Viking Press, Inc., 1953.
Seize the Day. New York: The Viking Press, Inc., 1956. (Contents: "Seize the Day," "A Father-to-Be," "Looking for Mr. Green," "The Gonzaga Manuscripts," "The Wrecker" [a one-act play].)
Henderson the Rain King. New York: The Viking Press, Inc., 1959.

RALPH ELLISON
Invisible Man. New York: Random House, 1952.

JAMES BALDWIN
Go Tell It on the Mountain. New York: Alfred A. Knopf, Inc., 1953.
Notes of a Native Son. Boston: Beacon Press, 1955. (Contents: "Autobiographical Notes," "Everybody's Protest Novel," "Many Thousands Gone," "Carmen Jones: The Dark Is Light Enough," "The Harlem Ghetto," "Journey to Atlanta," "Notes of a Native Son," "Encounter on the Seine: Black Meets Brown," "A Question of Identity," "Equal in Paris," "Stranger in the Village.")

Giovanni's Room. New York: The Dial Press, Inc., 1956.
Nobody Knows My Name: More Notes of a Native Son. New York: The Dial Press, Inc., 1961. (Contents: "The Discovery of What It Means to Be an American," "Princes and Powers," "Fifth Avenue, Uptown: A Letter from Harlem," "East River, Downtown: Postscript to a Letter from Harlem," "A Fly in Buttermilk," "Nobody Knows My Name: A Letter from the South," "Faulkner and Desegregation," "In Search of a Majority," "Notes for a Hypothetical Novel," "The Male Prison," "The Northern Protestant," "Eight Men," "The Exile," "Alas, Poor Richard," "The Black Boy Looks at the White Boy.")
Another Country. New York: The Dial Press, Inc., 1962.
The Fire Next Time. New York: The Dial Press, Inc., 1963. (Contents: "My Dungeon Shook: Letter to My Nephew on the One Hundredth Anniversary of the Emancipation," "Down at the Cross: Letter from a Region in My Mind.")

WRIGHT MORRIS
My Uncle Dudley. New York: Harcourt, Brace & Co., 1942.
The Man Who Was There. New York: Charles Scribner's Sons, 1945.
The Inhabitants. New York: Charles Scribner's Sons, 1946.
The Home Place. New York: Charles Scribner's Sons, 1948.
The World in the Attic. New York: Charles Scribner's Sons, 1949.
Man and Boy. New York: Alfred A. Knopf, Inc., 1951.
The Works of Love. New York: Alfred A. Knopf, Inc., 1952.
The Deep Sleep. New York: Charles Scribner's Sons, 1953.
The Huge Season. New York: The Viking Press, Inc., 1954.
The Field of Vision. New York: Harcourt, Brace & Co., 1956.
Love Among the Cannibals. New York: Harcourt, Brace & Co., 1957.
The Territory Ahead. New York: Harcourt, Brace & Co., 1958.
Ceremony in Lone Tree. New York: Atheneum Publishers, 1960.
What a Way to Go. New York: Atheneum Publishers, 1962.
Cause for Wonder. New York: Atheneum Publishers, 1963.

BERNARD MALAMUD
The Natural. New York: Harcourt, Brace & Co., 1952.
The Assistant. New York: Farrar, Straus & Cudahy, Inc., 1957.
The Magic Barrel. New York: Farrar, Straus & Cudahy, Inc., 1958. (Contents: "The First Seven Years," "The Mourners," "The Girl of My Dreams," "Angel Levine," "Behold the Key," "Take Pity," "The Prison," "The Lady of the Lake," "A Summer's Reading," "The Bill," "The Last Mohican," "The Loan," "The Magic Barrel.")
A New Life. New York: Farrar, Straus & Cudahy, Inc., 1961.
Idiots First. New York: Farrar, Straus & Company, 1963. (Contents:

"Idiots First," "Black Is My Favorite Color," "Still Life," "The Death of Me," "A Choice of Profession," "Life Is Better Than Death," "The Jewbird," "Naked Nude," "The Cost of Living," "The Maid's Shoes," "Suppose a Wedding" [a scene of a play], "The German Refugee.")